Contract & Consent

CONTRACT & CONSENT

Representation and the Jury in Anglo-American Legal History

J. R. Pole

University of Virginia Press Charlottesville and London

University of Virginia Press

Printed in the United States of America on acid-free paper

First published 2010

9 8 7 6 5 4 3 2 1

LIBRARY OF CONGRESS CATALOGING-IN-PUBLICATION DATA

Pole, J. R. (Jack Richon)
Contract and consent : representation and the jury in Anglo-American legal history / J. R. Pole.
p. cm.
Includes bibliographical references and index.
ISBN 978-0-8139-2861-6 (cloth : alk. paper) — ISBN 978-0-8139-2892-0 (e-book)
1. Law—England—History. 2. Law—United States—History. I. Title.
KD606.P65 2010
349.42—dc22

2009021510

For Janet

The door had been closed, and on the unventilated air were those traces of mustiness, that ghost of cigar smoke, to intensify the feeling of things past—upholstered furniture in old, old cracked leather; on the paneled walls in need of paint, old, old, tarnished gold picture frames containing old, old engravings that nobody would hang today—Sir Edward Coke in ruff and skull-cap; Sir William Blackstone, robed and bewigged.

—"On Noah Tuttle's Chambers," James Gould Cozzens, *By Love Possessed*, 1957

Contents

Preface

For a comparatively short book, this one has been a long time in the making. And for a book that has been long in the making, it leaves much remaining to be said. Its beginnings are difficult to locate, but its deeper roots might be traced to the legal and constitutional issues involved in my studies of the theme of equality, which emerged as *The Pursuit of Equality in American History,* the first edition of which (1978) was substantially rewritten and much enlarged for the edition of 1993. William E. Nelson's generous offer of a Goleib Fellowship at New York University Law School, followed by a semester at the Marshall-Wythe Law School of William and Mary College, gave me valuable opportunities for research and conversation, and an editorial invitation to write up my preliminary findings for a Forum issue of the *William and Mary Quarterly* (January 1993), associated with a semester at the Commonwealth Studies seminar, all helped to clarify my sense of direction. I am duly grateful for these opportunities.

English legal history as an established academic field may be said to have begun with the great medievalists of the mid-to-later nineteenth century. William Stubbs, bishop of Oxford, may now seem an old-fashioned guide, but to read Stubbs now is often to rediscover what he already knew. Maitland remains incomparable—even where he may have been superseded. More recent practitioners, whose names are familiar to scholars, are legal craftsmen of a caliber that I cannot expect to emulate. But they have influenced the writing of general history less than the subject demands, perhaps because they have tended (with exceptions) to be specialists in law rather than general historians for whom law is part of the structure of general history. And on the whole, much the same can be said of the historians of American law.

The chapters of this book, which have been composed over the years, constitute linked essays on overlapping and related themes. Unlike predecessors in "Anglo-American" law or legal history, they do not separate British and American legal history into "fields" as though they belonged to distinct or divergent areas of jurisprudence. Rather, they recognize and respect the interdependence observed by contemporaries. While they lean on each other for support, they can be read independently. Among issues I have not specifically addressed, that of gender may seem to call for explanation. But although the subject has certainly not stood still since *The Pursuit of Equality* was revised, I did not feel that I had anything of substance to add to the long revised chapter in the second edition of that book.

So far as possible, I have tried to report the "story" of the legal cases and issues recounted here while involving the more arcane technicalities of procedure only to the extent that they are necessary to understanding the outcome. But it was once wisely observed by Sir Henry Maine, and has often been repeated, that "law is gradually secreted in the interstices of procedure."[1] Much the same might be said of liberty. But procedure is often inseparable from substance; and the substance in such cases *is* history.

JRP
Oxford
October 14, 2008

Acknowledgments

The author wishes here to acknowledge the support of the Leverhulme Fund and the law firms of Slaughter and May (London) and generous personal support from Mr. Tim Clark; also of Getty, Meyer and Mayo (Lexington, Kentucky), for grants which have supported this research. I am also most grateful to Joyce Appleby, to my late friend Gerald Aylmer, Sir John Baker, Peter Dickson, Joshua Getzler, Daniel W. Howe, Joanna Innes, Maija Jenssen, David Seipp, Shannon Stimson, Warren Swain, Michael Thompson, and John Zvesper for comments and information on drafts in various stages (some hardly now recognizable); also to the Rare Books and Special Collections department and the Manuscript Reading Rooms of the Library of Congress, the staffs of Rhodes House Library, Oxford, the New-York Historical Society, New York Public Library, Historical Society of Pennsylvania, Harvard Law Library, Columbia Law Library, and Yale Law Library, and several others for their always generous help. I have greatly appreciated the assistance of Juliana Dresvina, Shruti Vidnyasagar, Yvonne Cornish, and Sarah Apetrei.

Earlier versions of individual chapters have been presented to seminars at Berkeley (political science), Harvard Law School, Oxford Modern History Faculty, Princeton University history department, University of Texas Law School, and Yale Law School, whose searching but generous comments have done much to improve the text. The intersecting paths of legal, political, and cultural history are strewn with traps, and my counsellors must not be held to have agreed with my views, nor are they accountable for errors that may have survived scrutiny.

I

Contract & Consent

Introduction

Reason and Custom

Time changes the face of things, origins become occluded, straight lines are bent, and in the words of W. H. Auden, ". . . History to the defeated / May say Alas! but cannot help or pardon." History, however, keeps one or two tricks up its sleeve, including the advantage of being unpredictable. A case in point is that of *Baker v. Carr,* in which, in 1962, the Supreme Court of the United States, under the leadership of Chief Justice Earl Warren, took responsibility for reverting to the first principles of the Republic, an unpredicted turn that led to the most fundamental decisions of the Warren era. The case came up from the supreme court of Tennessee, whose state constitution required the legislature after each decennial census to maintain equality of representation by redrawing electoral district boundaries. Decades of neglect to fulfill this obligation had led to gross disparities of representation between diminishing populations in the rural areas and the increasingly crowded cities. The Supreme Court saw this neglect as a constitutional violation calling for a constitutional remedy. But before that, the Court had to decide whether the issue was justiciable, that is, whether it fell within the powers assigned to the judiciary.

There was no precedent for direct federal intervention in a state's electoral system and the Court returned the case to the state judiciary. It was clear enough where this would lead. The Court was reclaiming the power to restore the original principle of the Constitution.[1] The state acted accordingly and direct federal intervention was averted.

Writing, however, had appeared on the wall. Only two years later, *Reynolds v. Sims* comprised a group which gave Warren, with an eight-to-one majority, the occasion for a direct announcement of constitutional principle. "Legislators," he declared, "represent people, not trees or acres; legislators are elected by voters, not farms or cities or economic interests." To the argument which had been made that certain interests deserved special consideration, he replied that it was "inconceivable that a State law to the effect that, in counting votes for legislators, the votes for citizens in one part of the State would be multiplied by two, or five, or ten, while votes in another area would be counted only at face value, could be constitutionally sustainable."[2] Warren's central argument was simple: as declared in *Baker v. Carr,* a constitutional violation required a constitutional remedy. That seemed clear enough. But Mr. Justice Frankfurter, joined by Justice Harlan in closely reasoned dissents, saw the problem through a more complex lens. The distribution of seats was a responsibility assigned to the legislature, not to the courts; by entering into questions of the design of electoral districts, Frankfurter argued, the Court would inevitably involve itself in partisan politics, in which it would be trapped by rival interests claiming to stand on rival interpretations of the Constitution. This insight proved to be prescient. That consideration, however, could not override the principle of political individualism on which Warren based the Court's finding. Setting aside the specially safeguarded equal representation of the states in the Senate, the Constitution acted directly on persons as individuals, not as members of groups, and derived its authority from a contract to which free individuals were supposed to have agreed at the formation of political society.

A legally binding contract must reflect the mutual understanding and intentions of the parties at the time it was made. Generations of landed and commercial transactions had made the process familiar. The principle of political contract which lay at the foundations of American government rested on the same authority; the individual wills must, of course, give their consent voluntarily, free from coercion or deceit.

The Warren Court's position thus derived from common ground with colonial Americans when they repudiated their allegiance to the king and followed by contracting to form a government of their own. But their commitment involved a paradox: when they stepped out of doors into the marketplace, town square, meetinghouse, or church, they took their part in collective, organically formed communities. But when they *theorized* about government, they perceived something different: a political society created contractually by the rational intent of independent individuals. In current psychological terms society in its political form was the creation of the human faculties of reason and will. For legal purposes the concept of will translated into intention. And the intention was to protect rights which already inhered by nature in every mature individual.

The town meeting of Concord, Massachusetts, explained the implications when it resolved on October 21, 1776: "We conceive that a Constitution in its proper idea intends a system of principles established to secure the subject in the possession and enjoyment of their rights and privileges, against any encroachment of the governing part."[3] In his brief but influential tract *Thoughts on Government,* John Adams approached the obligations of society on similar lines by distinguishing society from government; society, he explained, was from the nature of man, not from God. A curious distinction, since Adams would hardly have denied that the nature of man was from God; one had, however, to distinguish between man before and after the Fall, exonerating God from the natural consequences following from that unhappy event. The crucial point was that government was created by deliberate choice, which meant the aggregation of *individual* choices.[4] "The happiness of the individual," Adams declared, "is the end of man." It must be the individual's sense of his own condition that gave value to the efforts of society; the individual retained an unmistakable primacy of self-knowledge and self-interest. This distinctive emphasis on the individual—by which was generally meant the adult white male individual—was characteristic of the development of contractarian thought among Americans; the theme was a commonplace, repeated in innumerable tracts (though more so in secular tracts than in sermons). William Livingston, a governor of New Jersey, asserted that "governments in these states are in fact nothing more than social compacts for the mutual advantage of the individuals of whom they are composed."[5] The radicals who seized power in Pennsylvania in the spring of 1776 emphasized "the protection and security of the community" while recognizing that the community was composed of individuals. In Virginia a formulation written by George Mason and adopted by the general convention held in Williamsburg as early as May 6, 1776, declared that all men were "by nature equally free and independent, and have certain inherent rights, of which, when they enter into a state of society, they cannot by any compact deprive or divest their posterity."[6] In Massachusetts, after a draft constitution drawn up by the general assembly had been thrown out by the towns, and after a prolonged convention whose handiwork was circulated to and ratified by town meetings throughout the state, the Constitution of 1780 explained exactly how political society came into being. "The body politic," it declared, "is formed by a voluntary association of individuals; it is a social compact by which the whole people covenants with each citizen, and each with the whole people, that all shall be governed by certain laws for the common good."[7] When George Washington, as president of the Philadelphia Convention, transmitted the text of the draft Constitution to the Congress, he warded off anticipated objections by reminding the states of the principle underlying self-government: "individuals entering into society, must give up some share of liberty to preserve the rest."[8]

Universal assumptions about individual rights did not in themselves dictate the forms of the new Constitution, but they were wholly consistent with the logistics by which it would operate; Chief Justice Warren's argument would have been understood on both sides. It was no comfort to Anti-Federalists that, under the Constitution, individuals would be equal in voting power. They understood that very well. Their crucial objection to the Constitution, as they charged over and over again, was the threat of consolidation of power. The independence of the states would be swallowed into the maw of the new federal government. They trusted the states more than the federal government for the protection of the rights which they held dear and whose sources lay deep in the layered complexities of the common law.

In the chapters that follow I have begun by attempting to establish a connection between the issues outlined above and the common law of contract as it emerged as a crucial though contentious issue in seventeenth-century England. This has necessarily involved some attention to the arcane processes, and not least the writ system through which the common law operated, a system which was more familiar to the general public in that period than legal technicalities are now. While these essays are self-contained and each is devoted to a separate theme, they are unified by a common interest in the ways in which public law and legal institutions contributed to the social process. This may not appear to be a startling proposition until we reflect that most mainstream history, while quite justifiably absorbed in politics and power, and preoccupied with standards and costs of living, with land and commerce, with religious passions and conflicts, with cities and populations, with war, diplomacy, and finance, and—more recently—with families, gender, and minority interests, and other familiar themes, most of the mainstream of historical writing has been singularly neglectful of the history of law.

The neglect is periodically interrupted when spectacular state trials—the trial of the Seven Bishops in England under James II, the prosecution for seditious libel of John Peter Zenger in New York in 1735, the sensational General Warrants cases in England in the 1760s—throw normal politics into disarray and impinge on the distribution of power. But the law then seems to sink below the surface of events to run its own course without explanation of decisions which would affect the outcomes of future cases; the narrative of political or economic life offers no explanation of the law's own points of reference or criteria of judgment and why, therefore, the law could not be equated with the will or intentions of government—or, for that matter, of interests in the economy or the society which wanted the law to lean in their favor. That (for example) Lord Mansfield and his colleagues might, from the King's Bench, have nudged the common law in ways which promoted economic development and capital formation, not to mention the economic independence of women, seems to be a somewhat neglected consideration.

Law was sanctified by custom, and customs differed from one community to another. But customs frequently had to be mediated by the courts, which, from the Middle Ages down to the emergence of parliamentary sovereignty in the seventeenth to eighteenth centuries, in effect became the authoritative sources of law. And by a perverse and paradoxical irony, after the Americans had established a complex republican government under the protection of a written constitution, armed with a bill of rights which incorporated but added new provisions to the old common law, the unelected Supreme Court, by exercising the negative power over legislation, developed virtually law-making powers of its own.

The issues discussed under this heading overlap with those of a chapter devoted to the Anglo-American jury, the ancient institution on which devolved much of the responsibility for local administration. Much more than parliaments or assemblies, the jury system (though sometimes cruelly abused) integrated people with their government. The jury has always been extolled as the most basic protector of popular liberties; it is a central thesis of this chapter that the jury (at its best), so far from being separate and distinct from formal politics, is historically an organ of public opinion and thus of political representation. Such was prominently the case in 1651 when the London jury acquitted the Leveller John Lilburne; such was the case in 1984 when a London jury acquitted the civil servant Clive Ponting, who was charged under the Official Secrets Act for leaking documents concerning the Falklands War. (He argued in defense that he had leaked them to a member of Parliament, and Parliament was sovereign). These deep continuities explain the emotions aroused by proposals to "reform" the jury system; but antiquity is not self-justifying, and in many important respects, as this chapter explains, the modern jury would hardly be recognized as the same institution if brought face-to-face with its medieval ancestor. Comparable disparities have come to characterize the English and American jury systems.[9]

The explanations and clarifications which I have attempted in these essays are far from resolving the numerous problems, some of them highly technical, which surround Anglo-American legal history. But in some justification of the labors that have been expended in the cause, a beginning will have been achieved if legal issues are restored to their rightful place in the mainstream and current of Anglo-American history.

1

Where the Law Comes From

The Courts and the Making of Society

I. Law generates law, creating its own procedures, methods, unspoken assumptions which, taken as a whole, form a legal culture, in turn transfusing the political culture in which it grows. English and in time American legal cultures molded themselves primarily around variants of the common law, which Americans fashioned to reflect the needs of colonial cultures and their prevailing elites. Roman or civil law was occasionally cited in chancery courts, not so much as defining law, but rather as indicating legal principles. Lord Mansfield, who presided over the King's Bench for most of the second half of the eighteenth century, took steps to introduce equity or civil principles into many of his judgments in commercial cases. He never liked the common law so much, he said, as when it was like equity.[1] In England, other fields included the law merchant, whose precepts got absorbed by the common law during the eighteenth century, and also, notably, ecclesiastical law, of which a residue still, at the time of writing, survives in the bench of bishops in the House of Lords. This arrangement, peculiar to the relationship of the Church of England to the state, could have no constitutional equivalent under the Constitution of the United States.

The courts of high commission were swept away early in the life of the Long Parliament. Before that upheaval, the common law had been swallowing the other and lesser jurisdictions. Ecclesiastical jurisprudence covered those areas of life, such as marriages, births, deaths, and burials, which were the province of the church. The common law itself was much influenced by the canon or civil law, so that the two couldn't be easily disentangled; judges, law officers, and commentators, like the early seventeenth-century attorney general in Ireland Sir John Davies, who were steeped in civil law did not hesitate to borrow one from another.[2] At the foundations of the common law lay medieval commentaries such as those attributed to Bracton and Fleta, together with accumulations of casebooks, beginning with some three centuries of Year Books; but at its heart lay the idea of *reason.* The common law's method used both, applying reason to case history, accumulating in the process an ever growing mound of precedent. Precedent (sometimes spelled "president") was not in itself law. But it was *evidence* of law. It signaled directions even if it did not enforce conclusions. In the early seventeenth century, Sir Edward Coke, attorney general, chief justice, and later member of Parliament, injected his own brand of legal reasoning into the common law, well knowing that reason, which had always been in very high repute in the Western tradition of theology, and its cousin, philosophy, enjoyed exceptional prestige among the gifts of God to man. To understand the subsequent growth of the common law and at the same time to pursue its hold on the legal processes of England's Anglophone colonies, we must reckon with the concept of reason in those earlier generations.

Reason, then, was more than logical procedure, the ability to argue that if A was A, then B must be B: it was the faculty of the mind which was responsible for moral understanding, and could therefore control the unreasoning passions. Reason was the faculty through whose operation men and women might know the difference between right and wrong; and reason also told them why right was right and wrong, wrong. A telling Shakespearian example is the extraordinary exchange between Prospero and Ariel which may be interpreted as the moral climax of *The Tempest.* Ariel, in obedience to his master's commands, has rendered his enemies helpless, though conscious, and returns to report their abject condition; but then he touches Prospero with the affection of pity. Though understandably chagrined at receiving moral instruction from a spirit, Prospero relents: "And with my nobler reason, 'gainst my fury / Do I take part."[3] There were two distinct modes of thinking about reason, and both had political implications. For Shakespeare, reason was universal; and he was addressing audiences who understood it in that light. For his near contemporary Edward Coke, however, it was esoteric, almost cabalistic. Coke attributed to the common law a mode of reasoning that was cumulative, resulting from the application of human intellect to legal records and piles of casebooks assimilated through long years of study. It was also Coke who famously laid down that the common law could control acts of Parliament, a claim which—although there is little sign that it stood as a principle of English law—has often been held as a source for the American practice of judicial review. How, then, are we to understand Coke's rhetorical strategy? He is, of course, excluding nonlawyers from the mysteries of English law; and in the immediate political context, the most prominent nonlawyer is the Scottish Stuart King James I. To accomplish this political aim Coke draws on the immense moral prestige of reason: the design is masterly, for he implies that for legal understanding, the process of reasoning, on which all the human race relies, is available only to men of specialized training reeking of midnight oil. If this was the "reason" which Coke elsewhere described as "the life of the law" (translating the old Latin tag "Ratio est anima legis"), it seemed bound to conflict with the common law's other claim to authority, its respect for the customs of the ages.[4] Custom, it was true, was supposed to rely on reason; an unreasonable custom was not law, as Chief Justice Cushing of Massachusetts would later observe (significantly, still in force *after* the transit of power from England to its former colonies), but it could hardly be maintained that all customs were inherently reasonable. Coke's prestige did not protect his methods from his critics, notably Thomas Hobbes, who exposed these contradictions in his *Dialogue between a Philosopher and a Student of the Common Laws of England.*[5]

Law was doctrine vested in experience but untangled and brought to life by procedure. The practices of institutions will therefore form much of the subject matter with which this book is concerned. From the Middle Ages onward, individuals in their duties, obligations, and rights were, in Norma Landau's felicitous phrase, "imbricated" by law.[6] A lord or landowner held his own court, in which he heard the disputes, adjudicated the grievances of his tenants or villeins, and issued his commands. Everyone's identity, including his or her obligations and expectations, was in a sense *defined* by law. In Ben Jonson's cruel satirical comedy *Volpone,* the miserly master, "the Fox," plays a malicious joke on his avaricious heirs expectant by changing places with his servant, Mosca, "the Fly." But wearing Volpone's robes, Mosca seeks to take advantage of him. When the fraud is exposed (in a ludicrous trial scene ridiculing evidence against witches), both are severely punished, but Mosca's fate is the more severe because he has transgressed the bounds of his class in redefining his status, a maneuver subversive of society's moral order.

Traditional social order and its associated system of authority were periodically disrupted by events such as the demographic disaster of the Black Death, by baronial or royal wars as in the contest between white and red roses, and so forth; but it tended to reassert itself, and only began to crumble with the advance of commerce, the growth of towns, and the increase of the money supply in the seventeenth century. Many traces remained, and some still remain, in titles indicative of nobility or even in the word "landlord."

While different types of court presided over different spheres of jurisprudence, legal institutions of various sorts discharged many of the day-to-day offices of government, in addition to which the judges on circuit kept their ears open and acted as channels of communication to the central government. The role of the judiciary—and this is a keynote of the argument—was as much political as it was judicial, a distinction, indeed, which would not have been understood before the early seventeenth century. As we shall see, it was through complaints picked up by the visiting judges that the king's government could detect evidence of local maladministration or of economic or social discontent; while most people relied far more heavily on the courts for a hearing of their problems and grievances than on the remote and occasional sittings of parliaments. The successes of early parliaments were arguably facilitated by the habits and sense of community formed by the more frequent and regular county hearings of the royal justices. In a familiar phrase, the quarter sessions were affectionately known as the parliaments of the shires, an expression reflecting in judicial institutions a consciously representative capacity which modern constitutional theory does not adequately reflect. Together, their functions unified the administrative, instructional, and disciplinary responsibilities of government.[7] In their turn, the courts of Westminster did far more: periodically, as cases came before them, they took it into their hands to declare the legal principles on which the realm was founded.

Assisted, or hampered, by occasional interventions from Parliament, from the mid-fifteenth century the judiciary effectively controlled major areas in the development of English land law, than which nothing could be more fundamental to the character of the kingdom. Professor A. W. B. Simpson makes this point almost casually when in a discussion of the legal development of entails he refers to the judges' "nervousness about the monster they had created."[8]

Intervention by the courts to permit the conversion of an entail to fee simple seems to have been originated in Taltarum's case in 1472, when a need for judicial action was perceived to arise from the development of perpetual entails under the statute *De donis conditionalibus* of 1285 (a statute involving land inheritance). This seems to have been the first occasion on which the judges resorted to a legal fiction, a device of their own invention which had the effect desired by many landlords of barring an entail. Professor David Konig has described this step as a judicial repeal of a parliamentary statute, which he sees as a challenge in a political struggle.[9] As a result, landlords gained tax exemptions and the royal revenues suffered, while the courts had exercised an effective agency in national policy. It might, however, be more satisfactory to explain this case and its successors not as a clash between the judiciary and the legislature (to adopt American terminology), not as a conflict between institutions, but as a judicial modification of statute law in circumstances in which it was altogether more convenient for Parliament to leave the somewhat obscure technicalities to the courts. The involvement of the courts had other advantages. There might be no parliament sitting, and no one could know when or on what necessity a new parliament would be called. Judicial terms, by contrast, were formal, regular, and predictable, being at the same time independent of the sittings of parliaments.

The legal fiction sustaining the writ system was the pretense that an existing writ or form of words meant something which it had never yet been understood or intended to mean. By this invention the courts enabled themselves to amend the defects of the complex writ system itself, by which any sort of grievance or complaint had to be addressed through a particular writ appropriate to that question or "plea"; but more than that, as time went on, the courts empowered themselves to declare the law—and a declaration of the law, when the law was obscure or inapplicable to new circumstances, was indistinguishable from an act of lawmaking.[10] It is a primary consideration that throughout the centuries which we are pleased to call "the Middle Ages" a substantial element of English law flowed from the courts rather than from Parliament.

The "use" or "trust," by which an estate could be nominally transferred "in trust" into other hands while the original owner continued to enjoy the benefits of ownership and the estate avoided taxation on his death—this extraordinary invention, which kept countless properties intact, was a pure legal fiction (it was rediscovered and given a wholly new lease on life in the interests of Standard Oil, by John D. Rockefeller's lawyers in 1879). After much loss of revenue, Henry VIII moved to suppress this practice by forcing an unwilling Parliament to pass the Statute of Uses (1536). One effect was the restoration of the crown's common law rights to its great financial advantage; another was the institution of primogeniture. The Tudors, Henry VIII in particular, gave Parliament a great deal of work and thereby exalted its powers. Sir John Baker dates from these events the development of the distinction in lawmaking power between Parliament and the courts. This was a development of obvious potential significance. But it would be premature to diagnose a programmatic division of functions.

It was also by fictitious readings of conventional language that the courts enabled themselves to determine the character of an action and to make private issues public. Thus, when in another common fictitious device an injured party claimed that he (or she) had been assailed *vi et armis*—by force and arms, frequently a wholly fictitious complaint—or that property had been invaded, the effect was to allege a breach of the king's peace, thus bringing the matter into the realm of public law; the crown, if it chose, could then prosecute. The process would be judicial, the outcome political.

As Hans Prawlisch has shown, England's subjection of Ireland was accomplished in substantial measure through the agency of the courts applied through the instrumentality of the common law. Coke's objectionable but extremely able contemporary Sir John Davies, who served first as solicitor general and then, from 1606 to 1619, as attorney general in Ireland, advanced this process not only by systematically entrenching the common law but also by admixing civil or Roman law, with which he seems to have been more deeply acquainted than Coke.[11]

The English claim to Ireland rested on conquest. By contrast, England's settlers in Massachusetts held a charter from the crown, but took the precaution of keeping possession of that instrument when they sailed for American shores. The first rulers of the colony knew nothing of the doctrine of the separation of powers which their revolutionary successors regarded as the indispensable safeguard of republican government: that transition was one of the hallmarks of a revolution in government. The powerful magistracy which dominated the early years until modified by some of the elements of representation exerted state-making powers as far-reaching as any exerted by the courts in England.

II. The Founders' intention to create their own commonwealth in their own way could not have been more clearly demonstrated than in the invention of the New England town. As a unit of local government the town was much larger than the English parish, but it would be impossible to read the town meeting records without being struck by the sense they convey of a community: "our meetinghouse," "our school," "our highway," "our town."[12]

In their first attempt to lay down fundamentals for the colony, the General Court in the Body of Liberties of 1641 disposed of the relics of feudal tenure and introduced an approximation to partible land inheritance; soon afterward, the court promoted an ambitious iron-manufacturing enterprise in the Hammersmith works, for which they tapped the most advanced technology available in Germany and imported experts from England. But the greatest investment went into shipbuilding, in which Boston soon rivaled the most productive centers in the English-speaking world. Shipbuilding called for and stimulated a wide variety of special skills and promoted what later economists would call the multiplier effect. Cod fishing and whaling were internationally important activities; by mid-century New England was already becoming a maritime force in the English as well as the colonial economy. Numerous local economic enterprises were stimulated and capitalized, the towns taking responsibility for subsidizing sawmills, grist mills, and similar developments; and when Oliver Cromwell came to power in England, Massachusetts declared itself a republic—a view of its status not shared by its coreligionists in England.[13]

The common law as its seed took root in American soil had many curious and esoteric features and shared with England its most benign characteristic—its preference for liberty. In principle, this yearning to make of the very concept of law an instrument and agency of personal freedom was also England's most valuable but most controversial legacy to its colonies, on which they drew when asserting their own rights and liberties against British domination. American law, however, diverged from its English ancestry in the matter of personal freedom when the issue was slavery, and particularly slavery based on what was later called "race," and then, unable to resolve the tension, split apart within itself.

Virginia took a major step in the Americanization—or, we may say, "nativization"—of English law when, in 1705, the legislature (at that time dominated by the council) determined that property in slaves was to be of the same legal status as land, and could therefore be transmitted by inheritance.[14] Although slavery existed without, as yet, legal challenge in England, no such statute was introduced in England, nor would the common law have condoned such practice if challenged. In America, on the other hand, the southern colonies accommodated law to the dictates of a slaveholding and class-structured social order, maintained by primogeniture—which by the time of the Revolution, many planters were willing to assist Jefferson in dismantling. In marked contrast, New England preferred small properties and, after the elder son had received a double portion, partible inheritance, administered through the courts. It is a mistake to regard legal systems as dividing simply between England and the colonies. The differences between the northeast of the Continental colonies and those of the Chesapeake and southward were at least as great as between either and the domestic jurisprudence of England, and should be approached in their own historical contexts.

That the law leaned in favor of liberty was a dictum of Bracton's which did not necessarily travel abroad, but which English courts proclaimed to declare the liberty of countless villeins.[15] Villenage had declined steeply during the reign of Elizabeth I, and by the latter sixteenth century personal freedom had become the normal English status.[16] It was the same principle at work in the early formulation of codified—or, to use modern language, constitutional—law in Massachusetts, as contained in the Body of Liberties, reduced to writing (but apparently not printed) in 1641. Bondage might be imposed only on captives taken in "just warres." But also on those who might "willingly selle themselves or are solde to us"—to which were added those who were judged thereto by "Authoritie."[17] This language does not carry conviction as to its authors' liberal intentions, and African slavery existed, if only in small proportions.

However, as lifelong slavery devoid of any expectation of personal independence or freedom either for oneself or one's offspring became embedded in the labor systems of the transatlantic colonies, the benefits of the common law, of which the colonists were formally assured by the Board of

Trade in 1720,[18] became in some respects problematic for colonial planters. But divergences which severely strained common law principles began to develop critical implications when an English antislavery movement challenged the legal status of slaves in the British Isles. Although the circumstances differed widely, antislavery activists evoked the time-honored respect for liberty in 1772, in the celebrated case of *Somerset (Sommersett) v. Stewart.* James Somerset was an African slave whose owner, Charles Stewart, had brought him to England; but rightly fearing that his master intended to sell him, Somerset had run away. Stewart's agents recaptured Somerset and threw him in irons aboard a ship lying in the Thames and waiting to sail to Jamaica. Since owners of West India plantations and the more southern of the Continental colonies frequently brought their slaves with them for periods of residence in England, the issue of Somerset's legal status could clearly have far-reaching implications. Apart from the economic implications of any threat to the legitimacy of the labor force, the lifestyle of the planters was involved; men of new wealth extracted from the plantations by the labor of slaves valued the social status associated with domestic comfort and the self-satisfaction associated with the habit of command; some acquired seats in Parliament. The issue was opened when Granville Sharp, an intensely religious young High Church Anglican who devoutly believed that slavery was a sin which would bring divine retribution on the country, heard of Somerset's plight, which he seized as the opportunity for a legal challenge to the status of slavery in England. On the other hand, the West India merchants, with fortunes invested in slavery and the slave trade, were deeply concerned about the security of their property and took up Stewart's cause.

The epicenter of this challenge was to lie in the Court of King's Bench, presided over by the formidable Lord Chief Justice Mansfield; and it became Mansfield's anxious task so to construe the law as to combine justice for the individual with protection of the legal interests of the owners of this volatile form of property. The story of the action that followed has been told and retold many times, and in many variations, but the core of it can be recounted quite briefly. A witness of the kidnapping obtained a writ of habeas corpus which brought Somerset ashore and enabled his sponsors to begin proceedings against Stewart. The legal status of the action is seldom remarked on, but it is surely significant that Somerset's own name appeared on the docket: *Somerset v. Stewart.* As litigants, Somerset as plaintiff and

Stewart as defendant appeared as equals, implying a measure of procedural equality.[19] It appears that common law did not presume that the plaintiff's alleged slave status deprived him of the right to sue his master, and in a sense it recognized Somerset's humanity.

Stewart had acquired Somerset in Virginia, whose laws permitted slavery; but another country's laws could not have an effect in Britain, a conflict of laws element therefore entered into the issues; since for jurisprudential purposes, Virginia was deemed to be another country. The situation confronting Mansfield was both complicated and delicate. No records were kept, but estimates of the numbers of African servants in socially prominent English families, servants who, well-dressed like their English counterparts, are familiar figures in family group portraits of the period, vary from three thousand to fifteen thousand. Their legal status was uncomfortably described as that of "near slaves" or "slavish servants."[20] The first edition of Blackstone's *Commentaries on the Laws of England* in 1765 had adopted the "free air" doctrine that a slave became free on setting foot in England, a position he modified for the third edition to hold that "the master's right to his service may probably still continue."[21] Mansfield, who may have influenced Blackstone's revision, appears to have felt that a certain ambiguity was preferable to a general determination either way; a verdict for Stewart might be contrary to English law, while a verdict for Somerset might stimulate mass slave desertions and precipitate domestic confusion and even an imperial crisis. For familiar reasons, relations with the colonies were already under severe strain.

Lord Mansfield's intentions and motives have been the subject of much dispute. He personally detested cruelty and abuses of power and was devoid of racial antipathy. A young colored woman called Dido Belle, for whom Mansfield had an undisguised affection (observed with disapproval by the exiled ex-governor of Massachusetts, Thomas Hutchinson), was a member of his household. She was actually a daughter of Mansfield's nephew Sir John Lindsay; Mansfield provided generously for her in his will, in which he affirmed her freedom. That he should have needed to do so is substantial evidence that he did not think his decision in *Somerset* had ended slavery in England—and also that her color might prompt the suspicion that she might be mistaken for a slave. Although Somerset's case was often referred to as "The Negro case," it was not, legally speaking, about "race"—a category which had no legal meaning—and had only an oblique bearing on what would now be called race relations. This point had been established in common law some seventy years earlier, in *Smith v. Gould* (1706), in which Chief Justice Holt had bluntly dismissed the racial consideration as irrelevant: "[T]his action does not lie for a negro, no more than for any other man; for the common law takes no notice of negroes being different from other men." (In other respects, however, the case reinforced property in slaves.) In English law, then, being a Negro could not be held as definitive evidence of slave status. But in a deeper sense race was involved, since the presumption of slave status attached only to Africans or their descendants. Mansfield, fearing that a general declaration on the legal status of slavery, either one way or the other, would threaten dangerously divisive political consequences, tried by devious stratagems to persuade the parties to avert such an outcome by an out-of-court settlement. But a general declaration of principle was exactly what Granville Sharp *was* seeking. The issue between Sharp and Mansfield became highly personal. Meanwhile the West India merchants, who felt their fortunes and the prospects for future investment in this debatable form of property threatened, wanted the law defined.

The conflict of laws was easily settled. The laws of Virginia, where Stewart had acquired Somerset, and which recognized perpetual slavery, could have no power in England. The problem, then, was to define the status of slavery in the British Isles. Since the decline of villenage in the time of Elizabeth I, the subject had a ragged history; but Somerset's legal team, who all served without fees, were able to demonstrate that slavery had never been upheld under the common law. Slavery was not humanity's *natural* condition, and nothing in English or natural law could be held to make it lawful.

Stewart countered with the allegation that Somerset had deprived him of his lawful property by running away. Failing to bring about an agreement between the parties, under which one of Somerset's patrons would have bought his freedom, Lord Mansfield narrowed the issue to the validity of the "return" by Captain Knowles (master of the vessel) and Stewart to the habeas corpus. Mansfield, after having observed that the exercise of a master's power over a slave must be supported by the laws of particular countries, and "such a claim was never allowed by the Laws of England," at length concluded that the return was invalid because "no Master ever was allowed here to take a Slave by force to be sold abroad because he had deserted or for any other Reason whatever, we cannot say the Cause set forth by this Return is allowed or approved by the Laws of this Kingdom and therefore the man must be discharged."[22]

The judgment achieved Mansfield's immediate purpose: it freed Somerset; but only, it seems, because Stewart was going abroad and could not force Somerset to go with him. It did not free anyone else. But despite its technical limitation, the judgment did rest on the premise that slavery, which Mansfield, with uncharacteristic emphasis, described as "odious," was an *abnormal* condition that could only be sustained by positive law, and no positive law upholding slavery had ever existed in England. It has been observed that Lord Mansfield personally agreed with Somerset's counsel on this crucial issue for both England and its colonies.[23] It seems significant that, notwithstanding its narrow focus on the technicalities, and considerable doubts left by Mansfield's careful evasions and ambiguities, both sides interpreted the decision as being antislavery and the antislavery forces believed—and Mansfield must have suspected—but did he hope?—that they had won a famous victory. Somerset's principal counsel, Serjeant Davy, had cited from a seventeenth-century case the claim that no slave could breathe the free air of England, which would instantly set him free, language that was widely attributed to Lord Mansfield himself (from whom it would have been most improbable). Only a few years later, in *Knight v. Wedderburn* (1778), the impulse was sustained.[24] In the long run, the blow struck by Mansfield in Somerset's case resembled the action of a lever rather than a hammer. Both parties knew that the decision was never likely to be reversed.

The impairment to the legal status of slavery in the realm of England did not extend to the colonies, where it was parliamentary action that ultimately wiped slavery off the map. But the whole antislavery movement gained a momentum which carried through to the abolition of the slave trade; and there was a psychological dimension to these gains which is missed by sticking strictly to the legal arguments: Somerset himself understood the verdict in its broader sense; the news must have spread rapidly by the grapevine, encouraging slaves to take their liberty into their own hands—or legs—and, although slave kidnapping did not end in 1772, making more difficulties for slave owners.

The common law's newly confirmed inclination for liberty made its way across the ocean and resonated in New England, where in 1783 Chief Justice William Cushing of Massachusetts, having echoed the antislavery implications of Somerset, declared that in "our constitution of government all men are born free and equal." Every subject was entitled to liberty.[25] This judgment, however, could not have come from any court south of the Mason-Dixon line; American courts were remaking the law in the local image of their own social order.

The British had never been altogether comfortable when asked to base high policy on high principle. Neither British social structure nor the economic system was at stake in Somerset's case as they were in the Caribbean. English judges evidently did not feel that their powers extended to removing the legal foundations of slavery in the British Empire. It may, then, seem ironical that the might and sovereignty of Parliament, which had been invoked in the long struggle with the American colonies, had to be summoned up to abolish the slave trade in the British Empire in 1807, and slavery itself (officially, at least) throughout the empire in 1834–38. Whether this achievement would have been possible if the American revolt had failed in 1776 and the slave-owning colonies had remained within the empire is an interesting if unresolvable question. When the planters caught rumors that the abolition movement was gaining ground in Parliament, some of them began to prepare for secession from the British connection with a view to joining the United States. Nothing came of this, but if the Americans had remained within the empire one may speculate that a movement in the 1830s to abolish slavery through Parliament might have precipitated a very different American Revolution. While that must remain in the realm of speculation, there can be few aspects of a nation's life more fundamental than the difference between slavery and freedom. Parliament had declined to intervene when approached by the West India interests, and in the British Isles it was the judiciary, not Parliament, which had taken the first step to dissolve slavery's legal foundations.

These issues left a legacy which marked the sharpest possible divergence of American law from its English roots and its continuing English development. In England, slave status had no foundation in concepts of race and, though it continued to exist, was deprived of legal protection and gradually withered without being formally abolished. In America, where its legitimation was explicitly racial, and notably south of the Mason-Dixon line, slavery was maintained and protected by law. This was in all probability the most far-reaching and profound instance of the much talked-of process of the "Americanization" of the common law. It should be noted, however, that the positive law doctrine adduced by Lord Mansfield, though carefully wrapped up, did not depend on conventional common law reasoning, and did carry broader implications of the kind sought by Granville Sharp.

But the further American legacy of racial slavery was a racial caste system far more pervasive and intense than the residual if unpleasant color prejudice that survived in many quarters in British society. Americans, enjoying the freedom of access to each other described by Tocqueville's "equality of conditions," were divided by a caste system almost as impenetrable as that of the Hindus in India.

III. In the early years of George III's reign, the common law was also instrumental in protecting fundamental British liberties from the intrusion of government, thus, incidentally, validating the Whig belief that the chief danger to liberty came from the government itself. Both cases involved invasions of the private realm by government agents under the authority of a secretary of state. The first, and by reason of the principal's personality, the most famous, was that of John Wilkes, M.P. for Aylesbury, who published a satirical antigovernment newspaper, *The North Briton* (the title was a play on alleged Scottish influence on the youthful king), which the ministry regarded as seditious. In response to the allegation of No. 45, which attributed the king's speech to the influence of his mentor the Earl of Bute, the secretary of state, the Earl of Halifax, sent his agent, Wood, to ransack Wilkes's private apartments under a general warrant, which gave him power to search at random and seize anything he might find. Wilkes, along with his printers, was sent to the Tower. But Wilkes was a member of Parliament and claimed a breach of privilege as well as alleging that the general warrant was illegal. The result was *Wilkes v. Wood* (often called The Case of General Warrants, 1763), which came before Sir Charles Pratt, an old and radically minded Whig associate of Pitt, and now chief justice of the Common Pleas, who declared that the case was the most serious he had ever encountered in the whole of his practice. The government's claim threatened "the person and property of every man in the country"; the exercise of such a power by a government agent, thundered the chief justice, was "totally subversive of the liberty of the subject." The jury, thus guided, found for Wilkes, awarding heavy damages against the secretary of state both to Wilkes and to the printers who had been arrested with him. The case was widely reported in colonial newspapers, where Wilkes soon became a public figure.[26] But more was to follow.

By 1765 Pratt, now ennobled as Lord Chief Justice Camden, heard the case of *Entick v. Carrington*, which arose on a complaint of a search directed against the liberty of the press. The case, which therefore involved censorship as well as privacy, was to be of great historical importance. Camden searched in his books; but nowhere could he find support for the government's claim, nor warrant for press censorship, either in statutes or in the common law. The Licensing Act, which had expired in 1695, had not been revived. If Parliament had wanted to revive that act, it would have done so. Camden's language resounded with the voices of centuries of common law judges: "[I]f it is law, it will be found in our books; if it is not to be found there, it is not law. . . . And as for the argument of State necessity, or of a distinction that has been aimed at between State offences and others, the common law does not understand that kind of reasoning, nor do our books take notice of any such distinctions."[27] With these blows a Whig judge demolishes claims of crown (or, in modern terms, executive privilege). The principle is fundamental: governments and their agents are subject to the law. Already, after the earlier case, the House of Commons had followed the chief justice by passing a resolution declaring general warrants illegal; but in the Lords, Mansfield went further, saying that he would rule them illegal even if the House of Commons declared them legal. And Mansfield was not known for Whig principles. This remark may have passed little noticed in the general furore, but it was a remarkable reverberation of the power of the courts to override Parliament. Lord Camden meanwhile became a national hero, commemorated in portraits, pub names, and civic freedoms. Linked with his denunciation of the Declaratory Act in the House of Lords, he found a quick response across the Atlantic, where counties and cities were named for him from Maine to South Carolina. Taken together, *Wilkes v. Wood* and *Entick v. Carrington* may be considered flagship cases in the history of the liberty of the subject against governmental intrusion and in the broader history of press freedom. In the protection of the individual against what the Fourth Amendment to the American Constitution calls "unreasonable searches and seizures," they feed directly into the American Bill of Rights.[28]

The objection may be raised that the events of George III's reign cannot by ordinary historical methods be invoked to explain what had been happening in earlier centuries. But the continuity which is so unmistakable here is a continuity of which the judges are visibly aware and which they conceive it as their duty to preserve. "If it is law, it will be found in our books" was a concept that dated from a time whereof the memory of man ran not to the contrary; it is wholly compatible with Coke's concept of "perfection of reason."[29]

IV. Courts had always been busy places, buzzing with the ins and outs of local politics. The county courts were also, in a collective and cumulative sense, nationally important; for they were the scene of most of the weekly or quarterly work by which England was governed. But in order to understand their influence on the character of political life, and in America, even on the operation of the Constitution, we have to begin by unthinking two powerful modern phenomena: in Britain, the doctrine of parliamentary sovereignty; in the United States, that of the separation of powers. The modern situation in both these common law countries would have been completely unintelligible in the Middle Ages. Chief Justice Ralf de Hengham, presiding in 1305 in a case in which a serjeant (that is, a barrister) was seeking to enlighten the bench on the Statute of Westminster of 1285, admonished him with: "Ne glosez pas le statute. Nous le savon mieulx que vous car nous le feime" (Do not gloss the Statute. We understand it better than you, for we made it.).[30] This was no anomaly; counseling the crown was one of the duties as well as rights of the senior judges.

The gradual nature of the judicial response to challenges from social change arose from judges' sense of appropriateness; they spent at least six years in sorting out Slade's case, as we shall see in the next chapter, and it was not for another ten years that it appears to have been accepted as determinative.[31] The judges applied their reasoning to their accumulated legal knowledge with a basic concern to solve these problems in terms of the ethical, rather than what would now be called the economic, courses presented by social change; which is why we can say that no moral principle was sacrificed. But it would be a mistake to insist that the decision represented a choice between opposed principles, for we may doubt that such a distinction would have occurred to them. What we call economic problems *were* ethical problems; as it had been with Aquinas, so it essentially remained, that in the buying and selling of goods and services, the just price was the price most satisfactory to both contracting parties: the economic calculus is expressed in ethical language. Utilitarianism was not yet an available intellectual resource.

From time to time the habitual practices of the common law needed the attention of a diligent housekeeper. When this happened, the side opposed to change could be counted on to claim that the practices they were defending had the force of principles. On such occasions the courts addressed themselves to the problem by reaching into the common law for their arguments. This became particularly important when in the eighteenth century British merchants had established trading relations in India, where traditional procedures were liable to conflict with the needs of an expanding economy itself locked into the operations of a commercial empire. The common law assumed that the inhabitants of the realm were Christians, and that only Christians were worthy of its benefits. But the British had often done business with Muslims, and in India, merchants did not inquire as to the religious credentials of their counterparts. The credibility of a British bargain was severely tested in the case of *Omichund v. Barker*, which was heard by the King's Bench in 1744–45, a case which furnished an important example of the common law's internal resources.[32]

And it also tested the moral capability of the English judicial system. Barker was an English merchant who had swindled his Indian partner, Omichund, described in the court report as "Gentoo" (Hindu, presumably) out of the enormous sum of £7,000. When Omichund sued, defendant's counsel told the court that Omichund's case could not be heard, on the ground that English common law courts could only hear testimony sworn by Christians on the New Testament. Practice and principle were one; the tenets of the Christian religion must be upheld; many appalling consequences would follow if these fundamental principles were violated. However, the crown's interest and the political importance of the case were not lost on the government: Omichund was represented by the attorney general, Sir Dudley Ryder, and seconded by the solicitor general, William Murray—later, as Lord Chief Justice Mansfield, to preside over the bench he now addressed.

Omichund's attorneys relied on a two-pronged argument. The first, rather unusually for an English trial, called on extraterrestrial evidence: the New Testament, they argued, was not the only validation available for an oath, for the Old Testament recorded several incidents in which oaths were sworn, at least once when required by the Almighty. It would be iniquitous to suppose that oaths sworn in the Old Testament lacked power to bind their swearers. But, since Jesus had not yet appeared on earth at that time, the Christian religion could not have been an available resource. Ancient authorities including Feta and Bracton were also invoked; the medieval law seemed to have been more indulgent in these matters. In any case, what mattered was that the Hindus believed in one god, by whose name they committed their trust; in their own oaths they used a form very similar to "So help me God." This seems to have been an argument from expediency rather than principle; it implied that people who did not believe in one god might be swindled with impunity—a position the government would hardly wish to defend in other circumstances. Ryder also argued that there were precedents for the taking of non-Christian oaths, alluding to the views of Chief Justice Sir Matthew Hale in the previous century; that esteemed judge had regarded Jews as infidels but was ready to take their testimony on oath in court. The second prong was pragmatic. Britain had a commercial empire whose operations involved agreements with many non-Christian peoples. "It is of the greatest moment," the attorney general told the court, "that we should have commerce and correspondence with all mankind; trade requires it, policy requires it, and in dealings of this kind it is of the utmost consequence, that there should not be a failure of justice."[33] Judgment for Omichund; and the Court of King's Bench had demonstrated that the common law contained within itself the power to modify and adapt its own controlling principles. To modify, to adapt; but that did not mean to undo or disavow. The court could claim that it was merely extending the application of a principle more important than the formalities of procedure, for it was extending overseas the fundamental common law principle that anyone, no matter of what religion or rank, could be sure of a fair hearing and impartial justice in the king's courts. By admitting Omichund's case, the court extended the principle of equal protection to persons of non-European descent. The ruling is consistent with that of Chief Justice Holt at the beginning of the century when he had laid down that the condition of merely being a Negro could not be evidence that a man was a slave, because the common law did not recognize such distinctions.[34]

V. This then, was England, with a self-sufficient judiciary following its own procedures and assured of its own, "separate," powers. Allowing for the passage of space and time, the men who made the American Constitution were firmly convinced that a rigorous separation of the different branches or "powers" of government ascribed to distinct and separate *functions* was the only sure safeguard that a republican government could contrive against corruption or tyranny. What mattered was that the makers of law should not be entrusted with the power of either enforcing the laws or administering justice arising under them. The separate powers of legislature, executive, and judiciary should always be separately exercised, "To the end that it shall be a government of laws and not of men," concluded the declaration of rights appended to the Massachusetts Constitution of 1780.

From a point of view based on the principles and practices of the English common law, some of the American results were paradoxical. For it came about that the Supreme Court gradually acquired powers not only over the structure of the Constitution but over some of the most important aspects of American political, economic, interracial, and personal development, extending into aspects of personal intimacy far beyond anything that its founders had intended or had more than dimly envisaged. Much that had characterized the pervasive presence of the common law as administered by the senior judiciary in England flowed easily into the life of the law when that law sustained the American Constitution. Taking the historian's advantage of playing tricks with time, we can see the nature of that continuity with a clarity enhanced by some degree of historical understanding. By the mid-twentieth century, the laws which many states had passed in earlier generations were out of tune with public opinion and scientific capability, yet for reasons of religious bigotry and political ineptitude were difficult to repeal. The most intrusive of these laws dealt with such matters as contraception, abortion, and private expressions of sexuality. In the case of *Griswold v. Connecticut* the Supreme Court was invited to judge not the morals but the constitutionality of a state ban on the use of contraceptives.[35]

One way of dealing with this issue would have been to return it to the political process; was not this, after all, what the political process was for? The arguments for and against were far from novel; they could be traced to the late nineteenth century. But the Supreme Court justices may have sensed that state politicians could not be trusted to get the right answer, and determined to take the responsibility on themselves. This involved them in judicial researches through which they inferred a right to personal privacy, not from the explicit language of the Bill of Rights, but in what Justice Douglas, for the Court, styled its "penumbras and emanations." (This finding showed remarkable flexibility in a judge who always affirmed that in regard to press freedom, the First Amendment's "No law" meant neither more nor less than that—no law.) The knot was untied by the finding of a right to sexual privacy which was necessarily implied by the right to individual autonomy inherent in the Constitution, a right inhering in citizens not only of Connecticut but of the whole nation. But it solved the problem and effectively created a new constitutional law.

The next issue on the agenda was abortion, and the same doctrine soon sprang to life again in the celebrated case of *Roe v. Wade.*[36] In this case the Court overturned a state ban on contraception and introduced its own conditions, based on a division of the life of the fetus into trimesters, each with its individual qualities and in each of which the public had a different interest. These were two closely connected and prominent cases in which the Supreme Court depended on what has been styled a "decisional" right to privacy, meaning an individual's right to decide on his or her own will how to behave without intrusion by the state. The right to privacy may well be considered a reasonable inference from the First Amendment, especially in conjunction with the Third (security of the home), the Fourth (protection from "unreasonable" searches and seizures), the Fifth (against self-incrimination), and the Fourteenth (equal protection); the reasonableness of the inference depends on the established practice of the Supreme Court of construing the language of the Constitution to meet situations which the founders did not anticipate. The invention, in *Roe*, of three notional phases in the life of a fetus was a device akin to the legal fictions invented by English courts; they were no less necessary if the diverse American states were to be ruled by consistent constitutional principles. It may be an irony of history that the American system moved in this direction while the British had moved to parliamentary supremacy. But that did not detract from the fidelity of the Supreme Court to the responsibility it had created for itself to maintain at the basis of federal law a unique mixture of common law and equity.

Like the English courts of Common Pleas and King's Bench in earlier times, the American Supreme Court exercised on occasion a power to define the character of the nation: meaning that the Court could require any one of the states, or a group of them, to conform its social practices and public law to the principles of the American State as a whole—principles laid down by the Constitution. Such cases are apt to reach the Court out of intense political controversy, are well known, and call for little explanation here. The argument for present purposes, however, differs from the debates on social policy which are usually adduced. Some of the most consequential have involved the very character of the civic population. This was true of the pre–Civil War case of *Dred Scott v. Sandford,* in which Chief Justice Taney sought to put a definitive end to the controversy over slavery and its westward expansion by finding that, at the formation of the Constitution, a Negro had no rights which a white man was bound to respect, and that, in effect, nothing had since happened to change that situation.[37] Whether Taney was familiar with *Smith v. Gould* (1706), in which, as we have seen, Chief Justice Holt had ruled out the question of "race"—a term not then in its modern use—as having no bearing upon a man's legal standing, it is clear that his view envisaged a deep separation of American law from its English ancestry. Taney held this separation to have been in force by the time the Constitution was founded. But it is also clear—to cite one of many examples by which northern states moved toward abolition—from the opinion of Chief Justice Cushing of Massachusetts that this view would in fact not have stood the test of public policy in the era of the Revolution.

Notwithstanding four years of civil war, followed by the cluster of Reconstruction amendments equalizing (or affirming the equality of) all American citizens, by 1896 the Supreme Court laid down that racial segregation, imposed by one race upon the other, was consistent with the Fourteenth Amendment's promise of equal protection when the races were offered equal facilities.[38] Equal but separate. When this ruling was overturned in a different era and after two world wars, in *Brown v. Board of Education,* the Court was indulging in policy, not housekeeping.[39] White supremacists accused it of exceeding its constitutional powers, but that was not what they had said about *Plessy v. Ferguson* sixty years earlier.

Most of these cases, American and English, were widely separated both in time and in subject matter; there were some similarities, however, and the American racial cases involved issues not remote from the British cases on slavery in the British Isles. And they were remarkably consistent with each other in principle and method. Slade's case belonged to an earlier era, but appears in the light shed by these comparisons to offer a choice between Bacon's preference for domestic housekeeping and Coke's argument for developments in policy. Housekeeping would retain the traditional writ of debt to cover a contractual liability alleged by the plaintiff. Policy would insist that a contract—in the words Coke would attribute to the court—"implies an assumpsit." In either case, a contract, if it existed, was the product of the will and intent of the contracting parties. A "will" theory of contract was inseparable from the principle of legal obligation. The common law had armed itself with a theory and a method with which it could confront the future.[40]

VI. When the judicial system began to develop an English version of contract law, it needed, whether or not consciously, to work from some agreed concept of how contracts came into existence. Men and women often said things they did not, or did not fully, mean, made promises or avowals they would never keep. The underlying question was to establish precisely what type of undertaking, commitment, or promise constituted a contract enforceable at law. A valid contract could take place only when the parties to the agreement had understood each other's intentions or honestly thought they had understood them, and when these intentions related to some exchange by which each would in some way benefit. The will and intention of each party would then be committed. But the exact meaning of the commitment might still be in doubt, as in a case that ran from 1772 to 1775 in the province of New York. *Bland v. Yeomans* does not settle legal principles but is worth attention for the problems it illustrates. A landowner called John Bailey leased some land (which he held from Archibald Kennedy of New York City) for a term of years to a watchmaker, James Yeomans. Bailey later explained that he was in too much of a hurry at the time to record the original agreement in writing. It is not disputed that Bailey agreed that Yeomans might build a house on the site, which Yeomans did. But Yeomans died, not, apparently, leaving the house in his will. Bailey appears then to have occupied the house, because we now find that Elias Bland, as Yeomans's executor, claims that the lease was not executed in a form entitling Bailey to occupy the house; and further, that Bailey had conceded this point and had agreed to the drawing up of a new lease omitting that clause. So at least we are now dealing with written documents. Bailey explains that he had done this because Yeomans refused (presumably on general grounds against expansion of occupation rights), saying that this covenant ought not to have been inserted, and called it "a Roguish business." (So we have at least this record of Yeomans's opinion from before his death.) The executor now wanted the defendant, Bailey, to consent that the improvement made by adding the house be valued at the end of the term of the lease. Defendant refused, thinking this unreasonable, and contrary to the true intent of the agreement. This is the core of the problem.

The suit was taken to Chancery, because Chancery could order the fulfillment of the terms of contract. (An ordinary law court could only require repayment of the surviving debt.) The problem for the court was to determine the actual intentions of the parties when they executed the lease. Defendant claimed that the parties differed as to the terms of the lease after the agreement had been executed. The attorney general, John Tabor Kempe, for the plaintiff, replied that this argument was of no avail; this point had been settled in the House of Lords. (He did not name the case but their reference makes clear that the House of Lords would override a colonial court.) And if the defendant wanted to avail himself of the argument that the agreement had not been signed, he ought to have pleaded the Statute of Frauds and Perjuries. (Which, incidentally, had been passed in 1677 partly to correct the consequences of Slade's case by requiring written agreements for contracts in certain cases.) But he had not done that, and the contract must stand. The plaintiff's case rested on strict enforcement of contract, and when the defendant confessed the contract, the fact that it was originally unwritten is immaterial. (This comports with the common law principle, observed in Slade's case, that parol contracts have legal force.) The argument was supported by reference to Gilbert's (English) Chancery Records. It is to be observed in this connection that the fact that the case was being heard in Chancery made no difference to the common law principles of contract by which it was judged; Kempe elicited the admission from his opponent's answers that a court of equity would desire a specific performance of a contract made, the defendant being bound in conscience to fulfill his contract. Kempe also made the point that there was no conflict between law and equity, though Bailey contended that there was. (We observe that reliance on English precedents in no way detracted from, but rather assured, the pride and sense of security of freeborn Englishmen.) The essential key, however, to the legal identity of both the politically able adult male and the person whose economic standing might permit him to enter into a contract was his independence. The free man was he whose circumstances made him independent of the will of other men.

This concept, so far as it extends into practical life, implies the active presence of some element of the more general Western concept of individualism. The word "individual" with reference to a single person begins to appear in English in the first half of the seventeenth century. But by Continental standards, English development is late; no specialist knowledge is required to recognize that vital elements of individualism gave life to the art as well as much of the mercantile activity of the Renaissance in Flanders and Italy. It may at first sight seem redundant to attribute contracts to acts of will, but they do not in fact necessarily originate in the wills of those named as the contracting parties. Arranged marriages, which constituted one of the most socially important sectors of contractual activity, presume rather than proceed from the wills of the espoused.[41]

Nor does ownership of property necessarily confer on the owner genuine freedom to contract for its disposal. Entail of estates makes the owner a sort of tenant of his family's property; far from exerting an independent will, the seemingly powerful landlord is a custodian for the family in mankind's eternal vigil against the devouring force of time. We may discern glimmerings of a will theory of human action in the cult of romantic love, in which the parties are willing to enter into the contract of marriage by defying their parents or clans to satisfy their own ardor. But the fates of Paulo and Francesca, or of Romeo and Juliet, warn us of the obstacles that might be encountered in transforming a will theory of human motivation into a corresponding theory of contract.

Freedom of contract makes the individual responsible for his own economic (rather than emotional) actions, but in this the role of the law is not inevitable. Only in a society which lives by bargains and transactions does it become necessary to have laws which make the fair conduct of such transactions into matters of public interest. The law could if it chose completely ignore the arrangements of private parties. The law is not obliged to protect freely contracting individuals from the consequences of their own errors. An English judge, refusing to intervene to save the victim of a bad bargain, was to hold in 1750 that an unfair bargain was binding if freely and voluntarily entered into by the losing party; and a man is allowed by law to be a fool if he likes, said another English judge in 1876.[42] Chancellor James Kent of New York, who, admittedly, was concerned to protect the consistency of Anglo-American legal principles, made the position clear when he set down the famous *Commentaries* that traced the common law in its passage to and establishment in America: "The common law affords to every one reasonable protection against fraud in dealing, but it does not go to the romantic length of giving indemnity against the consequences of indolence and folly, or a careless indifference to the ordinary and accessible means of information. It reconciles the claims of convenience with the duties of good faith, to every extent compatible with the interests of commerce."[43]

On the other hand, the common law would not suppose that a contracting party willed his own damage; it would intervene to offer remedies against deceitful, fraudulent, or imposed contracts; these were liable to be invalidated because they could not have been true expressions of the will of the weaker party, who was not acting freely in the full understanding of the law, and would presumably not have agreed if he (sometimes she) had not been deceived, imposed upon, or coerced. To this extent the courts were committed to protecting the weak, and to ensuring that contracts and covenants conformed to consistent moral standards. If the common law's occasional compassion deserves a muted form of respect, its sentimentality was not a rule of law.

To the question, Where did law come from? any definitive answer was a metaphysical impossibility. And in American constitutional law—in its incessant search for fundamental principles, from different sources at different times—at its most metaphysical, it might be said to come from the negotiation of conflict not only between different interests but between different generations.

2

John Slade's Other Harvest

Common Law, Contract, and the American Republic

I. Ideas of contract are almost (though not quite) as old as the human activities of giving and receiving. If I give you this thing hoping or expecting that you will give me that thing, or even in return for something, that exchange is no contract; but if I give you this thing on *condition* that you give me that thing or do something for me, and you agree to the condition, there is a primitive form of contract. The essence is a promise.[1] But what constitutes a promise? And need the promise offer a reciprocal advantage? Legal advocates, philosophers, and judges had these and many other passages to negotiate before laws of contract with predictable applications had been formulated by English courts. The courts had to take their decisions case by case as they came up; there was no conscious aim, nor sense of historical direction. The law dealt with many contractual forms of agreement; these could comprehend agreement of a wide variety of unrelated types, ranging from land deals and marriage settlements to (increasingly) commercial transactions and insurance claims. English courts were not seeking the fulfillment of a social vision. Guided by practical necessity, they grappled with each case as it came to them, and by the turn of the sixteenth century, it was not so much a formal definition of contract that they had shaped, as a method for handling the problem.

Long before that, theology had its own form of contract in covenants made with God. In sixteenth-century England, Puritans began to develop the metaphor of a covenant with God as justification for their existence, and this became a dominant theme in New England, where almost every human relationship was generally held to be sanctioned by some form of covenant;

and since in Puritan usage covenant was interchangeable with contract, the idea easily assimilated itself to the political contract at the basis of society. As John Wise patiently explained in 1717, in *A Vindication of the Government of New England Churches*, people ranging freely without organized society must have come together, covenanting mutually first to form a society and then to establish a government (after having decided what form of government they wanted).[2] Wise claimed to be guided by Samuel Pufendorf, whose *De Jure Naturae et Gentium* had been translated into English in 1703, but the influence of Locke is difficult to miss—and Pufendorf had time to read Locke. Puritan theorists convinced themselves that their forebears had entered into a covenant with God, who had proved to be a tough negotiator but eventually agreed to limit the exercise of his own powers in exchange for obedience to his rules. As the eighteenth century advanced, however, secular explanations of the origin of social obligation gained at the expense of theology. In an important pamphlet in 1744, Elisha Williams cited "the celebrated Lock" and placed government firmly on secular ground.[3] It is significant that Perry Miller uses the expression "common law contract" to describe the origin of covenant.

An element of contract was manifest in agreements between a king and his people. A coronation oath could be invested with the stamp of contractual obligation, as could the (unwillingly) granted liberties of Magna Carta in 1215. Charles I was told, as his death sentence was pronounced, that he had violated his contract with his people.[4] But Charles spoke a different political language. A king, according to divine right doctrine, was God's representative, or vice-gerent, on earth; he was not invested with the right to strike bargains in the name of the Almighty; divine right did not lend itself to notions of contract. Nevertheless, the writings of Richard Hooker, the sixteenth-century theologian later invoked by John Locke as "the judicious Hooker" to give moral cover for his own more radical views, implanted in English minds the idea of an analogy between religious covenant and political obligation.[5] This was soil in which seed might flourish. But a more concrete kind of thinking based on more familiar experience was required before the idea of contract could enter into current political idiom. That was provided not by theology or philosophy but by the old, familiar, if often opaque English common law.

From the middle years of the sixteenth century the courts, from quarter session to quarter session, confronted dockets ever more crowded with essentially contractual complaints. The problem was complicated by the common law's procedure of describing grievances in terms of a battery of writs; success in court depended on pleading on the right writ for the type of case. These cases were private, not political, but if only through common usage, they opened a way for applications of contract language to the idiom of politics. The same Sir Edward Coke who wakened the sleeping giant of Magna Carta in Parliament's controversy with the early Stuarts, had earlier represented John Slade, a small farmer in Devonshire, in his complaint against Humphrey Morley, probably a local merchant. It was Coke, moreover, who wrote the first report of the case and insisted that, whatever writ was invoked, it was in essence a case of contract. The case arose from the perceived need to settle the underlying and not particularly edifying rivalry between the courts of King's Bench and Common Pleas. King's Bench had been attracting business away from Common Pleas by proving hospitable to contract cases brought on the writ of *assumpsit* in place of the conventional writ of *debt.* But although assumpsit had been in occasional use since the 1530s, its application was not firmly established. (Morley had presumably expected to be able to fend off a writ of debt, and this may have been why Slade's attorneys were tempted to the trial of assumpsit.) The battle over John Slade's modest spring harvest became a battle of writs. Apart from the reluctance of many learned men of the law to give up using the writ of debt, assumpsit itself gave rise to disagreements, principally because doubts arose as to whether it correctly described, any better than debt, the nature of the transaction that had taken place. These highly technical arguments gave little clue as to whether there might be wider issues.[6] For these we must look in the wider world beyond the courts. In fact the case was historically remarkable because of the difference in scale between the formal issues of law and the wider political and even cultural consequences of the decision.

The story begins in November 1594, when John Slade sowed his eight acres with a mixture of wheat and rye in the prospect of a spring harvest, having no reason to anticipate that he would soon make legal history. With the first shoots of spring in 1595, John made a bargain with Morley, who verbally agreed (there was no written record) to purchase the crop. This agreement, if proved, was clearly a contract; custom did not require a signed deed. The giving and taking in such unrecorded, face-to-face transactions normally took place on the spot, but this one was to be completed on the feast of St. John, at the end of June; in giving a future date for completion, this was what the law called an executory contract. But when the crop was ripe, Morley refused to fulfill his bargain. Slade, with an unsold crop of diminishing value on his hands, began an action to recover his loss by suing Morley on a writ of trespass on the case on assumpsit. The trespass meant that Morley had done him a wrong, while the assumpsit was based on Slade's claim that Morley had assumed an obligation to pay for the crop. Morley, according to Slade, was therefore in his debt for the sum agreed. But Morley replied, "Non assumpsit," meaning not necessarily that he denied having made the agreement, but that he denied that his failure to complete his bargain constituted a legal debt.

The case of *Slade v. Morley* might seem to the layman's eye like a commonplace dispute turning on at best a misunderstanding or at worst a dishonest promise, to be resolved only after debate about a legal technicality; but things are not always what they seem: Slade, a modest small farmer, was represented by the attorney general, Sir Edward Coke; and for Morley, when the case was fully argued, appeared among others the great Sir Francis Bacon. More is afoot: a high public interest grows out of a private grievance. The lawyers had seized the opportunity to fashion a case to determine points of law whose effects would extend beyond the scope of Slade's spring harvest. That more was at stake than the produce of Slade's acres was clear to the legal community. The formal issue of law was resolved in the oft-quoted words of Coke's own report (though Coke's far from limpid language demands tenacious scrutiny), beginning with the first sentence: "Every contract executory imports in itself an assumpsit."[7] The structure of this opening places contract first, verbally because conceptually. Coke does not say that every assumpsit implies a contract; he says the opposite. This meant, as regarded the facts, that the court recognized that the agreement between Slade and Morley was a type of agreement the violation of which would create an obligation of debt. If the language reflected the absence in common law of a writ or any general theory of contract, it is obvious that the courts knew a contract when they saw one. The Westminster judges had taken an important step toward creating such a theory by establishing contract as a formal obligation. It is a mistake, however, to infer that they were allying themselves with a particular interest, nor is there any reason to think of them as pursuing a social or economic agenda.

After pleadings in Sergeants Hall and Exchequer Chamber, during which all the justices at Westminster were consulted, judgment was announced on

November 9, 1602, when Chief Justice Popham effectively upheld the claim of assumpsit. But behind this battle of writs, giving interest and even a kind of belated urgency to the whole proceeding, lay the deeper issue of the management of contract in a rapidly expanding economy.[8]

Slade's case against Morley soon acquired a paradigmatic significance whose language translated with surprising rapidity into the way men argued about the foundations of the state. The case generated a literature at which both Slade and Morley would have undoubtedly been astonished. Legal scholars have wrestled with the technical complexities, from which historians have drawn different inferences. In the outcome, the Court of Common Pleas seems to have yielded to the political necessity of clearing the air rather than actually losing the legal argument. Although these arguments testify to the significance of Slade's case in the eyes of the legal profession, the present purpose is not to add to the legal debate but to pursue its more political implications, which cannot have been fully understood at the time. The dynamics of the debate would eventually cross the Atlantic.

Such a claim could not have been possible if Slade's action had stood alone, or had come earlier in the history of the action of assumpsit. The judgment, however, concluded by providing the common law with a unification of the existing contractual remedies; this is what was achieved by bringing them under the heading of this one writ of assumpsit. Chief Justice Popham's announcement in fact was not universally popular; but once it had been absorbed, the historic function of Slade's case came to be more than merely symbolic. Its contemporaries would not have so excited themselves and so extended their resources for light or trivial reasons, and the case may be taken as a catalyst for a new intellectual process—a politicization of contractual discourse. Since the lawyers had no cause to keep these matters to themselves, it seems altogether probable, especially in such a litigious community, that the discussions spilled out into taverns, markets, theatres, churches, parlors, and London's crowded streets. (The coffeehouse was not yet known.)

This development, a form of political popularization, can be traced from a fundamental contemporary assumption about human nature. Human psychology was thought to be a composition of faculties, each making its own contribution, and that of the will being a free and independent agent. This free and independent will continues to authorize human action when, nearly two centuries after Slade's case, Americans convert their political status from that of dependent colonies to independent states. On giving those states new constitutions, the colonists justify their actions in terms of individual rights. The protection of these rights was held to be the fundamental purpose and justification of the State; but the State's very existence was held by the most influential political thinkers to have derived from mutual, individual *contracts* among the people. Such contractual proceedings would underlie any form of republican government the Americans might choose, though they could not determine what form any ensuing government would take.

After their dismal experience under monarchy, it was agreed on all hands that American governments must be republican. But the term was nowhere defined. All manner of states, from Sparta and Athens in the ancient Aegean, to Venice, the Netherlands, and the Swiss confederation, could claim to be republics. James Madison, writing as Publius in *Federalist* 51, laid down as fundamental that "in republican government, the legislative authority, necessarily, predominates."[9] That was why other forms of constitutional law were required to circumscribe this predominance. But legislative power came from the English Parliament via the colonial assemblies packaged in the form of the representation of historic English communities such as shires and boroughs. American constitution makers were not wholly content with these origins. They rested their case on consent, and for them, political consent required political contract.

It must be said at once that the idea of contract was far from standing alone among the sources of republican government; nor had anyone fully worked out the logistics of this original process of contracting, which most writers took literally. The contractual basis of American constitutional law was affirmed early in the life of the Supreme Court in the case of *United States v. Isaac Williams* in which Chief Justice Oliver Ellsworth opined that Williams, who had sought to renounce his American citizenship, had no right to do so without official permission because "[a]ll members of the civil community are bound to each other by compact. . . . One of the parties to this compact cannot absolve it by his own act."[10] This was no mere abstraction. The principle of contract was familiar from the transactions of the market to every man and woman who bought or sold or rented land or goods or services, and the law was based on the assumption that contracting parties acted from free, independent, and individual wills. All this despite the apparent anomaly that, at the time of *Slade v. Morley*, there was as yet no general theory either on the law of contract or in linking contract to the state; essential ingredients were only beginning to come together.

Any connection between this local English lawsuit and the principles that would later guide American constitution makers may seem tenuous and remote. But eventually the connection leads toward the particular kind of republican theory which begins with the individual's sovereignty over his own person (a male attribute); on this basis, free and equal individuals were thought to have acted independently but in unison in creating political society, and thence establishing a government. When that end was reached, the gleam of a connecting thread between Westminster and Philadelphia may be faintly glimpsed.

The *Slade* judges were not planning a political coup. However, the clarification of the availability of assumpsit must have made a sensible difference; one economic consequence was to make executory contracts safer for the major risk taker in these transactions. For an expanding and increasingly mercantile economy this was a significant shift of balance. The value, however, was only incidental to the immediate contest.

II. Professor A. W. B. Simpson credits contemporary critics with perceiving the judgment as "a deliberate judicial change of law." From the point of view of political theory, it is equally important that this "change of law" did not come down from the hands of Parliament: it had taken place entirely within the judicial system. It would be anachronistic to regard such judicial lawmaking as fulfilling a calculated judicial agenda. If such changes in the legal regime were needed, where else were they to come from than the courts? Elizabeth notoriously disliked parliaments and in her later years avoided summoning them whenever possible. The institutional tension became acute; neither private litigants nor wider national interests could afford to await the pleasure of a crotchety and aging queen. As for the courts, in their own way they were in their element. If, in "finding" law where none was known to exist, they were essentially making law, it was procedure with which they were quite at home. The common law through its own internal processes had administered the "uses" which protected the interests of landowners often at the expense of the crown, had made carriers responsible for the safety of goods in their charge, had generally raised the level of responsibility for cures, repairs, and services, and in 1602 produced what was in essential ways an already mature law of contract.[11] It should be noted, however, that common law courts refused to enforce uses, which were administered instead by chancery, church courts, star chamber, or exchequer.[12]

The "internalist" or self-generating common law has often been seen by lawyers as one of its most endearing features. Yet, except by specialists in legal history, its constitutional significance is very commonly neglected. Slade's case would be worth its place in the literature as a leading example of the internalist principle. The technicalities on which the arguments rested, which have not here been described in all their detail, were not trivial; in fact the outcome, with all its economic and social implications, turned on them; but the result, having been reached, led far beyond them.

One singular feature of English law was that it was largely incomprehensible to the common people. In spite of its widespread ramifications, its proceedings were recorded in medieval Latinized French. The common law was inaccessible to common men, and indeed, as Coke was at such pains to insist, to anyone who lacked legal training. It is hardly surprising that James I, a Scot with no background in English law, was among those who wanted to see the law simplified. So did many of the common people whom it affected.

These obscure procedures and their esoteric language did not enhance public affection for the legal profession or "pettifoggers." Theatregoers, who were much more familiar with legal themes than they are now, must have responded to Hamlet (and Shakespeare spoke from personal experience) when he satirized the lawyer's pedantries: "Where be his quiddities now, his quillities, his cases, his tenures, and his tricks?"[13] And paradoxically, this obscure legal methodology, by establishing its own institutional separateness, merges almost imperceptibly into the more recent concept of legal "autonomy." For the lawyers were carrying on, in a barely accessible private language, debates which would affect the kingdom's future. In this light, legal autonomy has enjoyed a very long life, and this contributed to the assurance with which the judges went about their traditional business; but these occasional tensions do not constitute reason enough for regarding the judiciary as committed to an agenda for the extension or perpetuation of their own power, or for anticipating a power struggle with either crown or

Parliament. No sectional interest claimed the common law of England for itself. The courts mediated the cases that came before them with an assurance born of their schooling and their books.

No parliamentary initiative had been necessary to give the country, or subsequently its colonies, an adequate law of contract. The common law's internal self-sufficiency was an essential, well understood if not entirely unchallenged element of its power. The questions that were being asked in the early years of the seventeenth century called forth expressions of the thought of its practitioners and exponents which did not appear in the case reports, but were never more eloquently expressed than in 1615 by Sir John Davies, formerly attorney general in Ireland. Prefacing his *Irish Reports*, Davies wrote that the law was "like a silk-worm 'that formeth her own web out of herself' only." In the same preface, Davies also gives serene expression to the English lawyer's sense of the law's permanence and supremacy. "The customary laws of England . . . doth far exceed our written laws, namely our statutes . . . that when our parliament have altered or changed any fundamental points of the common law, those alterations have been found by experience to be so inconvenient . . . that the common law has in effect been restored again."[14] The connotation of the word "inconvenient" in legal language was much stronger than it is now, referring to some fatal inconsistency which might deprive the law of its authority. It was the duty of the courts to avoid that sort of distortion, and it was also their duty to engage in the work of "restoration" to which Davies referred.

Davies's greater colleague Sir Edward Coke develops the same theme: "[T]he common law is that which was in England before any statute was enacted. It was grounded on the general customs of the realm; it includes in it the law of God, and the customs of the realm. It is founded upon reason, it is the perfection of reason, acquired by long study and experience, and refined by learned men in all ages."[15] The keynote of the law, its essence, was reason; Coke later insisting that the common law was "the absolute perfection of reason."[16] But Coke's concept was of a specialized "artificial reason" only to be "acquired by long study"; it was remote from the common man's mode of thought.

Contract's peculiar leverage on the English legal system was the gift of the common law itself, acting on private individuals, unwinding its own thread. It was to exert its subtle influences on a wider constituency, but that was to be for the future.

This further strand to be unraveled from the silkworm will here be called the *will theory*, which is implicit in the concept of contract. But to avoid confusion it should be distinguished from the formal theory of the same designation, which historians have discerned taking root in the later eighteenth century, and maturing by the mid-nineteenth. This theory, much older in its early formulation than the English common law, could be traced to the *Institutes* of Justinian. It provided a methodology for ascertaining the legal consequences of an agreement, but it might for present purposes be better renamed as an *intent theory*.[17] Justinian insisted that to make a contract, the intentions of the parties must match; agreement, a meeting of minds, was essential, not mere promise, and each party's agreement must be voluntary. This principle, which may be said to have been rediscovered by Lord Mansfield, who presided over the King's Bench from 1756 to 1788, did not supersede the will theory but incorporated it; the original, independent will was the force that drove the agreement.

The will, or newly named intent, theory was in frequent use, and all too frequently gave rise to problems of interpretation. This happened whenever the courts had to decide the meaning of an actual testamentary will in cases where the language led to contradictory applications or consequences which the testator could not have meant or even where certain formalities had been omitted. In these cases, Mansfield attached importance, wherever possible, to the express intention of the testator. In disputes over contracts, which often involved questions of what the parties had thought themselves to be doing, the same principle attributed all the legal consequences and implications of an agreement to the mutually understood intentions of the parties at the time it was signed. This might seem simple enough; neither side was free to change his mind about the original meaning of the words; but the words were not always self-explanatory, nor could it always be certain that both parties had understood the written document in the same sense. One party might now say, "When I said that, I didn't mean it in the sense you are now giving to it." Or, throwing more obscurity into the situation, "That is not what I would have meant if I had known the meaning, or consequences, which would be imputed to it." The deception practiced by Morley on Slade had probably been a consequence of a speculation on "futures," and Morley's verbal agreement with Slade may have been associated with a silent mental reservation to allow for the flux of the market. According to the doctrine of will or intent, the court must cut through all this occlusion and get at the first, mutual intent without which there could have been no agreement. But in Slade's case this might well have meant relying on what Slade had understood Morley to mean. (This does not impair the theory, since Morley must have known the meaning in Slade's mind. Obviously, Slade would not otherwise have made the contract at all; and Morley's intent to deceive, if known, would have lost him the case.) A century and a half later, however, the principle of intent or will seems to have been understood in relation to the increasing number of disputes arising in commercial agreements made when long distances separated the contracting parties in time and space. In a rather British way, practice preceded doctrine, in a manner not out of keeping with common law jurisprudence.

This was common law in its true element. The courts behaved in much the same ways on either side of the Atlantic; a characteristic and well-documented example from late colonial New York demonstrates similar principles in the colonies as in England. In 1772 *Bland v. Yeomans* came before the province's Court of Chancery (but proceeding on common law principles).[18] James Yeomans, a watchmaker, had built a house on land leased to him by John Bailey, who, after the former's death, sought to reclaim possession by challenging Yeomans's right to build under the original agreement. That agreement, though not signed at the time, was accepted as valid by the original parties because it represented their mutual intent. Here was the will or intent theory in full flower; but the problem for the court, some years later, was to determine what exactly the contracting parties, one of whom was now dead, had agreed on when they appeared to have been in agreement. (It may have been because one of the original parties was dead that the case went to Chancery). The attorney general of New York, John Tabor Kempe, relying on a settlement in the House of Lords, impressed on the court that the issue was to determine that point of mutual intention; his frequent citations of English cases from collected reports demonstrate that where differences of opinion or recollection had developed, abstract reason alone did not suffice: specific, preexisting rules of procedure must be applied in determining the parties' will. But that was the problem. The attorney's notes unfortunately do not give us the court's answer; this case history only demonstrated the difficulties of getting at the parties' intention in a particular situation. A more fundamental principle sustained the legal argument and depended on a common understanding: that when the original intention had been established, it would be binding because it was the voluntary product of a meeting of equal, uncoerced wills. This is the original and better-called will theory, a philosophical principle that makes an agreement a contract. The principle might seem obvious, but its applications were not. One party to a property negotiation frequently possessed more information than the other, or more time, or, having more choices, was better placed in bargaining power. (These things have changed very little, though they are subject to more intense legislative regulation.) But that was where the essence lay: in a hypothetical equality of bargaining power. Each side must be equally free to refuse.

Markets and consequently routine contractual obligations were even older than the common law; their legacy survives in such English place-names as Chipping Norton, Chipping Camden, Cheapside, and Chepstow (compare with the anglicized Danish Copenhagen, meaning "market harbor"). Since the thirteenth century (and in all probability, since Anglo-Saxon times), English law had permitted free men to enter into their own contracts in dealings about land or goods.[19]

The most important type of contract open to them was marriage, but this was the province of the ecclesiastical law of the church. The principle was the same: the individual was free to marry or to refrain, but not to vary the meaning of his or her mutual contract. This gradual transition to the will principle from contracts controlled by feudal status reflected the emerging significance of the expression of individuality. Every transaction was based on a presumption (once again) of the equality of each personal will. This, the only true equality, had acquired respectable sanction since the first quarter of the seventeenth century from the powerful influence of Hugo Grotius, whose great work, *The Laws of War and Peace*, appeared in 1625 and, written in Latin, was available to all educated Europe. Not only in knowledge of the facts but in freedom of choice, he said, "there ought to be a kind of equality between the contracting parties."[20] Grotius was one of the most powerful influences in breaking the ground for the rationalist style of systematic thought that we associate with the idea of Enlightenment, comparable in jurisprudence with Selden and Hobbes, and with Descartes and Spinosa in philosophy. For many reasons besides his influence on the essential necessity of fidelity to contracts, Grotius, as his thought sank in, became the leading external influence on the formation of Whig thought in England.[21]

At the time of Slade's case, although contract was an old custom, the problem of finding a newly effective legal application was on many minds besides those of Slade, Morley, and their advocates. Very soon afterward, ideas of contract became an idiom, escaping from the pleadings and technicalities of the courts into the wider discourses of English politics and social relations. Slade's case did not work in intellectual isolation; but that long-drawn-out lawsuit, surrounded by controversy, dramatized the issue as no previous event or treatise had done. The connection is too close for pure accident. Whatever the merits of different writs, it became clear in the next few years that in 1602 a corner had been turned.

It was a turning, as we have seen, that led into early Jacobean London. The theatre, which lived by public goodwill and intelligent appreciation, could hold an audience by nod-and-wink references to events and issues in the public eye; and in such a litigious society it was to be expected that legal themes and terminology would feature in knowledgeable dialogues. In the theatrical world, revenge tragedies were always popular; and *Hamlet,* as it happened, was written and first staged during the Slade arguments. Like much drama of the period, the play conveys direct comment on legal themes, all of it expressing some degree of discontent. In his most famous monologue, Hamlet instances "the law's delay" as one of the burdens that might lead to suicide.[22] In the graveyard scene, Shakespeare catches popular resentment about the law's esoteric language and arcane procedures from the viewpoint, first of the unlettered laborers, and then of the educated aristocracy. The gravedigger gets his technical terms wrong ("But is this law?" "Ay, marry is't; crowner's quest law"; i.e., coroner's inquest law), no doubt arousing educated laughter in the seated galleries of The Globe;[23] but the sardonic realism of his social comments would not have escaped them either. (What a shame it is that great folks are at liberty to drown themselves and still have Christian burial while us little folks are condemned.) Shakespeare's absorption with legal terms takes a different course in the sonnets. The tone now is a blend of passion with touches (depending on the subject addressed) of a melancholy irony. The method was a metaphorical application of legal technicalities to do with the possession, or, significantly, the leasing out, of landed property to the theme of personal, if not erotic love.[24] Shakespeare read as much law as could be found, and he certainly spent time in the law courts. (The time by boat from Southwark to Westminster was probably shorter than it is now by bus.)

But Shakespeare was far from being alone. Only a few years later, Ben Jonson's use of legal terms and themes was even more insistent; he differed when, as in *The Alchemist*, he shaped his plots out of shady characters who employed legal terminology in the course of their business. (The ironic comment is thus supplied by the audience, who see that the characters are rogues.) It is all the more interesting that Jonson introduces into the dialogue of *The Alchemist*, which was registered in October 1610, a direct reference to the most recent and most technical theme of legal debate—the very theme which had been at the center of Slade's case. Subtle, the alchemist, is hesitating about a contract (now a prominent subject for satirical comment) with other characters of dubious repute:

> Face: I am sorry
> I ere imbarqued my selfe, in such a businesse.
> Dapper: Nay, good sir. He did call you.
> Face: Will he take, then?
> Subtle: First, heare me—
> Face: Not a syllable, lesse you take.
> Subtle: Pray ye, sir—
> Face: Upon no terms, but an assumpsit.
> Subtle: Your humor must be law.[25]

Significantly, this esoteric common law writ requires no explanation for the London audience. In his later play *The Staple of News* (1626), Jonson builds much of the action around law and familiar abuses of law. Other cultural indications of an interest in contractual relations even occurred during the witch craze, which was fermenting throughout Jonson's time, and the language of contract contributed to the increasingly popular notion that witches entered into contracts or compacts with the devil, or with his agents in the form of other evil spirits. In a world at least as full of evil as of good, such alarming possibilities had taken shape in anxious minds for years, but with much more prominence on the Continent; in 1604 they took legal shape for the first time in England with the passage of the statute which made it a felony, among other things, to make a compact with any evil spirit.[26]

This Act followed the accession of James VI of Scotland and I of England. Soon afterward, Shakespeare composed his Scottish tragedy, *Macbeth*.[27] In a complex but significant coded message, the plot cleared the air of any taint of usurped lineage by exhibiting the tyrant's destruction and including a flattering prophecy of Scotland's royal future; but at the same time it hinted at the fate of a king who attempted to rule without the law. The role of witchcraft, whereby the protagonist colluded with the Weird Sisters, was instrumental in Macbeth's self-induced fate. For King James and his contemporaries, as Sir Frank Kermode has pointed out, the Weird Sisters were not mere fantasies, and a man's decision to deal with—or in other language, to enter into compact with—the forces of evil belonged to life and not to fairy tales.[28] Meanwhile, Christopher Marlowe had earlier created the classic English version of the popular story of Faust's contract with Mephastophilis. Contract as an act of free will was also central to Jonson's version of the Faust theme.[29]

It seems wholly in keeping with this high level of popular interest not only in litigation in general but in current common law usage that the idea of contract should have entered into the discourse of politics, not as a distant metaphor but as a concrete statement of a legally binding obligation. "Heightened popular consciousness of contractual ways of thinking," Luke Wilson aptly surmises, created the "background noise" in the pursuits of "lawyers, law students, justices, parliamentarians, playwrights, and merchants."[30] Political ideals intersected with popular theatrical culture in *The Tempest,* Shakespeare's last play, which was first staged in 1612—actually in the Middle Temple, and using for a stage the great table which still stands in the dining hall. The plot lands the characters on an idyllic, nameless island, circumstances which gave Shakespeare the opportunity to give an old courtier, Gonzalo, the expression of a utopian vision (a presumed comment on More's *Utopia* as too good for human nature). Subjected from the sidelines to cynical comment from members of the Neapolitan court, Gonzalo pronounces his ban on the sources of corruption—learning, commerce, feudal relics and all their works:

> No name of magistrate;
> Letters should not be known; riches, poverty,
> And use of service, none; contract, succession,
> Bourn, bound of land, tilthe, vineyard, none;

And later he crowns it all with "No sovereignty."[31]

Contract and titles to land were inimical to harmony and goodwill. But Gonzalo by this time was a little late for English politics; the language of contract had entered into the controversy between the parliamentary opposition and James I—an issue involving the fundamental character of the English monarchy. The issue was squarely put before the court and the people when, in February 1609, Sir George Carey raised the stakes in the debate on the prerogative by introducing in the House of Commons the question of whether the monarch's relation to his people was a contract, binding the king as much as the people.[32] It was not a theme which a divine right monarch was likely to regard as a suitable topic for debate among his subjects. James probably appreciated it no better when one speaker likened the relationship to a contract of marriage.

Such language had not been heard when Elizabeth was on the throne. But this was the year in which began the negotiations between the Commons and the court over a proposed agreement to define the character of the monarchy: the king would renounce certain prerogative rights to revenues, the Commons would vote the supplies the king desired. Lord Salisbury introduced a well-drafted settlement which he called "The Great Contract," a designation the more striking in that it came from the court, not from Parliament. By July 1610 Sir Edwin Sandys, returning to the theme, hoped for "a happy resolution of the contract, which is not a private contract, but with the whole kingdom."[33] Such an agreement would have impaired James's successors' claims to divine right and would therefore have permanently affected the character of the English monarchy. Negotiations dragged on while debates sounded out higher principles. By November the whole negotiation had failed.

But King James had not been able to keep the concept of contract out of the language of politics. His son, no more disposed to conduct negotiations with the people's representatives, reaped the consequences. Ideas of contract as the binding and legitimating sanction to political relationships were revived in several forms by the pamphleteers of the 1640s. In the influential work of Henry Parker, Parliament took its place as the agency of the people's consent, but Parker was not an advocate of the individualizing basis of political obligation; for him the consenting agent was always communal. Philip Hunton came closer to political individualism by arguing that moral obligation is structured by the human will; more radically, he tried to superimpose a contractarian theory of the justification of the state onto an Aristotelian constitution.[34] All of this implied an interest in legitimacy through contract; none of it could be said to have anticipated Thomas Hobbes.

In contrast to his rivals, Hobbes based the commonwealth on the will of the individuals—or rather, on the willing submission of those wills—who until that moment were ranging about, predatory but apprehensive, in a state of nature. Here was true evidence of equality: all men were equally vulnerable and equally subject to fear. That was the great enemy which civil society was designed to overcome. The process of creating civil society and establishing sovereign authority involved two steps. By the first, the people put their relationship with each other, and created the state, on a contractual basis; by the second, they conferred their natural right of self-rule on the sovereign.[35]

Their mutual agreement, first to form a commonwealth, and then, collectively, to entrust absolute power to an individual or (less likely, one feels) to a corporate body, but in both cases to a sovereign, was an upheaval in the application of contract. The aim was simply to create a legitimate basis for sovereignty in some form of consent; but it was vital to Hobbes's thesis that the sovereign (as with Bodin) should be free of legal constraints; the sovereign made no covenant with the people. He could not be called to account. But contract, which authorized the original consent of the people to forming civil society, was fundamental: it lay at the basis of the original act of state formation.

Having first to define his concept of contract for the ordinary reader without legal training, Hobbes used the language of everyday experience: "buying and selling with ready money, or the exchange of goods, or lands."[36] That was how people understood contract and that was the example Hobbes offered them. This account has recently been described as "ostensibly" based on the common law, but a deeper debt is traceable to Christopher St. German's account in *Doctor and Student,* published in the 1520s.[37] The question of attribution has some bearing on the present argument. Hobbes undoubtedly knew *Doctor and Student,* a fundamental text for anyone writing about law, to which he alluded in the 1660s; and there is no need to doubt that he bore it in mind when writing *Leviathan* (working in exile, he may not have had a copy to hand); but there are still stronger reasons to think that he first became conscious of the issue of contract as a young man, and from recent experience rather than from an already antique text. His student years at Magdalen Hall, Oxford, coincided with the ferment which politicized contract just after Slade's case. Moreover, his definition of contract took care to explain executory contract, which had surfaced in that case;[38] time might pass before the fulfillment of the terms, he said, but if that point was understood, there need be no disagreement about completion. The likelihood that Hobbes had in mind the practical working of the common law as known to his contemporaries rather than St. German's much earlier tract is enhanced by analysis of the order in which he states the objects of contracts. Buying and selling goods with money takes precedence over transactions in land; whereas St. German puts land first and refers mainly to land transactions, as was the experience of his day. It is unlikely that Hobbes would have reversed St. German's order, and done so without explanation, if St. German's earlier book had lain open on his desk. Hobbes does not introduce the common law of contract by way of mere illustration or analogy; it is the substance of his argument; and if we are prepared to define as citizens those who have rights to give up or withhold, Hobbes is using the legal principles of contract to define the basic condition of citizenship in the commonwealth.

Whatever form they might assume, contracts of government had traditionally been collective. The people, or defined groups of people, had made a binding agreement with a ruler through chosen representatives or "attorneys."[39] In the first of all such recorded transactions, as reported in Genesis, the Lord made his covenant first with Abraham, and through him with the people of Israel.[40] But this was hardly a prototype for secular government. It was to be perpetual, it was to be obligatory, but in no real sense could it be called voluntary. Nor could any act of faith make of it an agreement between equals. In Europe, the Protestant Reformation had, earlier in the sixteenth century, revived ideas of religious covenant. For Hooker, a divine covenant may have served as a sort of Platonic prototype for human government. The Puritan saints, arrived safely in New England, expressed themselves in archetypal language at Salem in 1629: "We Covenant with the Lord and one with another, and doe bynd ourselves in the presence of God, to walke together in all his waies, according as he is pleased to reveale himself unto us in his Blessed word of truth."[41] This was clearly both individual and voluntary; but it seems to have been based on the previous existence of civil government, which was in fact a general characteristic of covenants ecclesiastical. And by 1629 it takes its stand as a salient example of the recent generalization of ideas of contract. Individuals had assented, but individual wills were absorbed in and subordinated to the group.[42]

It was Hobbes who adapted the idea of contract to gather up the wills of a random multitude of individuals voluntarily collected into a moral whole to form an ecclesiastical and civil government. Individual rights did not cease to exist, but they lost their operational value, to repose in the supreme authority of the sovereign; at the very least, no civil authority existed to which a plaintiff could appeal.

Covenants or contracts were now at large. Locke, upward of thirty years later, also defines obligational relationships as contracts, the foremost being that of husband and wife. Marriage is a contract, but also a sacrament; still more, it is an intensely private relationship, involving many facets beyond the scope of law. Locke, then, could use the concept of contract to convey more than what the law would enforce.

But there is also a fundamental political issue in which he follows Hobbes, though with differences of tone and emphasis. Of the original coming together of the people to form a social and political order, he speaks of "compact." According to Cowell's law dictionary, *The Interpreter*, first published in 1607, compact and contract were interchangeable expressions, the one defining the other. More recently, probably since the eighteenth century, contract has come to suggest a more formal and legally defined relationship.[43]

But Hobbes, who was quite inventive enough to make words do what he wanted, had also given them the same meaning: "[W]hen a multitude of individuals come together to form a commonwealth, they covenant to let the will of one person represent and stand for the will of all."[44] Locke's intention is as plain as with Hobbes: the people—meaning adult men, no doubt—who enter into the first compact, the compact of society, do so as free individuals possessed of equal wills.[45] Their use of the concept makes it clear that Hobbes and Locke were fully aware that they were employing a will theory of contract, and imported that theory into the foundations of the state. This development was by no means entirely new; it is, however, much more explicit than the idea of consent in the original formation of a kingdom or commonwealth than had been envisaged by Sir Thomas Smith in the reign of Elizabeth I.[46] Later utilitarians would claim Hobbes as a predecessor; but his authoritarian system was not one that liberal republicans would wish to be made responsible for. Allowing for the contractual origins of the Hobbesian commonwealth, it was Locke rather than Hobbes whose individualist principle found its way into the strand of political thought which flourished in the American colonies, to become one of the philosophical foundations of the Republic.

Both in his self-acknowledged and widely read *Essay Concerning Human Understanding* and in his long-unacknowledged *Two Treatises of Government*, John Locke maintained a consistent commitment to the principle of the adult male individual's sovereignty over himself. Without depriving others of their rightful dues, individuals were entitled to live for their own sakes.[47]

Although Locke shared with Hobbes a figurative dependence on a primary state of nature, he did not regard men in that condition as so impoverished, brutalized, and threatened that they survived, if at all, in perpetual fear for their lives. That more irenic turn justified Lockeian man in claiming that government, which he or his forebears had created, existed for his own benefit and that of his contemporaries; and that by the same token he was entitled to make demands on government, judge its performance, and call it to account in a manner not available to his Hobbesian predecessor. He could in fact claim that government existed by virtue of a contract of which the people remained the judges.[48] And in 1776 that is what Lockeian man did in the American colonies.

III. Behind that event lay a combination of the political and the ideological strands which gave unity to the Anglo-American Whig tradition. The tradition had older origins than its Whig name; it had not originated in the Glorious Revolution, but that crisis brought the issues out with an extreme prominence which colored all subsequent colonial attitudes. The abrupt departure of James II, which the Convention Parliament chose to construe as an abdication, gave rise to a renewal of the contentious debates on whether the English monarchy reigned by virtue of an original contract. Several Whig members endorsed contract theory in the debate of January 28, 1689, in which Sir Robert Howard declared, "The constitution of our government is actually grounded upon pact and covenant with the people." But they encountered much Tory and Church of England opposition, and in the interests of unity, they abandoned their attempt to leave their mark on the Bill of Rights; that charter turns away from the formalistic road, making no reference to a contract between monarch and people. England was too congested with relics of feudal obligations, of complex and ancient land tenures, of corporate privileges, guilds, antique institutions, and local customs to accommodate such a radical philosophy of politics. And so official

English history passed on its triumphal course with barely a nod toward the theory of an original contract of government. To this there was, however, an important exception to be noticed in a moment.

It would be a mistake to ignore Locke's wider intellectual legacy. In the mid-eighteenth century Sir Jeffrey Gilbert, Lord Chief Baron, wrote a treatise on the law of evidence whose epistemology was permeated with Lockeian ideas.[49] A negative but cogent indication of the penetration of Locke's theme on the origin of government was evident if only in Gilbert's skepticism of social contracts for which all the evidence rested on memory. Lack of documentation had, it seems, not previously been considered a defect in the theory. Whig doctrine survived to achieve its most lasting success through the historians and publicists who succeeded in attaching contract theory to their justifications of the Glorious Revolution, with which they also associated Locke's *Second Treatise*. (Until Peter Laslett proved the earlier dating for the composition of the *Two Treatises*, the conventional date of publication in 1690 gave plausible reasons for believing that Locke had written to justify the revolution.)

Apart from Locke himself, the most influential medium of transmission took shape in the polemical writings of John Trenchard and Thomas Gordon, who attracted much attention through the years 1720–23 with a long series of epistolary publications under the title *Cato's Letters*.[50] This literary eruption was sparked by the bursting of the South Sea Bubble. The government's role in that affair convinced the authors that the country's moral foundations were seriously threatened by the mixture of official corruption, authoritarian politics, and ecclesiastical privilege fostered by Walpole's administration; they discharged batteries of old Whig arguments, among them the concept, or myth, of the original contract. Cato, whose authors made no claim to originality, derived his principles from Locke's moral psychology; the basis of the state's authority was the consent of the independent individual. Cato took it as common knowledge that men had entered voluntarily into society from a previous state of nature to secure certain protections and improvements. "That Right which, in the State of Nature, every Man had, of repelling and revenging injustice . . . is transferred to the Magistrate, when Political Societies are formed, and Magistracy established" was one of many statements to this effect.[51]

The state of nature was no mere figure of speech; it progressed from the language of political philosophy only a year or so before Trenchard and Gordon got to work, to gain alarming credibility and wide readership in Daniel Defoe's epic, *Robinson Crusoe*. Alone, lacking tools, and with a diminishing supply of gunpowder, Crusoe described himself as reduced to "a meer State of Nature."[52] Soon afterward, on discovering cannibalistic savages on the island, Crusoe is reduced to a fearful condition more resembling the state of nature as seen by Hobbes. The language of political philosophers had clearly penetrated into public circles and literary speech.

Naturally enough, it had also penetrated into legal discourse. The government's most effective way of inculcating both doctrine and policy into the people was to be heard at the opening of the assizes throughout the country, when the judge, who represented the nation's government in London, issued a charge to the grand jury. The formal purpose of the charge was to instruct the grand jurors in their duties under the law. But this was often interpreted to involve indoctrination in the principles on which English government rested. Very soon after the Glorious Revolution, in 1690, the Earl of Stamford told the Leicester grand jury that the monarchy was not of "meer divine right but of human consent." Men were by nature equal, and government could only be established by consent, express or implied. Deep into the following century, and no doubt in response to Jacobite rumblings, the theme of contractual consent appeared again at the beginning of grand jury charges.[53] Thus the Westminster grand jury will not have been surprised to hear in 1728 that the origin of government was in contract—followed by a long lecture on the Whig provenance of ancient and medieval history. These charges insistently repeated the theme of contractually derived government; from the judge the message passed to the substantial landowners and merchants who formed the grand jury, and from them throughout the county.[54] In this sense, ideas of contract can certainly be said to have made their way into the official record known as "history."

On its home territory, the wider claims of the old commonwealth theme made little impression outside the most radical wing of old Whigs; but it was otherwise in the colonies. To understand this we need to grasp experienced reality before ideology. Although colonial societies were too various and too subtly differentiated to be described under one character, they had in common certain nascent republican characteristics; of the far-flung Hanoverian dominions, the American colonists were in their social character the least suited to be subjects of the more authoritarian powers of European monarchy. One feature ingrained in their character was a psychological susceptibility to threats of corruption, moral degeneracy, or governmental intrusions, which they readily perceived as portents of intended tyranny. Much of Cato's argument was concerned with the needs of dissenters from the Church of England, but in Lockeian strains he called readers' attention again and again to individual responsibility. These arguments, directed against the creeping threat of corruption, and borne in repeated reprintings in England and reproductions throughout the colonies, reached out to a mentality almost overprepared to receive them, and were reflected in some of the colonists' own more influential publications. This psychological climate contributed to Cato's pervasive influence in both crystallizing and energizing what the more reflective colonists thought about such leading political questions as the nature and obligations of government.

Under the widely diffused influence of Locke's thoughts on education, which derived a consensual attitude to government from the consensual relationships between parents and children, some of the leading colonial spokesmen may well have been psychologically prepared to transfer this domestic consent to the larger arena of their political life.[55] But this thesis, attractively though it has been argued, leaves altogether too many questions unaccounted for, and offers no explanation of variations of the supposed effects, or of widespread colonial loyalty to the crown and indifference and even resistance to the colonial leadership.

Four score and seven years after the Glorious Revolution, the leaders of colonial resistance, under the aegis of the Continental Congress, declared the colonies to be independent states. During the dispute with British authority they had relied on the rights of British Americans under the common law, laced later on with dashes of natural law (which in any case the common law was supposed to include). To claim no more than continuity with the authority conferred by their colonial past would no longer have served their purposes. There was no getting away from it: they had renounced their allegiance. They were setting up new governments. Contrary to much of their own better judgment, they needed a theory. But here their problem solved itself; they *had* a theory, for they knew how governments came into being and how the manner of their birth justified their existence.

When the Virginia legislature entrusted George Mason with the task of drafting a bill of rights to declare the principles that were to guide them in creating a new government, he had more than a century of doctrine behind him, and his people's political education was reflected in his language: "that all men are by nature equally free and independent, and have certain inherent rights, of which, when they enter into a state of society, they cannot by any compact, deprive or divest their posterity."[56] This apparently simple statement embodied ages of received wisdom, but it also expressed carefully deliberated choices. With these words, Mason and the House of Burgesses, representing all of political Virginia, rejected Hobbes but embraced Locke. The rights thus claimed for posterity would soon become, in Jefferson's "unalienable" rights, the public philosophy of the United States. In Massachusetts, four years later, after prolonged debate in the towns as well as by the state convention, the preamble to the new constitution was even more specific: "[T]he body politic is formed by a voluntary association of individuals. It is a social compact, by which the whole people covenants with each citizen, and each citizen with the whole people."[57] Pennsylvania's bill of rights replicated section 1 of Virginia's.[58] The concept was pervasive; in 1787 George Washington, who would have been the last to claim for himself any originality of thought, in a covering letter transmitting the draft federal Constitution to the Congress, observed that "all individuals entering into society, must give up a share of liberty to preserve the rest."[59] And the debt to Locke could not have been more explicit, for a crucial argument of the *Second Treatise* appeared in similar language: "[B]ut though Men when they enter into Society, give up the Equality, Liberty and Executive Power they had in the State of Nature, into the hands of the Society, to be so far disposed of by the Legislative, as the good of the Society shall require; yet it being only with an intention in every one the better to preserve himself his Liberty and Property."[60]

The familiarity of these elemental propositions should not obscure their historical and contextual significance. The philosophy they implied may seem to later generations to represent a political equivalent of the "naïve" paintings of Edward Hicks or Grandma Moses: intense moral seriousness serving a one-dimensional social vision. Locke may have been conscious of employing a form of extended metaphor, but the evidence of these formal pronouncements suggests that many of the men in American public life believed, or professed for political purposes to believe, in the individualist will theory which would underpin constitutional authority in America; whether they took literally the notion of state formation by contract out of the state of nature, they subscribed to it in language that they handed down to later generations. They had good tactical as well as moral reasons for this thesis. For it presumed the moral autonomy of the independent individual, who was sovereign over himself; and only one who possessed this self-sovereignty could assign it in a compact of government. The basis of this principle was the doctrine of the sovereignty of the individual over his own person.

Certainly, colonial spokesmen who sang from the same music sheets as their British sources showed every sign of reading their texts more literally than their originals—an aspect of colonial lag, which is no more remarkable in political ideas than it was in other forms of expression such as clothing, architecture, or domestic style. Moreover it was important to make the language simple enough to be understood far beyond the circles in which it was proclaimed. The wording of these highly public declarations, which aimed to arouse a surge of popular support, resulted not from some distant recollection of a historic English original event but from actual replication of the principles of contract, as Mason and his colleagues believed themselves to have derived them from Locke.

This claim to authority was also deeper and older, reaching for the long thread of the common law, and drawing out from that tangled mass what it needed of contract. At some risk of imposing a simple, unilateral scheme on complex, historically derived situations, it looked directly to the mature (if male) individual as the fundamental element of the social order. This was the basis of the contract of government, and was to be the basis of the American Constitution. Anti-Federalists opposed it for the reason that Federalists supported it: because they clearly understood that the new government would bear directly on the individual citizen.[61]

There was nothing inevitable in this arrangement; other formations such as private property, geo-economic interests, even religious or ethnic groups, might have been recognized as elemental building blocks of the constitutional order. As the Constitution emerged, only the states remained under the new federal order to represent the principle of an alternative political basis. America's powerful brand of individualism flowed from various sources; in turn, they both fed into and were invisibly sustained by the individualism of the Constitution.

IV.

It would be fanciful to suppose that the theory of contract could alone support the idea of republican government. Slade's case may have proved to be a catalyst for the intensification and thence the generalization of ideas of contract, and to have reflected the common law's major contribution to the tradition, but it stands in a wider context of political practice in which representative institutions played an increasing role; America would have had one or another form of republican government if the case had never been brought to court, or had ended differently. Neither Sparta nor Athens in ancient times, nor the medieval or renaissance city republics of northern Europe or Italy, had defined citizenship in terms of the law of contract. (John Locke and his contemporaries knew this perfectly well.) Such a concept as that of an original, government-creating contract does not appear to have been known to these republics. It was unknown to Machiavelli, who himself looked back to the Roman Republic. This strand of creative political thought was, on the contrary, a product of English common law married to English and later to American experience. It derived from sources independent of parliamentary or representative institutions; it implied not only the consent of free and equal wills but that they be responsible wills, capable of understanding their transactions and keeping faith with their neighbors.

Unfortunately, in the years immediately following independence, several of the newly empowered American states, for all their republican characters, failed to show the respect for contract that they should have learned from the law itself, if not from their proclaimed principles. It was in response to the excesses alleged against state legislatures that the Constitutional Convention at Philadelphia placed the sanctity of contract under the protection of constitutional law. Locke, whose commitment to the public welfare was indissolubly connected to the interests of private property, would not have had any difficulty with that (whatever he might have thought of the separation of powers). He himself was convinced of the primacy of legislation, and therefore of the legislature.[62]

Yet this proved to be another connection in which his intellectual reach exerted direct influence on American political consciousness: exactly the same point is emphasized by Madison at a crucial stage in the development of his institutional argument in *Federalist* 51 where he explains the need for departmental defenses precisely because "in republican government the legislative authority, necessarily, predominates."[63] If Locke's *Second Treatise* was not open on Madison's desk as he wrote, it can only be because it was fully present in his head.

To claim exclusive possession for the common law heritage would be a presumption apt to invite an action of trover and conversion. Even older ideas of contract had been known to students of law at least since Justinian's *Institutes,* to which allusion has already been made. Anglo-American republican theorists were eclectic enough to acknowledge a variety of sources ranging from the ancient Aegean to eighteenth-century France. Ideas of contractual obligation in various forms were familiar enough among opposition thinkers on the European continent. But, as we have seen, they generally contemplated collective obligations collectively undertaken. The idea owed less, if anything at all, to the sense of individualist responsibility which had gained such unusual momentum in the Anglo-American tradition.[64]

That tradition required of the subject or citizen a decent respect for the concept of law, and a willingness to conform to its rules. Without this much virtue, a republic could not be expected to survive very long; Montesquieu, widely read in the colonies following the English translation of *The Spirit of the Laws* in 1752, had emphasized that republics depended on virtue. For the makers of the American Constitution virtue was a secretion binding the elements of the structure. But there was probably not one among them who believed that disinterested virtue could be relied on to outweigh self-interest, where the pursuit of self-interest might lead to personal advantage. And there are in *The Federalist*'s eighty-five essays only a handful of passages in which the authors express a hint of confidence that America possesses the virtue necessary to sustain a republic; at best it might shore up the complex institutional arrangements by which ambition was to counteract ambition.

V. The concept of divine right, which had thrown its shadow across the path of Edward Coke and his generation, has given way to that of contract, itself not invented, but formulated for the English world by common law procedures supported by common law reasoning. A further, equally fundamental step was the invention of the state, an intellectual fiction akin to the legal fictions by which the common law maintained its ability to surmount new problems. But this intellectual fiction was allied to a concept, that of the political action of the will, which actually entered, and may even have enlarged, the principles of contract; and this lay at the conceptual foundation of the republic, which owed its authority to govern to the fact that it officially subscribed to the idea of the continuing consent of individual wills. This was what Jefferson and his colleagues in drafting America's Declaration of Independence intended by the claim that a government owed its just powers to "the consent of the governed." Just as the original contract was believed to have brought the commonwealth into existence, so the viability of the state was to be sustained by the qualities that went into its observance.

It would be presumptuous to suppose that England was the only begetter of the contractual view of authority, or that these events were without earlier precedent. Magna Carta, indeed, had contractual provisions; but Magna Carta had lapsed from active English political consciousness until it was revived by Coke. In Spain, however, Philip II, by no stretch of the imagination a democratic monarch, had been sharply reminded by rights-conscious Catalans of the limits of his authority when he tried to impose an order on a company of shipwrights, only to be told that his relationship with that province was defined by contract.[65] But England had never imitated Spain; its people had discovered, or rediscovered, the principle by the internal processes of their own common law.

Although American legal thought absorbed infusions from Europe in the generations succeeding American independence,[66] state formation was not an area in which Continental philosophers appear to have defined the issues.[67] In any case they achieved little penetration of the web of English legal philosophy until English lawyers and philosophers were ready to listen to them. This attitude was absorbed in time by the increasingly professional legal class in the colonies. Before the mid-eighteenth century, colonial lawyers were coming self-consciously under the influence of the English case reports as well as the classical English authorities. Not only the writs and processes, the quiddities, the quillities, cases, indentures, tenures, and tricks but the principles enshrined in the common law's conventions and procedures, and most significantly the law of contract, were active agents in forming the political education of British Americans. That education lay at the foundation of a new and newly sustainable idea of the state, and infused the thinking that went into the ideology of state-making in the era of the Revolution. The most persistent, pervasive, and ultimately formative influence on the individualist character of the American idea of the state seems to have been the Anglo-American common law.

Since the first stirrings of the artistic experiments which developed with the Renaissance, many aspects of individualism, from the artistic and the spiritual to the economic and material, have attracted the attention of historians and philosophers.[68] The sense in which the satisfaction of individual aims actually becomes the object of society and government reached an early prominence in the United States; through English translation in 1840, Alexis de Tocqueville first familiarized English readers with the word "individualism" itself. The translator was apologetic: the word, he admitted, was strange and sounded alien. American dictionaries were the first to give the word "individualism" a favorable connotation.[69]

Although these principles have gained in familiarity, the legal aspects of individualism, though often implicit in the others, have attracted less attention among historians. But a social order sustains itself through its law no less than through its customs, its politics, education, religions, morals, and sports, and this must be no less true of an individualistic order than of a society of more communal values. Contract has always presented problems of interpretation and priority; individualism is a broad idea which has no inherent tendency to emphasize equality as an attribute of individuals; the concept is susceptible to an obvious internal tension, the demands of dominant elements in society having often created an agenda for the law without necessarily laying down a clear set of legal principles. At formative periods, such demands have been dominant enough to act as determinants of social or economic development. In common law societies, conflicts over contract have presented these problems to the courts, whose early formulations enshrined certain fundamentals: contracts are made by the will and intent of free individuals, and to that extent, in principle, these individuals are recognized as equals. Needless to add that these principles have often been bent by private interests and have often fallen short of fulfillment, and in many respects the common law protected privileges which were far from egalitarian in any modern sense. Such principles do, however, depend on values as well as procedures, and individualistic values go far to explain the constitutional foundations of the American Republic. The determinations of the courts have done much to shape the law, and the law has shaped as well as reflected society.

So we return to where we began. As we have seen already but for the sake of completeness must now repeat, when, in 1962, the Supreme Court of the United States, whose existence was not even contemplated during most of the period under discussion, decided the case of *Baker v. Carr,* it did nothing less than open the opportunity to restore the American Republic to its own first principles.[70] That case raised the fundamental question of justiciability—whether legislative disputes fell within the province of the courts. The Supreme Court decided in the affirmative and returned the case to the state judiciary of Tennessee. Shortly afterward the similar cases grouped as *Reynolds v. Sims* gave Chief Justice Earl Warren the opportunity to pronounce the constitutional principle.[71] These decisions were fundamental in the literal sense because they restored a corrupted system to its republican foundations; they put into effect a doctrine well understood by the Founders, that a republic must be returned periodically to its founding principles in order to survive as a republic—a principle well known to the republics of the Italian Renaissance in the injunction *ridurre ai principii.*[72] It does not follow that the foundation thus established will dictate the forms taken by the constant mutations of political power—that is another story, long, complicated, and tortuous, which we do not intend to pursue. Sufficient to the day is the judgment thereof. And it was sufficient to have established that the Constitution owed both its origins and its sustaining principles in large measure to the contractual basis inherited from the English common law.

3

Sedition and the Jury in London and New York

I. The English judicial system, and with it the jury, became involved in almost every phase of the series of political crises that afflicted England during the first century of American colonization. The irrepressible Leveller John Lilburne was twice, in 1649 and 1653, subjected to political trials for alleged offenses against the state and twice acquitted by irrepressible London juries. His supporters struck a commemorative medal bearing the legend "John Lilburne, saved by the power of the Lord and the Integrity of the Jury." A Leveller pamphlet appearing in the same year included this right of juries to judge law as well as fact in a long list of political demands.[1] The distinction, as we have seen, was not new; but it had very rapidly acquired new political significance. Coke had earlier laid down the lawyerly doctrine that the jury was to determine the facts, leaving it to the bench to declare their legal meaning.[2] In view of Coke's extremely specialist concept, according to which the law could be known only through many years of erudite study, he was bound to regard legal interpretation as being beyond the powers of lay members of the jury. Coke's determination to get the law right did not imply any disrespect for the idea of law as the Englishman's birthright; the important thing was to keep the matter in the proper hands. The idea of a distinction between law and fact as a principle dividing judge from jury was not apparent to medieval legists, but developed gradually with developments in the concept of proof, involving, as we have noticed, more tangible ideas of verification.[3] What was new by the mid-seventeenth century was the conceived division of political power which it represented. As Lilburne's medal shows, the issue flared into political controversy when the authority of rulers was challenged, particularly when that authority stood on shaky ground.

But it does not follow that lawyers were necessarily taking sides politically when they sought to protect the prerogatives of their profession. When (as in Lilburne's case), the charge was treason or seditious libel, the politics of the charge necessarily entered into the legal distinction. Radical opponents of the regime claimed that juries spoke with the voice of the common people, from whom they were drawn and to whose ranks they would return when the court adjourned. It is hardly going too far to say that, at least to the end of the eighteenth century, in both the English kingdom and the American republic, the issue of the trial jury's claims to determine law as well as fact was the critical theme of dispute whenever the courts became involved in struggles for authority in the state.

The problem was incisively analyzed by Sir John Hawle, whose treatise *The Englishman's Right*, published, as noted above, in 1680 in the form of a dialogue between a barrister and a reluctant (but unusually well-educated) juryman, no doubt modeled on Christopher St. German's *Doctor and Student*, became a textbook for what may be called the popular or Whig position. It is evidence of his lasting influence that he was acknowledged a century later by the editor of the fourth edition of Blackstone's *Commentaries*. Hawle was politically active as a Whig member of several parliaments during the 1680s to the 1700s and became solicitor general under William and Mary; but the canon of Whig political thought, which concentrates on contract, representation, and consent, ignores his contribution. His book proved incidentally that lawyers did not all think as members of an endangered elite when their profession engaged with politics.

In a sustained attack on the idea that the work of the jury ought to be or could be confined to finding the facts of the case, Hawle argued that the distinction between "fact" and "law" was logically indefensible. The issues were not necessarily political. Experience, he observed, showed that the jury often judged both, as for example in a homicide, "whether it is *murther, manslaughter per infortunia or se defendendo.*" These were distinctions in which "facts" could not be separated from "law" because the legal category would itself define the facts. Are not the parties' states of mind to be regarded as facts? The jury can hardly reach a verdict on the facts without making a finding in law. This kind of finding, extending to both fact and law, will be called a general verdict. The judge will have given technical instruction on points of law and if necessary will have informed the jury of precedents; but the verdict belongs to the jury. It was Hawle, moreover, who shrewdly pointed out that if a jury were really confined to declaring fact, it would return a verdict of "done" or "not done." The word "guilty" in itself implied a moral judgment; a verdict of "guilty" or "not guilty" was in itself a judgment of *law*. J. M. Beattie has shown that the trial jury often decided whether the case was murder or manslaughter.[4]

The charges that politicized the issue, with profound constitutional implications, were those involving treason or seditious libel. Hawle had anticipated the problems much as they were to recur a century later. Suppose, he proceeded, a man is accused of treason for failing to remove his hat when passing the king's statue. The evidence—the fact—is simply that he did not remove his hat. The verified report of that omission tells us nothing about the frame of mind in which he walked past the statue. He might have not realized what he was doing or neglecting to do; he might have been lost in thought; or he might have been making a political point. Would you find him guilty of treason? Hawle's juryman thinks not, because he would not think the omission constituted treason.[5] The jury, Hawle might have said, must apply both heart and eye. At the village level, this moral agency of juries is suggested by the fact that they would often forgive sheep stealing in bad times; and in capital cases, judges would collude with juries in the cause of leniency.[6] Hawle's barrister is concerned to convince the reluctant juryman that his duty is essentially political. The technical argument involving law and fact in the same bundle had the ulterior purpose of strengthening the independence of juries in a period of threat to freedom of expression. Hawle cited Fortescue on the role of juries in maintaining the people's liberties, and Coke on the duty of fearless attachment to doing right according to the law. "The end of juries is to preserve men from oppression," says the barrister, and Vaughan's recent judgment in Bushell's case is played into the argument. The judgment was certainly not regarded as irrelevant then. But the situation now had a topical urgency. Certainly English government was unstable when Fortescue instructed his monarch in the 1460s, but the problem of rivalry for the throne between baronial houses, serious enough to precipitate civil wars, was nevertheless different in character from the threat feared by Protestants from the impending succession of the Catholic James II. The language had changed much less over some two hundred years than the political realities. Hawle and others were insisting on a more specifically political responsibility for the jury. Vaughan's judgment established the principle of jury independence and the fundamental principle that the jury's verdict must be accepted by the court (and Hawle repeated Vaughan's point about local knowledge, which refutes the notion that this function had become anachronistic).[7] But contemporaries had reason to fear that the struggle might begin again at any moment. The trials of Lilburne some thirty years earlier had brought the issues into sharp focus; the bullying and imprisonment of juries by tyrannical judges in the 1660s, not to mention Judge Jeffreys's notorious "bloody assize" penalties on Monmouth's partisans in the West Country were recent memory. Hawle was in effect codifying for the future the general principle, already proclaimed by Fortescue, that the jury was the people's instrument in protecting their liberties whenever and by whomever threatened; and in modern circumstances this claim made the jury an instrument in the process of political representation.

Juries either in England or in the colonies had no personal commitment to involving themselves in the refinements of complex technicalities, and willingly relinquished that power to the judges. The same principle held good in late eighteenth-century Virginia, where the future chief justice John Marshall acquired his extensive legal experience, and the view that judgment on law belonged to the court was apparently prevalent.[8] At a moment when the same issue was about to come to a politically charged head in England with Fox's Libel Act of 1792, republican Virginia perceived it as essentially a matter of the scope of the legal profession's responsibilities. It may be considered a tribute to the tenacity of the legal mind that a century and two revolutions after Hawle, the legal community had not been deflected from its self-appointed prerogative, nor does this seem to have been considered an affront to the rights of the populace; and in civil suits, which came to involve complex commercial and insurance transactions, and in disputes over feudal technicalities affecting land titles, the jurors (whose habitual deference to their social superiors was periodically spiced with a lively sense of their own worth) frequently needed guidance from the bench. The trial judge played a part that was remarkable for its reticence. In Virginia, according to Henry St. George Tucker, a professor of law writing in the 1840s whose father, the famous St. George Tucker, had held the post of chancellor, the judge normally refrained from intervention, and did not follow the practice of summing up the evidence for the jury's guidance, as was done, he remarked, in England "and in some of our sister states."

Even in colonial days a Virginia jury would have regarded such an intervention as an invasion of their privileges.[9] His father had a less flattering opinion of the moral quality of Virginia juries. Many local jurymen, he wrote in his notebooks, made a habit of loitering about the courthouse door in the hope of being called for jury service and getting their expenses paid; many of their verdicts had to be reversed on appeal.[10] By contrast, in thinly populated colonial North Carolina, the judicial system was frequently embarrassed by the failure of nominated jurymen to turn up at all at the designated place and time; legislative sanctions brought little improvement.[11] In the early decades of the nineteenth century, beginning in North Carolina in 1795, southern states began a trend which the North soon followed of passing legislation to prevent judges from presenting the jury with an evaluation of the evidence they had heard.[12] It seems likely that this movement was intended to block the noticeable trend on the part of judges in the late eighteenth century to imitate their English brethren by dominating the court and developing a political agenda.[13] If so, it may have been a manifestation of the hostility to elitist privilege associated with what came to be called Jacksonian Democracy.

II.

The Anglo-American jury's moral agency never extended to making substantive law; it was more likely to be concerned with what was *not* law, or what it would not enforce as law. These negatives could hardly stand as precedents. But even in this limited capacity they do suggest another consideration in respect to the jury's political function. Political representation, whether it was representation of estates or interests or even of individuals, was inherently in some sense *interest* representation. Members of any particular parliament were to guard or advance the interests of their boroughs or counties, of their landowners or merchants or yeomen; this was what they were called to do. In this political sense, however, the jury was supposed to be disinterested. In the sense of protecting the liberties of the people, yes, it was engaged in protecting or promoting their interests; but this was not the same as actually promoting concrete religious or economic programs by introducing or lobbying for legislation. It was when Parliament acted in the *national* interest that it claimed the title of "the grand inquest of the nation."

The trial jury was more often called to take part in political struggle in

England than in the colonies, however. In such turbulent times as those of the later Stuarts, the jury might be charged with a burden of constitutional significance. Only seven years after the appearance of Hawle's tract, James II proved Hawle's point by committing the archbishop of Canterbury and six bishops to the Tower for petitioning the king against an order in council requiring them to promulgate the king's Declaration of Indulgence. That James's desire to extend religious toleration to Catholics and Dissenters should have encountered opposition which precipitated a struggle for individual freedom was a historical irony probably not appreciated by any of the participants. The government accused the Seven Bishops of seditious libel on the principle that any expression tending to bring the government into disrepute was seditious. This doctrine proved to have great stamina; the same charge would be brought in the United States against critics of the administration of President John Adams in 1798–99. A change of regime had done little to mitigate the character of the law, whether of kingdom or republic; nor did the First Amendment's ban on congressional acts to restrict the freedom of the press afford additional protection to editorial liberty. In the United States no less than in George III's Britain, it was in seditious libel that the issue of fact and law came to a head and the courts contested the jury's claim to determine both fact and law. In the bishops' case, the King's Bench was divided, which must have encouraged the London jury to bring in their celebrated verdict of "not guilty."[14]

Between the trial of the Seven Bishops and the flurry of prosecutions under George III, the most important jury trial in the Anglophone world in which the law of seditious libel was used as an instrument for punishing press criticism of government occurred in 1735 in New York, when John Peter Zenger, the printer of an opposition newspaper, was prosecuted for attacking Governor William Cosby. Unfortunately for the governor, Chief Justice DeLancey, whom he had recently appointed as an ally, made the tactical blunder of banning Zenger's attorneys from the court, holding them in contempt for their attacks on the governor. This exercise of judicial power was a product of the colonial situation; no English judge would have been likely to go so far (with the possible exception of the notorious Judge Jeffreys—but even he was acting in the wake of a rebellion). But the chief justice of a colonial court had no need to fear being called to account by an independent superior like the lord chancellor. Like many abuses of authority, DeLancey's ban was also a blunder. The vacant brief was immediately offered to the famous Philadelphia attorney Andrew Hamilton, who rode posthaste to New York. According to the chief justice, the role of the jury was restricted to the fact of publication; it was for the bench to decide what constituted a libel. This was conventional ground; he would have been upheld in England. But Hamilton was ready for these familiar arguments for judicial authority: this was a classic instance of the fact versus law issue, raising the question of legal consequences if the allegations proved to be true. According to the court, publication of a truth could be a libel; the damage, not the truth or falsehood, made the difference. Hamilton replied that, on the contrary, in libel, truth was a defense, and the jury's duty, as ever, was to determine the truth. This argument extended the issue of fact from the bare question of publication to the question of what the publication alleged, Hamilton's point being that this was also a matter of fact for the jury. In a brilliant dialogue with the chief justice, Hamilton had seized for forensic purposes and turned against its official defenders the conventional legal principle that the jury determined only "fact"; for as Hawle had argued fifty years earlier, the definition of "fact" *included* the question of the truth of the alleged libel. The question for the jury, argued Hamilton, was not only whether Zenger had published the offending articles (which he undoubtedly had) but whether, in publishing, he had committed seditious libel. Departing from strict conventions of common law, Hamilton also advanced the daring argument that the jury could claim a higher prerogative in the colonies on account of their more popular form of government. In describing the jury as the representative of the people, Hamilton made adroit use of a popular English convention. In principle, as addressed to colonial circumstances, the precedent could have been seen as a step toward "Americanization"; but the opportunity does not seem to have been taken as a precedent. It was probably of more tactical importance that Hamilton also deftly introduced into his argument an allusion to the trial of the Seven Bishops with a hint that the prosecution of Zenger was a similar act of tyranny. These arguments satisfied the New York jury, who achieved historical fame by acquitting Zenger.[15] A negative form of the process of turning the judiciary into an instrument of political protest had occurred in Boston following anti-impressment riots in 1747. The provincial council wanted to prosecute the rioters, but no action was taken. Just as the militia had refused to intervene during the disorders, it had to be recognized that the grand jury would have refused to make a presentment.[16]

The use of the judiciary as an instrument of policy was resumed in the 1760s. The New England coast was the scene of skirmishes between local crowds and customs officers, followed by trials in which it is hardly an exaggeration to call the New England coastal juries an arm of the resistance.[17] Even normal domestic litigation was infected by the imperial crisis. This point is particularly well illustrated in the prominent but private New York case of *Forsey v. Cunningham*, in 1765.[18] Forsey had taken a writ for assault and battery against Cunningham, and the case was tried before a jury, who awarded Forsey the enormous damages of £1,500. Controversy broke out when Lieutenant Governor Cadwallader Colden agreed to hear Cunningham's appeal to the provincial council. Colden's decision turned on an interpretation of royal instructions, on which he acted against the unanimous voice of the council.[19] The spectacle of a crown officer taking the decision out of the hands of the local jury struck many New York citizens as an unprecedented threat to their liberties. The public outcry had no relation to the merits of the dispute, and was almost certainly fuelled by sensitivities inflamed by the Stamp Act.[20] Colden's presumption of judicial authority drew criticism from the Superior Court, the grand jury, and even the legal profession in New Jersey and Pennsylvania as well as New York, where the grand jury congratulated the judges for defying the lieutenant governor.[21] The central importance of the issue of fact and law was the theme in 1769 of a letter copied by the *New-York Chronicle* from the *Political Register* of London. By signing himself "Britannicus," the author claimed the jury's power to find law as well as fact as a traditional bastion of British liberty, which from the colonial point of view was also American liberty. The author seems not to have been a lawyer, for he thought the restriction of jury power to finding the facts had only recently been asserted. "O what can tend more," he asked, "to overthrow our laws and liberties? For if this pernicious doctrine should be allowed, juries would be so far from being a security to the subject, that they would be then a snare." With the jury confined to finding the facts, the judge, a royal officer, could impose what punishment he chose. He added a warning that juries should be careful to act only on a grand jury indictment, not on an "information," which might emanate from the crown.

The importance of the general issue of the English right to trial by a jury of the vicinity had gained urgency from recent British legislation which appeared to threaten Americans with transportation for trials in London.[22] Historians have given varying degrees of prominence to the colonists' fears of threats to these constitutional rights in the building up of colonial anxieties and resentments. Britannicus had pointed to the danger hidden in the doctrine which confined the jury to the facts. In the context of conflict between the British and the colonies, the policy of taking law finding out of the jury's hands was a policy of locating it in the hands of their oppressors. As we have seen, this theme had a long history, dating at least from the pugnacious seventeenth-century English radical John Lilburne; it was not the most prominent of influences, but certainly added its weight to the general suspicion of British intentions. Historians with their sights focused on the broader constitutional controversy involving taxation, representation, quartering of troops, and other familiar grievances have neglected the implications of this by no means trivial issue.

One reason why colonial spokesmen themselves failed to deploy this argument more emphatically may well have been that many of them were lawyers, and it divided the legal profession. Lawyers, after all, were trained in the law; in ordinary jurisprudence the courts themselves held conventional views. In an undated case involving a writ of trover and conversion in the 1750s William Kempe (father of John Tabor, who succeeded him), attorney general of New York, explained that the court was to direct the jury in the matters of law "arising from the Evidence"; the jury was to have regard for the court's direction. But this was not enough to satisfy the attorney general; it left too much to the jury, "for what is a conversion and what is not a conversion is a matter of law, and not proper for a jury who are ignorant of such matters." Kempe went so far as to say that the court should set aside a perverse general verdict given against the direction of the court.[23]

This regression to the older ideas of English judges may seem surprising in a colonial, even though a crown officer; but it is a mistake to regard all issues as reflections of an incipient imperial conflict. This was not a case of the crown against the people; rather it reflects a profession asserting its dignity and self-assurance, or claiming its territory. Such exhibitions of self-esteem, however, could never persuade the increasing numbers of dissidents, and may have contributed to the legal profession's unpopularity. The stubbornly persistent issue of the jury's power in libel bore a heavy charge; it involved the right of citizens to criticize their government and thus touched on the wider issue of press freedom.

Governments had rarely appreciated the advantages of hostile criticism, but criticism of government had become an American habit, and American governments proved no less sensitive than did their predecessors. Controversies on this theme not only survived the transition from British rule to reappear under American self-government, but in fact persisted through the transition from Federalist to Jeffersonian administrations. But Anglo-American law was far from self-explanatory. In February 1789 Chief Justice William Cushing of Massachusetts sought the opinion of John Adams in a long letter replete with references to Coke, Blackstone, and the Seven Bishops. By the law of England, he observed, a civil action for damages required that the libel be false as well as scandalous; it ought to follow from this language that the truth of an accusation might be pleaded in defense. The indictments against the bishops, which were criminal actions, did conform to law by accusing them of a libel that was *false* as well as scandalous. By analogy with the civil principle, the case, then, turned on the truth or falsehood of the assertion that the king had acted illegally. Mr. Justice Powell had held that to make the petition a libel, it must be false (a defense followed by Andrew Hamilton in Zenger's trial). He held the position of the bishops true and right; so it appears that in his view truth could be pleaded in mitigation. Mr. Justice Allybone had taken the view that a private man writing about the government was an intruder and a libeler. Happily, however, the jury had set them all right. But a single jury verdict did not overturn the law, and the law of England still held (where Lord Mansfield had placed it, though Cushing did not say so) that the truth could not be pleaded in bar of indictment. Where, then, did it leave Massachusetts and the constitutional protection of the liberty of the press? Cushing found the English position incompatible with the liberty of a republic; citizens must be free to criticize their rulers. "Why," he asked, acknowledging Gordon (coauthor of *Cato's Letters* in the 1720s) but distantly echoing Milton's *Areopagitica*, "need any honest man fear the truth? The guilty only fear it." Adams agreed that it would be safest to let the jury hear evidence as to the truth of the allegations, "and if the jury found them true and they were published for the Public good, they would readily acquit." The motive of publication was to be a consideration—which was consistent with Thomas Erskine's emphasis on *intent* in the prominent English trial of the dean of St. Asaph, as will appear in a moment; but the jury would be the judges of motive, vindicating their brief as society's moral agents.[24]

The issue was played out in similar terms on both sides of the ocean. The passage of a century more or less since the trial of the Seven Bishops produced remarkably little change in the issues of principle. When Lord North's government charged the printers John Almon and Henry Sampson Woodfall—the latter was "Memory" Woodfall, the famous parliamentary reporter who preceded Hansard and, not being allowed to take notes, committed the debates to memory—with sedition for publishing Junius's *Letters* critical of government policy in the American colonies, Almon's jury convicted, but Woodfall was found guilty of publishing *only*. In this trial Lord Mansfield once again laid down the traditional rule that the jury was to find only the facts, leaving the court to determine whether the material was or was not libelous.[25] But in spite of the lord chief justice's formidable personality, interrogation from the bench failed to elicit a verdict that the publication complained of was seditious as charged.[26] The government would not yield the point, and in 1783 began a prosecution of Dr. William Davies Shipley, dean of St. Asaph, who had published an allegedly seditious pamphlet written by his brother-in-law. The trial was remarkable principally for one of Thomas Erskine's most brilliant and passionate defenses of freedom of the press and conscience. The prosecution was again frustrated by a jury which would only find that the defendant had in fact published the offending material, while refusing to condemn the material published. On being asked the jury's finding, the foreman answered:

> Guilty of publishing only.
>
> Mr Justice Buller: I believe that is a verdict not quite correct. You gentlemen of the jury must explain one way or the other, whether you find the meaning of the innuendoes.

Interrogation of the jury as to the meaning of their verdict was continued with Erskine (for the defense):

> Would you have the word *only* recorded?
>
> One of the jury: Yes.
>
> Mr Justice Buller: But I must tell you the law is this: if you find the defendant guilty of publishing, without saying any more, the question of libel or not is open to the consideration of the Court; But if you say he is guilty of publishing only, it is an incomplete verdict.
>
> One of the jury: We certainly mean to leave the question of libel or not to the consideration of the Court.

Mr. Erskine: Do you find the sedition?
One of the jury: We give no verdict upon it.
Mr Justice Buller: When you understand your verdict yourselves, I will take it in the manner you state it. If you say guilty of publishing only, there must be another trial, because the verdict will be imperfect.[27]

The informality of the jury's proceedings (Mansfield had gone home while they deliberated, and they called at his house to deliver their verdict, where he interrogated them individually), the inconclusiveness of their consultations, their lack of unanimity, and the way one of the judges sought to interrogate their individual opinions all emerge as side products of this report. The record makes it clear that the medieval and early modern procedure by which the jurors could be individually interrogated by the bench could still be adopted when the verdict was unclear or controversial; even at this seemingly late date, the transformation of the jury was incomplete. But the government did not risk a second trial.

III.

On both sides of the ocean, Whigs, country party adherents, radicals, and opponents of strong government were committed to the view that juries existed and had always existed to represent the people. Although the people were never clearly defined, they seem to have had one constant characteristic: they were never in power, and their powerlessness rendered them perpetually vulnerable to repressive government. And in cases charging sedition or libel, the people were essentially present in the jury, who had a right to enter into questions of law; no judge could take this power from them. There was one way, however, in which the moral agency of the jury could be seriously impaired. Dissatisfied litigants could always complain that the jury was packed. There was probably no period since the jury had become a separate entity at which particular juries were wholly free from the opprobrium of this charge; we have noticed Shakespeare's hint on the subject. Yet jurors were subject to social restraints; at the end of the session, the jury dissolved and its members had to return from the assizes and live with their neighbors, and must have been subject to local opinion.

Spokesmen for liberty always preferred the jury to any other form of defense. There were, however, authorized forms of jury selection. They took shape in the "special" and also in the similar "struck" jury, which received parliamentary approval in 1730, and both of these were designed to try supposedly special cases.[28]

The struck jury consisted of the names that remained from a large panel after both sides had struck out a statutory number which they were entitled to challenge. The method could be used for either criminal or civil trials. The special jury, which was a form of struck jury, was selected on the basis of the perception of a need for qualified individuals, usually merchants and professional men, to hear complex cases involving such matters as insurance disputes and conflicting interpretations of contract. Lord Mansfield worked from a limited register of available specialists, for whom he had great respect and with whom he developed familiar and informal relations, sometimes dining with them. Together they worked out the lines on which common law accommodated itself to the interests of a mercantile economy.[29] The law officers of the crown, including William Murray (later Lord Mansfield) when he was attorney general, were not above designing jury selection with a view to securing results for the government in prosecutions for seditious libel.[30] The refusal of London juries, at least on certain historic occasions, to bow to pressure from the bench where the liberty of the press was at stake is all the more remarkable; it might be said that they were inscribing a first amendment into the British constitution in broadly the same period in which Americans were setting down their own in writing.

These acquittals plainly failed to impress Jeremy Bentham, whose tract *The Elements of the Art of Packing* attacked special juries as "a special engine of corruption," designed to subvert the freedom of the press. Corruption and influence reduced special juries to obsequiousness and subservience; the libel laws had destroyed press freedom.[31] Bentham obviously knew of the famous acquittals during his own lifetime, but no one could count on acquittal, and the possibility cannot have counteracted the silence-inducing influence of what is now called the freezing effect. An exemplary case of the political use of a selected jury occurred in New York in 1766. Serious land riots had broken out in the Hudson Valley. The issues were internal; no British interest was involved. But when the rioters were brought to trial, the authorities feared that an ordinary jury could not be relied on to convict; feeling too much affinity for the defendants, it might have failed to protect the interests of the great families of the Hudson Valley. The case was tried by a special commission assisted by a struck jury. The desired result was obtained.[32]

The colonies had no Jeremy Bentham but they did find a well-informed critic of jury abuses in Cadwallader Colden, lieutenant governor of New York at intervals in the years before the colonial revolt. Colden bitterly blamed the local lawyers for corrupt management of the jury system, leading to biased verdicts. He did claim, however, that one such verdict had been corrected by a jury. He also wrote a sustained critique of the subservience of provincial judges to a bullying governor in his long account of the regime of Governor Cosby, and here he implicitly praised the New York jury when he observed that the governor expected from a judge what he could not hope for from a jury.[33]

IV. The jury as moral agent and protector of liberty was not riding in privileged immunity above the political battle; its role could often be fulfilled only as a party in the struggle. The number of tracts that appeared in the generation after the English civil wars devoted to explaining the jury's duties and justifying its political functions is itself an indication that this old bastion of the fundamentals of English liberty was under threat from overmighty government. In witness whereof, some of these works, as we have seen, were kept alive by reprintings for generations after their original publication.

Four or five years before Fox's Libel Act of 1792,[34] which significantly claimed to declare *existing* law by settling full power on the jury to determine law as well as fact, jury trial was the issue at the center of some of the most forcible objections to the draft Constitution of the United States. Many Anti-Federalists animated their demand for a bill of rights with the grievance that the Constitution failed to provide adequate cover for the fundamental English right of trial by an impartial jury of the vicinity. (The specific provision for jury trials in criminal cases in Article III applied only to the area of federal jurisdiction, presumably not at that time expected to be the scene of much criminal activity.) Eventually, after strenuous debates in the first Congress, the Fifth, Sixth, and Seventh amendments were designed either expressly or by implication to call for indictments by grand juries or resolution of conflicts by petty juries. But Anti-Federalist positions on the issue contained a paradox. If they needed a bill of rights to protect individual liberties, cases arising under a bill of rights were inherently likely to land on appeal on the desk of the judges; but some Anti-Federalists regarded judges as potential agents of an ever more powerful central government. The political role of the jury as the popular element in the judicial hierarchy was to protect the people from such incursions; several of the most prominent Anti-Federalist spokesmen joined issue with the proposed Constitution on the grounds that the powers to hear appeals conferred on the new national judiciary would threaten the people's precious right to jury trial. "An Impartial Examiner" was one who sniped at the new court as a "high prerogative court," an expression which likened it to the notorious English Star Chamber.[35] Yet other Anti-Federalists, however, appeared to welcome the implicit power of the new Supreme Court to review congressional legislation. The general question of judicial review had attracted so little notice in the Convention that no debate was addressed specifically to the issue; even Luther Martin, a vociferous critic and later Anti-Federalist, seemed to accept in principle that the Supreme Court would have power of review.[36]

When the members of the Convention decided to discuss the future of the Union in profound secrecy they took the risk of losing touch with their constituents' sentiments. Once the draft Constitution was out, they soon learned that they had badly misjudged the extent and depth of public hostility, and came close to losing the debate. Americans knew about justice and understood that most of it was a local affair; they objected on practical grounds that the distance of the federal courts would impede suits by private persons; "Brutus," among others, insisted that justice must be brought to every man's door. The ancient tradition—for here were Anti-Federalist voices celebrating English rights—of trial by one's neighbors was a theme for "A Federal Farmer," for the Pennsylvania Minority, and for "Agrippa" (John Winthrop of Boston). "Centinel" and "Brutus" echoed a familiar theme when they contended that the Supreme Court's power to hear appeals would take away the trial jury's right to give a verdict on the facts. Publius, the pseudonymous author of *The Federalist Papers*, who took up criticisms of the Constitution as the debate proceeded, delayed a reply to this batch of accusations until *Federalist* 83 (out of eighty-five), long after the issue had been settled, and then with arguments invoking the balance of probabilities rather than with the intense conviction that marked most of his argument. In the event, though jury trial was not supplanted under the Constitution, the Supreme Court began under Chief Justice Marshall to take advantage of opportunities to develop a centralizing agenda.

The jury was the lowest element of the judicial hierarchy but it was also the broadest. So far from being formally separated from the other branches of government, the essentially political character of its role was a theme of widespread agreement and approval;[37] it did not come under criticism as a violation of the separation of powers. But this led into a less frequently cited conclusion that its role could also be on a constitutional footing with that of the courts; John Marshall would say in *Marbury v. Madison* that it was emphatically the office of the judiciary to say what law was;[38] but he omitted to note that that principle did not logically exclude the jury from the same function, and certain Anti-Federalist spokesmen said emphatically that a jury also had the duty of bringing in an adverse verdict if they thought the law in question was unconstitutional.[39] The western Pennsylvania politician William Findley went as far as to argue that the jury was a "sitting constitutional convention."[40]

The jury, as representative of the people as a whole or of the immediate locality, never lost its obligation of moral agency, which always required sensitivity to problems of interpretation. The Fourth Amendment, with its protection against "unreasonable" searches and seizures, presented juries with a new set of problems and obligations; for it fell to these ordinary citizens to decide on the criteria of reasonableness in any particular case.[41] By a historical irony that was certainly not intended, these issues would eventually pass on appeal out of the hands of the people's representatives and into those of an unelected and often unrepresentative Supreme Court.

Notwithstanding the jury's role as representatives of the popular interest, juries on both sides of the Atlantic could convict as well as acquit. It would be overindulgent to suppose that Fox's famous act brought an end to political prosecutions or convictions. The record of repression under Pitt, followed by numerous sentences of transportation for various radical activities and working-class combinations in the early nineteenth century, testifies that juries were generally unable or unwilling to defy the government.

Nor did American juries prove themselves reliable protectors of the more vulnerable. In 1809 the state of New York experienced its first encounter with collective action by the artisan class. A group of cordwainers, as shoemakers were then called, had combined to protect their wages. Jeffersonian democracy or republican principles were not now the theme of the debate; the state determined to suppress this dangerous trend and behaved exactly as the British would do under the combination laws. The authorities, however, faced the difficulty that there existed on the statute books no law against collective economic action. But this did not inhibit the prosecution, who overcame the absence of a chargeable offense by falling back on the English common law of conspiracy; this policy relied on an implicit assumption that, after more than a generation of American independence, the common law remained a seamless Anglo-American fabric which the Revolution had done nothing to sunder. This was probably the first occasion on which the common law had been invoked by an American government for the purpose of controlling the economic freedom of American citizens. The defense ridiculed the prosecution's reliance on English law, which they denounced as a feudal relic without legitimacy under America's republican government; but the jury of propertied New York citizens was no longer called on to identify itself with popular rights against the crown or its agents, and found for the prosecution.[42] This trial suggests that the concept of "Americanization" might be splintered by the clashing of divergent interests, no longer sheltering under the protection of republican liberties.[43]

A few years earlier, newspaper records suggest that all the Republican and opposition editors prosecuted for political dissent under the Sedition Act of 1798 were convicted.[44] It began to appear that the American jury had been domesticated rather than liberated by the introduction of the Republic.[45]

When the American Constitution was in its infancy, James Wilson, a Philadelphia lawyer and leading nationalist and now a justice of the newly constituted Supreme Court, gave a course of lectures at the College of Philadelphia, one of which was devoted to the jury, which (though admitting to uncertainty as to its origins) he eulogized as being "in the nature of things." The jury's moral agency was Wilson's central theme. It was clear to Wilson as to other lawyers, and had been since the Middle Ages, that the jury's task was to find the truth. He recognized that the definition of "truth" for the purposes of the law might include intention; but to this principle he entered the important reservation that, in forming their opinion on the law, juries were not free to exercise discretionary powers but must adhere to common law rules; and this involved observation of precedent (on which they would obviously need to be guided by the judge).[46] However, Wilson, borrowing from a cluster of European Enlightenment thinkers, notably Pufendorf, Burlamaqui, and Rousseau, advanced the concept of the nation as a "moral person"; and he took this claim further by maintaining that the power exercised by the people through their participation in the legal system was an exercise of delegated sovereign power (a rare use on his part of the concept of sovereignty).[47]

This was a sophisticated development of the concept at the center of the present argument: the jury as moral agent in the integrative political process. Juries, Wilson admitted, were liable to error, but they were not liable to building their errors into a system, as could happen when judicial error became sanctified as precedent. Juries, randomly chosen and constantly changing, could not develop an esprit de corps. These remarks may have been intended to answer the earlier Anti-Federalist claims for the jury's power to review legislation.

Whether the lawyer and the politician contended with each other in Wilson's mind, he conceded to the jury the right of determining legal questions. But the concession was guarded: "The discretionary powers of jurors find no place for exertion here; these powers they possess as triers of facts because, as we have already observed, trial of facts depends on evidence; and because the force of evidence cannot be determined by any general system of rules. But law, particularly the common law (echoing Coke), is governed by precedents, and customs, and authorities, and maxims: those precedents, and customs, and authorities, and maxims are alike obligatory upon jurors as upon judges, in deciding questions of law." After admitting the doctrine he attributed to Lord Hardwicke (though he could have found it in many other sources: the attribution no doubt added dignity) on the distinction between findings of fact and law, Wilson concluded in favor of "harmonious co-operation."[48]

In the same year, in reaction against the party warfare that had raged internally ever since the adoption of the radical, unicameral constitution of 1776, Pennsylvania revised that constitution. Anticipating by two years Fox's Act in Britain (and *The New York Times v. Sullivan* by 174 years!), the new constitution permitted the defense to plead truth in prosecutions for libel of public men in connection with their performance of their duty.

One consideration notably missing from these debates on the character and qualifications of the trial jury was that of age.[49] Jury service may have been thought of as a right; it may have been valued as a privilege; but in a locally self-governing society where the affections of the people at large underwrote the social order, jury service by properly qualified people was also an obligation. To be properly qualified required the exercise of reason, in the same sense as in voting. We may define the qualification in question as "political reason." To define only certain components of society as possessing this power was, by definition, to exclude others. Women, together with children under a given age (known to the law as "infants"), were subject to this general exclusion; in America after gaining independence, the increasing domination of white democracy excluded people of color. Meanwhile, definitions of competent age swung from possession of property or social status under monarchical regimes to maturity as seasoned by seniority when republican ideas were ascendant. England, with some periodical variations, and colonial American provinces could call on boys of fourteen to take up these responsibilities. The Constitution said nothing about the age of voters or jurors, leaving these questions to the states; but it excluded citizens under twenty-five from election to Congress, and fixed eligibility for the Senate at thirty. The president must be upward of thirty-five. The men who wrote these provisions, however, were in general in their thirties or forties and were working against a background of appreciably lower expectation of life than would prevail in succeeding generations.

No institution in either England or early America more intimately linked men and women with the manner of their government than the jury, which is the most ancient of institutions shared by England's and America's peoples. Until the development of popular elections and office-holding bureaucracies, the jury over many centuries served some of the purposes of political representation, although it was necessarily a reactive agency and could not have its own agenda. By taking the sting out of innumerable local grievances and conflicts of interest, however, the jury through many premodern centuries made a significant contribution to social stability in both England and America. In any one case, it was charged to seek the truth of the facts alleged. But in Francis Bacon's historic formulation: "'What is truth?' said jesting Pilate, and would not stay for an answer."[50] What we agree to call "truth" often proves to be an outcome of conflicts of opinion, perceived by contending parties as conflicting truths; the quest has always begun with the need to determine the facts alleged—the "what actually happened"—of the case (or in civil suits, what were the parties' intentions). But that is only the first step. Determining what actually happened often proves to be a problem in itself. To unravel it requires interpretation. What we call the fact, as we shall see, is itself frequently defined by law. And the jury has acquired its identity in a prolonged struggle to determine both fact and law, in which it has often served but sometimes thwarted the higher powers of government. But that is as much a *political* as a judicial function—a consideration crucial to the present argument.

Two coiled strands, the principle of fact-finding and the principle of evaluation or "guilt," have served as keys to the jury's aims, its very *raison d'être*. To assess the outcome, it will be necessary to take issue with one of the embedded assumptions concerning the character of both English and American government. Of the three vertical columns representing the "powers" of government as set out side by side in the American Constitution, the jury is not separately named, though its functions identify it as a subset of the judiciary. But juries were more than that. For they had also been integral to the essentially political representation of the community, or of its dominant interests, in a manner more commonly associated with assemblies, parliaments, or legislative bodies. To make its own contribution to the moral character of the society from which it is drawn, the jury has also had to keep itself independent of the bench, and at certain periods this function has also set the jury at odds with the national government. In each of these great areas of jurisprudence, deep consequences will turn on the jury's capacity to preserve its independence. Much of its history will prove to be the record and product of this central tension.

These features gained new prominence in the English constitutional struggles of the mid-seventeenth century. Though historians have seldom credited the jury with a critical part in those turbulent events, the jury's normal, everyday role in the administration of the county necessarily involved it as an agency of politics—giving it the character of a positive moral agency rather than that of a witness (whether active or passive, on which more later). But here the petit or trial jury has to be distinguished from the grand jury, which has also had a representative character but has often been more implicated in government's purposes and policies.

In tracing the jury since its inception in Anglo-Saxon England, and since its migration and development across the Atlantic, we confront a paradox on both sides of the ocean. As a quasi-representative institution, making its contribution to the manner in which society governs itself, the jury will represent local interests and often one local interest against another. But this purpose of representation—that is, representation of interests—calls the jury's impartiality into question and will sometimes come into conflict with the demands of justice as implied by moral agency. Justice however should by definition be superior to the outcome of competition between discrete and conflicting interests. To the extent that the jury has historically succeeded in reconciling conflicting interests, it has served the important purpose of integrating people into the political order. That process I have elsewhere called "the sociology of consent"[51]—a designation intended to distinguish it from the political theory of consent. But although the jury is a branch of the judicial arm of government, it could never be arbitrarily separated from the other elements of the political structure. In maintaining its integrity in the court, it has frequently had to define itself in relation to the judge, who was a more overbearing figure in England than in the colonies.[52] To understand the conditions which nourished the jury's independence, we must be willing to *unthink* the more recent plan of the separation of powers. It is significant in this connection that neither Locke nor Montesquieu, who both influenced thinking about government in Britain's American colonies, treated the administration of justice as belonging to a separate or independent branch of government. It is a more recent development.

These considerations around the turn of the seventeenth century belonged to the world of William Shakespeare, who was acutely aware of fluctuations in the atmosphere. In Sonnet 29, which begins: "Mine eye and heart are at a mortal war, / How to divide the conquest of thy sight," he sets up a lawsuit between heart and eye to settle a dispute as to which of them has the better title to the loved object. The humorous mockery of the setting frames a more serious moral tension. To decide this title he impanels "A quest of thoughts, all tenants to the heart."[53] "Quest" is short for inquest, or jury.[54] But this jury strangely enough consists of thoughts, and we do not need to look beyond the text to observe that the jurors are all tenants to one of the parties to the suit; so we are at once introduced to the art of jury selection, better known as packing. But still, why a quest of thoughts? The function of thought is to reason; so the jury is required to apply its reasoning powers to a philosophical dispute involving the faculties of perception and emotion, subjects that interested Shakespeare for other reasons than the law. Since neither heart nor eye can benefit without the other, the outcome proves to be an eminently manageable compromise. But Shakespeare is not making fun of the jury as he does of country justices and constables; he knew law and court proceedings well enough, in fact, to make fun of the reasoning in a famous lawsuit that had occurred soon after his own birth.

That case involved a suicide by drowning. Suicide, of course, was a mortal sin and a civil crime. Since a suicide's property could not be inherited, but reverted to the crown, the widow, Lady Hale, had a heavy property interest in the manner of her husband's death. The law, as illustrated in *Hamlet* in the gravediggers' scene, has all the authority of "crowner's quest law."[55] Shakespeare's audiences were evidently expected to appreciate nice legal ironies. Returning to the sonnet, the coroner was evidently sitting with a jury, which illustrates the jury's practical role in settling disputes with a moral dimension. Legal commentators repeatedly emphasized the jury's moral agency by appealing to conscience. Shakespeare's view of the jury's responsibility was in perfect harmony with more formal statements of the early modern era. Sir Thomas More declared that a juror must hold "a sure and certain persuasion & belief in his own conscience," adding that the conscience must have been "induced reasonably." More than a century later Chief Justice Sir Matthew Hale repeated that "it is the conscience of the jury, that must pronounce the prisoner guilty or not guilty." And jurors had to bring their consciences to bear in assessing the credibility of witnesses.[56] In giving justice, it is significantly the jury, not the judge, that here serves as the crucial agent. The jurors are required to draw on their moral sense as well as their knowledge of the terrain, which collectively are here presumed to qualify them to resolve problems both linguistic and metaphysical. All this, of course, was the jury as it should be, not as it invariably was. But its prolonged survival suggests that it more habitually served than failed its moral constituency.

Prolonged survival gives a retrospective feeling of inevitability, leaving scant room for possible alternatives. But that was not always the way it looked. In the thirteenth century, a variant procedure known as "trial by witnesses" might have thwarted the further development of trial by jury. F. W. Maitland once speculated that this was a real danger to the survival of jury trial as it came to be established. But he did not pursue the question of whether this might have been a variant of the jury-as-witness, or why it withered.[57]

Unlike the English church, the jury has not experienced an imported reformation. Unlike the monarchy, it has not been subjected to invasive changes of dynasty.[58] Writing in defense of juries after the civil wars, an old Leveller claimed that William the Conqueror, though he did away with many English customs, did not dare to lay hands on the jury, for "the people would never bear it."[59] This must be the basis of the jury's claims to superior antiquity. But formal continuity over many centuries has masked fundamental internal changes, more gradual but ultimately hardly less profound than a change of dynasty or a reformation. As the body entrusted with responsibility for finding solutions for local problems, a prototype of the jury of presentment—effectively, the original of the grand jury—can be found in late Anglo-Saxon England. This body had the duty of hearing complaints and allegations before deciding whether to pass them on to the petit or trial jury. Anglo-Saxon law appears to have given rise to a basic change in legal principle marking the transition from a social order in which a crime was a private injury, calling for private redress, to one in which crime became an injury to society as a whole, involving the king's peace and calling for punishment by society. This transformation has been described by Patrick Wormald as "a marked switch in later Anglo-Saxon law."[60]

Most of that law as it affected everyday life was derived from custom; and custom, often varying from one county to another, was the seasoned timber to which Henry II applied his powerful centralizing energy at the assizes of Clarendon in 1166 and Northampton in 1178, to which the common law is commonly (though not exclusively) credited.[61] The jury, whose character as representing the local community was vital to the performance of its duties, was already both a practical and a highly economical instrument of county administration. Information furnished and verified by jurors answered the questions from which Domesday Book was compiled.[62] Nor were the jury's functions confined to trials or official inquiries, but extended to adjudicating in a variety of local disputes and problems; by drawing them all into a share in the control of their local affairs, the jury nourished a mutual loyalty within the local community, and of the community toward the crown. (It could also, of course, nourish local disputes and antagonisms.) If its administrative functions have long since been taken over by government agencies, its original and fundamental purpose as an agency of justice has survived centuries of social, political, and legal change. But just as with social problems, the jury's criminal jurisdiction could raise such questions as whether the intentions behind an act were part of the act itself; if, for example, the definition of an act includes the actor's intentions, can the act and intentions be formally separated and separately judged? But—as Maitland was early to make plain—juries were also liable to reflect the inequities of power in society. Throughout the entire period under review, moreover, juries were constantly subject to various forms of intimidation, bribery, perversion, and manipulation. All these questions were to be hammered out in the course of controversies about the jury's proper role. Sir John Fortescue's oft-repeated passages on the excellence of the jury system, uttered in the mid-fifteenth century, were qualified by the frequent use of an "ought" rather than an asserted "is."[63] The medieval royal council administered much justice, much of it criminal justice, and when reports got around that bribed or partial jurors had acquitted some notorious criminal, lawyers and representatives accepted the need for a masterful court "which does not stand upon ceremony, which can strike rapidly and have no need to strike twice."[64] It would be a cruel injustice to all too many innocent victims to sentimentalize the jury as invariably honest or disinterested; by the early eighteenth century Alexander Pope, hardly a committed social reformer, but who in his youth had much opportunity to observe judicial manipulations, could coin the cynical couplet, when observing signs of oncoming evening,

> The hungry judges soon the sentence sign,
> And wretches hang that jurymen may dine.[65]

But juries also notoriously refused to render verdicts that would entail the death penalty, and often showed sympathy amounting to solidarity with rustics and common people accused of social, rather than genuinely malicious, crimes. Once again Shakespeare had been aware of the issue:

> The jury, passing on the prisoner's life,
> May in the sworn twelve have a thief or two
> Guiltier than him they try.[66]

Throughout the medieval and early modern periods, juries were known to make adjustments in the supposed value of items of stolen property in order to avert the death penalty, which fell at a value of twelve pence.[67] After the Restoration, in a period of transformation in landownership, aggressively self-serving landowners, whose possessions often resulted from recent family amalgamations, felt threatened by the lesser tenant farmers and yeomen they were crowding off the land; the result was the passage of a long series of repressive acts beginning with the notorious Game Laws in 1672. Offenses against property increasingly incurred capital punishment. The legal principle, though certainly not new, was established with new clarity:

private property outweighed human life. Throughout the following century, poachers and agrarian raiders, blacking their faces beyond recognition and known as the "Blacks," carried on a species of guerrilla struggle against the repressive Black Act. Law itself was molded into an instrument of one economic and social interest—or "class"—to subjugate another. In a later generation this would be called class conflict. Common law was summoned to the interest of statute as weapons of class interest.[68]

To enforce the law the landowners needed reliable institutions of justice, and notably the jury system, whose cooperation, however, they could not count on. Douglas Hay, in a now famous article, recorded that the farmers and tradesmen who made up the panels of common jurors at quarter sessions and assizes were often among the poachers. Law enforcement became a difficult, even a dangerous, business. A steward, preparing a prosecution, complained in 1791, "There is no answering for a Common Jury (who must Try the Indictment) as they have in general a Strong Byass upon their Minds in favor of Poachers, being professed Enemies to all Penal Laws that relate to the Game."[69] It was for this reason that Parliament removed most game offenses from the jury's authority and made them triable by justices of the peace or judges sitting alone. When the London tradesmen, shopkeepers, and the like who composed most trial juries in the city reacted with acquittals in many notorious cases (to some of which we shall come presently) throughout the eighteenth century, during the wars of the French Revolution, and subsequently in the economic disorders that followed the peace, they may have been an early manifestation of what E. P. Thompson once suggested was an English dislike of being pushed around; but this may itself have been driven by a well-judged collective sense of self-preservation.[70] Jurors were entrusted with the fate of their fellow men. The responsibility not merely for finding fact but for finding, and in the process defining, *guilt*, or assigning culpability, particularly in capital cases, was charged with a moral dimension from which juries could not conscientiously disengage themselves.

The changes that have taken place in the composition, methods, and to some extent the functions of juries have in some respects conflicted with this essential role of community moral agency; but in other respects, rather, they have enabled the jury to maintain those attributes. We have already seen, however, that moral agency has not always been translatable as social neutrality; procedures such as (for example) physical sequestration, an essential feature of the modern jury, have not invariably served to neutralize the social values, not to say prejudices, which jurors bring with them into court.

V. By the 1590s and 1600s, when Shakespeare's sonnets were written, assorted English adventurers and religious dissidents were on the verge of setting out to plant colonies in America, where they would revive, reinvent, and even transform many English institutions. Notwithstanding frequent claims for origins in Magna Carta, the English jury had a fitful reawakening in the colonies. In Massachusetts, juries were impaneled early, but were not consistently summoned, and in the seventeenth century most charges civil and criminal were heard by magistrates.[71] Connecticut, in contrast, instituted jury trial from the beginning, with provision for a majority verdict; the grand jury came in somewhat later.[72] Both Massachusetts, in its Declaration of Liberties of 1646, and Rhode Island, in its code of 1647, drew on—or rather, copied—the recent English handbook Dalton's *Country Justice;* these codes protected the jury from threats from the bench in ways that clearly anticipated Chief Justice Vaughan's famous ruling in Bushell's case, in 1670, which laid down the principle of jury independence.[73] In England this judgment represented a reversion to first principles, similar in principle to Chief Justice Warren's decision on one person, one vote in the United States Supreme Court in *Baker v. Carr* in 1962; in the colonies, it was an *initial* statement of the same principles. This was one of the ways in which the colonies resembled medieval England, though it was medieval England without feudal tenures. In England, the jury, which had probably by now been in existence in some form for more than seven hundred years, was entering into a gradual process of transformation; yet, once restored to active life in the colonies in the first two or three decades of the eighteenth century, it would remain recognizably the same institution on both sides of the Atlantic. The colonists' surest safeguard against tyranny was to incorporate the birthright of Englishmen into the bedrock of their own laws.

Magna Carta itself does not ordain a jury system, and later claims to that authority were exaggerated; but it does say that every free man (*liber homo*) is entitled to trial by his peers. Since the early English kingdom, certainly in Norman times, a free man had been known as one who had a right to be heard in the king's court as well as the lord's. Under the aegis of Magna

Carta, trial by one's peers in a society strongly differentiated by rank must mean trial by a body of men, however selected and constituted, who were of the same rank or order as the accused; but it appears to exclude unfree men, who were numerous in the laboring ranks of the feudal order. Sir James Holt has noted that medieval interpretations of Magna Carta were strikingly varied; in 1215 the concept of "liber homo" was extensive—we might now say "democratic." But social stratification became more detailed and specific in the fourteenth century.[74] The barons and clergy who drafted Magna Carta were familiar with the general character of the jury as a local institution, but the concept of trial by one's peers would later have been related to a more specific rank; changes in social structure rather than decrees or statutes thus shaped the language of Magna Carta into an authority for the right to jury trial. The year 1215, however, was portentous for another reason: it saw the Fourth Lateran Council's decision to forbid the clergy from taking any part in criminal trials by ordeal; it was now held impious to subject God to human interrogation. The practical consequence of abolishing trial by compurgation and ordeal was the immediate need for a new procedure for finding the facts in a case and determining whether these facts amounted to guilt or innocence. In England, where the concept of trial by one's peers had been formulated, this, after a short period of intense consultation between 1215 and 1219, gave an additional impetus to the function of the jury in criminal trials;[75] and this is where their duties came to include the obligation not only of determining the facts alleged in the case but of finding what the facts meant in law. As has already been suggested, this question would often be a matter of *opinion* rather than of immediate and certain knowledge; but opinion might be contentious, since it called for the exercise of judgment. This difficulty was clarified as early as 1230 in a statute of Westminster which defined the responsibilities of the jury by giving it the right to render a general verdict, covering both the facts and the law relating to those facts, in which they were to seek the counsel of the justices. But as Sir John Baker has observed, it was the emergence of the jury that really forced a recognition of the possibility of a distinction between fact and law, leading in turn to refinement in the principles of law. This made technical difficulties for the lay jury; not surprisingly, trial judges were soon giving directions to the jury on points of law.[76] Five hundred years later, when British subjects in the American colonies, confronted by the threat of juryless vice-admiralty courts, invoked the right to trial by jury as derived from Magna Carta, they were not far from the mark; and they stood in a line with English radicals including—perhaps starting with—John Lilburne, twice tried on charges of sedition and twice acquitted by London juries.

Trial jurors are now supposed to meet in a state which may be called *circumstantial ignorance.* In the modern United States, owing no doubt to the dominant influence of and tactical latitude permitted to attorneys in the courtroom, a prospective juror may be struck off the panel by virtue of the slightest connection with either the personalities or circumstances of the case, or even on an attorney's hunch.

Medieval jurors were not a board of independent but silent adjudicators. They were *witnesses* sworn to the truth,[77] and the quest for the truth made them responsible for seeking information on their own initiative and bringing their critical faculties to bear on information which they had themselves gathered in the community. Medieval jurors were expected to know the who's who of the case, including the accused. They could send for witnesses; they could interrogate. Jurors were expected to know the personalities, often the personal histories, of litigants and prisoners; in cases where bastardy was alleged, inheritance of property was likely to be at stake and the jury's local knowledge could be decisive. It was possible for members of the relatively early jury to sit separately in the courtroom, to ask questions of witnesses, even to offer individual opinions without any violation of their oath or of court protocol. Some of these functions, as we shall see, long survived the medieval period. So long as jurors were not related by blood to the accused, all these activities were consistent with the search for truth, and compatible with that sense of fairness which we have designated as moral agency. The fundamental difference in the modern jury is the rule that it must take into consideration *only* evidence heard in court and under oath. A verdict may be invalidated when a juror possessed of specialist or personal knowledge introduces it into the jury's deliberations. James Oldham begins his Selden Lecture on the self-informing jury by instancing a recent homicide case in which two of the jurors were shown to have been nurses who had improperly injected medical knowledge into the jury's debate.[78] This rule, which began by applying to judges early in the twelfth century,[79] had been gradually translated to the jury by the eighteenth century. This distancing of the jury from the *locale* represents the most distinctive example of the transformation from the medieval to the modern jury; for the earlier jury's qualification rested precisely on the opposite condition, their local *knowledge*, both of persons and circumstances.[80]

The modern distancing of the jury is also somewhat at variance from the assumption of colonial Americans that a person accused by the crown could best be assured of a fair trial in the friendly ambience of his neighbors, the colonial assumption being that a local trial would safeguard the accused against being carried away for trial (possibly on charges of treason) in England. It was a claim adhered to by the colonists with great vehemence.

VI.

The transformation from the medieval to the modern jury has been credibly linked to advances in scientific method and the law of evidence, as the concept of evidence came increasingly to depend on reliable verification.[81] Verifiability undoubtedly became a criterion of validity with the development of scientific experimentation in the seventeenth century. But this cannot be a complete explanation of so complex a process, where the benefits of recent science were, after all, very unevenly distributed among the population. The concept of verification would no doubt have been more likely to rule out supernatural evidence, particularly when it was unsupported by material or repeatable tests. But in Salem, Massachusetts, in 1692 the court hearing testimony in the notorious witchcraft trials accepted "spectral" evidence, according to which a person might be there (in spirit) and not there (in body) at one and the same time. Such an intellectual mirage deprived the defendant of all viable means of defense, both by the evidence of the senses and by the new, scientific concept of evidence available to educated people, because it automatically failed the test of being capable of refutation. An almost universal belief in witchcraft would actually weaken the impact of the criteria of verification. Holders of such beliefs had no reason to fear because they had no reason to anticipate the advent of the Enlightenment.

There is no point either in England or in the Anglophone colonies at which medieval snaps into modern. If the process cannot be dated with precision, the explanation is at least partly that the great transformation was never as complete or decisive as has commonly been supposed. A justly celebrated date in the history of rational modernization is 1670, when Bushell's case gave Chief Justice Vaughan the opportunity to win a place in the canon of English liberties by vindicating the autonomy of jurors, exonerating them from being punished, as frequently happened, for rendering a verdict contrary to the court's instructions. But his opinion (which is by no means easy to follow) included as one justification of the jury's independence that its members might possess personal knowledge, unknown to the judge, enabling them to evaluate the evidence heard in court. This cannot be called a "modernizing" argument; on the contrary, it looked back to the medieval fact-finding role of jurors, who, as we have seen, were expected to be self-informing and to bring to court the results of their own inquiries.[82] Clearly, the "modern" jury either had not fully arrived or was not conceptually exclusive; perhaps few were aware that any change might be taking place.

The canonical status of Bushell's case has been challenged, moreover, by the claim that Vaughan's invocation of the neighbor-witness tradition was "wilfully anachronistic."[83] But this is a misreading of the then current consensus. A new aggressiveness on the part of the common people may have owed something to the new politics of the Restoration, but judicial pressure on criminal trial juries was commonplace. Juries were regularly fined for disobeying the judge's instructions; judges clearly considered themselves entitled to make up the jury's mind and to punish them for noncompliance. The concept of moral agency was obviously neither attractive to those who bore its burden, nor even universally recognized in principle; political tension between the bench and the jury appears to have been common. When juries took personal risks by exercising lenity—known as "pious perjury"—or by the rendering of verdicts against the manifest weight of the evidence, and in defiance of the judge's directions, the concept of the jury's moral agency was itself on trial. On less controversial occasions, however, the medieval view still survived, as for example when a juror who made it known to the judge that he wished to give evidence from personal knowledge would be permitted to step out of the jury box to do so.[84] Either the oath he had already taken as a juror must have protected his evidence, or he was newly sworn as a witness.

Bushell's case takes its place in the political history of the judiciary as a move to restrain the domination of the courts by crown-appointed judges. Vaughan had in any case made available for future generations a definitive affirmation of the jury's historic role—to exercise *independent* judgment. But the opinion failed to put a stop to the practice of judicial bullying; Judge

Jeffreys's brutalization of his juries in the 1680s was notorious. Notwithstanding Chief Justice Popham's assertion of precedent in Slade's case as long ago as 1602, it is clear that precedent had not acquired definitive status. Vaughan, however, had added for good measure that a judge might err; and, if a judge was to find the facts, why should not the jury do so? To regard this opinion as nugatory simply because it relied in part on a practice—that of jury as witness—that was currently falling into disuse is to overlook equally significant contemporary evidence: this emerges in a tract published in 1680 by Sir John Hawle defending the jury which specifically invoked Bushell's case to justify the jury in the armament of English liberty.[85] The argument really turned on the question of why the jury was there at all.

A very thorough answer to doubts about the jury's place and value had already appeared in 1666 in the form of a complete guide to the conduct of jury trials by a member of the Inner Temple. Giles Duncombe's *Tryals per Pais* (subtitled *Methodically Composed for the Publick Good*)—a trial, that is, in which the prisoner was tried by the "country" or county—covered every aspect of trial procedure, citing numerous examples and cases. "[A]nd to find out this Truth no way is like to this of Juries," the author declared, making his work as much a manifesto as a guide, for jurors were presumed "to have a better knowledge of the fact than any others." Anachronisms were becoming thick on the ground; once again, the jurors were assumed to possess the advantage of superior local knowledge. If, however, the introduction of local knowledge were already anachronistic in the Restoration period, one would expect the neighbor-witness theme to have been excised from subsequent editions of *Tryals per Pais,* a comprehensive guide to current procedure. But a series of edited and updated reprints, containing much new material, continued to reproduce the same passage unchanged. And so did further reprints in 1718 and 1739, although these were expanded to contain new information about evidence, with many new citations.[86] The book also contained a long list of grounds for challenging prospective jurors, exhaustive enough to have satisfied a modern court. The untidy truth is that the neighbor-witness function died a very gradual death, to be buried in an unmarked grave.

Bushell's case arose from an issue of free speech and religious freedom; the accused were Quakers who had defied the law by preaching in public. The charges brought by the government were inherently political, and the case necessarily implicated the jury in the most fundamental of moral issues.

This was no abstract exercise in speculative moral philosophy; the verdict called for high principle and great personal courage. In no sense could the jury, as an integral part of the judicial system, be separated from the operation of the political system as a whole. Without conferring new constitutional powers, the transition from the medieval to early modern jury left the criminal trial jury "virtually absolute" in its power to determine the defendant's fate, says Professor Thomas Green of the later medieval period.[87] Bushel's jury at least made its contribution to that authority.

Interrogating contemporaries will do little to explain the transition, if only because contemporaries were only dimly aware that it was happening. Clearer and more authentic results will appear by seeking explanation of the transition in the internal dynamics and procedures of the court. Advances in scientific method would assuredly erode habit, and eventually even diminish prejudice; but reconsiderations in the philosophy of law or justice would be more likely to have *followed* from changes in practice and procedure. Change needs to be explained; explanation *follows* change. In seeking reasons for changes in the jury's role, the first place to look is in the courts.

The conduct of the courts was controlled by the judges, and the judges wanted to get through as many trials as possible in the day. Through the seventeenth and eighteenth centuries it was unusual for a routine trial to occupy more than half an hour. In judicial theory, the defendant had no need of counsel because the judge was there to conduct a fair trial; the judge would act the role of counsel for the defense, which rendered defense counsel superfluous; but the objection to the presence of lawyers in truth owed more to the consideration that they would inevitably complicate and protract the proceedings. By the eighteenth century the unsatisfactory nature of this way of doing justice, with its obvious disadvantages to poor and uneducated people trying pathetically to defend themselves in court, led to a relaxation; lawyers were already permitted to act when the judge considered that a point of law was involved, and from the 1730s it became general practice to permit defendants on felony charges the services of counsel. But the practice only became a legal right by statute in 1836. And it had been very unevenly absorbed in the colonies at the time of the trials conducted in New York in connection with the allegations of slave conspiracy in 1741, in which accused slaves went unrepresented and not one slave was acquitted in a jury trial. But on the other hand, in this as in many respects, as we have seen elsewhere, colonies differed from one another as much as from

England, and a promise of representation by counsel in New England codes of law in the early seventeenth century anticipated English practice.[88]

Once the jurors had withdrawn to deliberate, they were locked up and deprived of food or even drink until they had reached a verdict, a great inducement to speedy unanimity; at least, this seems to have been the practice during the fourteenth and fifteenth centuries, for which we have the records of the Year Books, and there is no clear indication that the procedure changed. Isolation made the jurors virtual prisoners of the court but gave them enormous discretionary power, since no one, not even the judge, could know where they got their information or how they reached their verdict.[89] The requirement of unanimity, which seems to have been undisputed, added appreciably to the jury verdict's authority. But once the trained lawyers entered permanently into the trial process, it was their interest on either side to control the evidence on which the case would be argued and the outcome of the trial would turn. As they developed their role, the lawyers amply fulfilled the fears of the judges by extending the hours and days of time spent in court, in the process making trials more formal, more driven by rules, and, inevitably, much longer. Once the principle was established, moreover, that only evidence produced on oath in court could be considered by the jury, the modern system was irrevocably in control. But the development was necessarily ragged and imperfect and subject to contrary instances. Exceptions to the rule occurred irregularly and at great distances. In 1796 the Supreme Court of South Carolina ordered a retrial because members of a jury had exchanged personal information after withdrawing from the court. These items presumably fell foul of the requirement that all evidence be given on oath.[90] There was a marked outbreak of jury interventions in a series of forgery trials at the Old Bailey in 1818–21; jurors seem to have been animated by hostility to the Bank of England, which suggests that their stance was a case of the representation of local class interests rather than the old-style sympathy with the historical underdog. At the same time they took the opportunity to perform a public service by using their privileges to subject the bank to public scrutiny—an unusually aggressive assertion of the tradition of moral agency. It was thus only gradually, and not as a result of intention or policy, that the development of the adversarial method—essentially an internal common law process before it was backed by statute—forced the jury into the role of passivity and silence which, as we have noticed, is its mode today.[91] Advocates trained and hired for the task took over the responsibility for protecting the interests of the accused for the understanding of the court.

VII. The composition of the jury, which has always been—and is still—admitted to have considerable bearing on the outcome of a trial, was designed to express a subtle mixture of elements; if the verdict was to be reached impartially as demanded by the law's sense of justice, that impartiality was to be achieved, not by studious distance from the characters and circumstances involved, but by a substantial admixture of relevant elements of the community when composing the jury itself. The demands of impartiality and, particularly since the adoption of the American Constitution, the development of an elaborately articulated separation of powers have sometimes obscured the fact that the medieval and early modern jury had always been known and expected to be a highly political animal with consciously representative functions.[92] This aspect—its representative character—actually antedated and remained more prominent than the representation in Parliament of the local community, the shire or borough. Yet none of these changes detracted from the jury's essential obligation of moral agency. As the mind of society changed, learning painfully to be both more skeptical and in some ways more humane, jurors' honest credulousness, often supplemented by simple religious faith, was gradually supplanted by the growing confidence in scientific verification—however imperfect and random it may have often been, and, of course, verification in turn depended on more impersonal procedures. But these changes did nothing to diminish the need for the many kinds of social office that were elemental to the jury's historic role. In order that English society might cling to the freedom, and the principle of equality before the law, which its legal exponents claimed for their countrymen, the jury had to adapt to the changing standards and expectations of the society of which it was itself an element; the real key to understanding the great transformation is not to see it as an inexplicable anomaly, but to recognize that it enabled the jury to survive vast social changes while remaining a secular moral agency. But the concept of moral agency had itself to undergo refinement and sophistication. Without these adaptations, both functional and psychological, the jury would eventually have withered away.

The community which sent a member to represent its interests in a medieval or early modern parliament had much in common with the same community as reflected in an assize jury. They were likely to be drawn from the same sort of people. Since 1429 the qualification of jurors had been set by Parliament at a forty-shilling freehold, which, surely not accidentally, was the same imposed for parliamentary electors in 1430. The quarter sessions were in many respects the county's principal public event. When the court assembled, there was a general coming together, social, economic, sporting, and political as well as legal. The concept of the *representativeness* of the judicial process, already implied in the work of Thomas A. Green and Cynthia Herrup, has more recently been deepened with more specific reference to the jury in Marianne Constable's account of the legal recognition of "other" communities.[93] Medieval and early modern England's prosperity depended on imports, exports, and financial operations which required the presence of permanent resident alien communities; inevitably, disputes arose both within such groups and between individual members and their English hosts. As far as internal disputes were concerned, the English authorities were generally content to leave matters to be resolved within the alien community; kept among themselves, alien ideas of justice or procedure did not affect the host community. But litigation could also involve an alien against an English person, and to ensure fairness in such cases, the Statute of the Staples in 1353 gave the affected alien community a right to be represented on the jury.

The statute did not alter common law or other English procedures, but it implicitly recognized that different communities had their own customs, views, and moral codes, which were entitled to consideration by English law. Aliens would also know the facts of a situation within their own communities. As Constable has pointed out, members of such "other" groups were not being treated as individuals but were identified by membership of their own community. It was fitting that a person be judged according to the laws and customs of his (or her) own country. There was policy as well as humanity in this procedure; the goodwill of alien merchants had its value to English economic well-being and the crown's revenues.

In more political words, then, aliens deserved some kind of representation. But here we are speaking a political rather than a legal language; a litigant was normally to be represented by his attorney, not by the jury or by officers of the court. The foreign communities, however, had no access to the political recourse of parliamentary representation. But even for the natives, the county court offered opportunities for the cut and thrust of *personal* representation which came much closer to home than that of the distant, relatively infrequent, and inaccessible meetings of a parliament, usually summoned because the king needed a vote of supplies. The political business of the county was effectively transacted at the assizes, whose character as instruments of political representation was well understood; not for nothing were they known as "the parliaments of the shires."[94]

The court continued to perform many functions of local government, issuing or refusing licenses, ordering the repair and maintenance of roads and bridges, and generally addressing itself to transgressions against the moral tone and religious observances of the county. The assizes also served as a meeting ground between judges from Westminster and the people of the shire in their various ranks and with their communal or personal concerns, grievances, and demands. The judges, on circuit from the center of government, were able to take soundings of local opinion as well as promulgate government policies. For such occasions, when the court had assembled, a grand jury of twenty-three men summoned by the lord lieutenant of the county was impaneled from a group of substantial landowners and merchants. Presiding over the session sat the judge, the one officer of the court who represented no section of the local community. Notwithstanding a measure of judicial independence, the judge was an officer of the crown and until the Act of Settlement in 1701, liable to dismissal by the crown.

The formal purpose of the solemn charge with which the presiding judge opened proceedings was to instruct the grand jury in the duty of presenting indictments for crimes of varying degrees of gravity, and to inform them of the differences between felonies and misdemeanors, and other points of law, frequently laced with warnings of the sins of godlessness, drunkenness, disorder, and sexual licentiousness by which the county was in imminent danger of attracting the wrath of a vengeful deity. Sin, which put the whole community at risk, was high on the catalogue of crimes, the more so in the seventeenth century; the sins of the flesh did not lose their opprobrium, but yielded categorical primacy to the advance in the mid-eighteenth century of greater concern with the sinful character of economic offenses. Forestalling, regrating, charging unfair prices, and unfair dealings in the market, all medieval market offenses, became more prevalent; though described in market language, they were still *sins*, and therefore likely to provoke God's anger. The religious meanings underpinning society's moral order gave way to more frankly secular concerns only gradually from the seventeenth to the mid-eighteenth century. Judges varied their language and emphasis from time to time, but the charges are more striking for their consistency and continuity than for any dramatic departures. We shall notice in due course the recurrence of these themes in America. On both sides of the ocean, the grand jury considered the evidence brought up on complaints from members of the community; whenever they were satisfied that there was a case to answer, they were to draw up an indictment for trial by the petty or traverse jury in the next phase of the session. But that was not all. It fell to the grand jurors to act as a sort of schoolmaster to their neighbors. Their moral surveillance had important political dimensions; any sign of discontent, subversion, or rebelliousness was to be made the subject of indictments.

The charge to the grand jury was an instrument whose importance is undervalued when historians concentrate their attention exclusively on the power of the crown and the development of Parliament or assemblies. Lines of communication between the central government and the populace were essentially limited to two major organs. The most important was the church. When attendance was compulsory and when priests received instructions from Lambeth Palace, always in close communication with Whitehall, the sermon and the notice board on the parish church door were probably the principal means of transmitting government policies and of inculcating general principles, obligations, and loyalties into the people. The other, and hardly less important channel, however, was the grand jury. The judge's charge began as a homily on fundamentals. At the Staffordshire quarter sessions in 1587, the judge instructed the grand jury in the importance of the connection between the rule of law and the necessity for obedience, a doctrine, as Christopher Brooks points out, which firmly endorsed the claims of divine right monarchy.[95] At the opening of the Norwich quarter sessions in 1606, the grand jury received from Sir Edward Coke a veritable education in constitutional law, religious doctrine, and economic policy. The chief justice expounded the king's title to the throne, explained and justified the recusancy laws (against nonattendance at church), and warned the jurors against the error that religious toleration would bring peace; he then went on to pursue his own passion for free trade by telling them to root out monopolists.[96] The grand jury also concerned itself with social conditions, on occasion in hard times ordering local magistrates to provide poor relief.[97] Grand jurors were the men of influence and authority among their rural and civic neighbors; the channels of authority ran down from them throughout the county. The interaction between judge and grand jury was usually respectful and harmonious, and both in England and America the grand jury often authorized publication of the judge's charge.

In the wake of the Revolution Settlement and particularly after the Hanoverian succession, presiding judges often expounded political philosophy, amplified by lessons in English history. In 1690 the Leicester grand jury heard from the Earl of Stamford that the monarchy was not of "meer divine right, but by Human Consent."[98] Men were by nature equal, said the earl, and government could be established only by consent—express or implied, this was a recurrent theme. The common law was founded on consent:[99] "The authority of our Kings has no other foundation than ye Rights of ye People have . . . I mean ye Law under ye King."[100]

The origin of government was in contract, as Westminster heard in 1728,[101] at the beginning of a long disquisition on history ancient and medieval; invoking Bracton and Fortescue, the judge reminded the grand jurors that the laws of England were the subject's birthright. The essential need to inculcate loyalty to the Hanoverians, undoubtedly prompted by Jacobite rumblings and the recent rising of 1715, reflected the importance of the connections between the Protestant religion, constitutional and political stability, and good government; but these oft-repeated and strenuously Whiggish views, which emphasized the bill of rights and the principle of consent found in representative institutions commonly believed to have existed before Parliament, could from a social standpoint be deeply conservative. They overlooked, or intentionally averted attention from, the divisive implications of changes in the laws of England such as the recent Black Act or even, from a constitutional view, the passage of the Septennial Act in 1716.

Toward the end of the century, the rise of radicalism and the news from France brought forth some of the most explicit political indoctrination of the whole period. But the tone had now changed. "Unlawful meetings and assemblies for altering the laws and changing the Constitution" were denounced by William Mainwaring, Esq., before the Middlesex grand jury in 1792; adding that the *purpose* made such an assembly unlawful.[102] Sir William Ashurst in Middlesex also in 1792 denounced pamphlets currently circulating which disclaimed any idea of subordination, while in Dublin, Robert Day, Esq., departed from Lockeian precepts to extol the blessings of *inequality*, a theme repeated by Charles Harvey, Esq., in Norwich in 1793.[103]

Sir James Eyre, lord chief justice of the Common Pleas, went as far as to say that even to seek the reform of Parliament was high treason.[104] Differing personal opinions found expression in these charges. In a philosophical address to the Gloucester grand jury in 1797, Rev. John Foley analyzed the distinction between the social and moral causes of poverty, urging the need to provide care.[105] Five years later he was recommending manufacturers provide employment for discharged soldiers and sailors.

Many of the social and economic changes of the era can be traced in the record of concerns which came before the grand juries of England, Wales, and Ireland. (Scotland was not involved in English jurisdiction.) Throughout these records, the representative role of the jury system is always visible and often explicit. There is no sense that the functions of the judiciary ought to be physically separated or morally distinguished from those of political institutions; they are all interdependent and often interlocked. Thus in 1751 the Norfolk borough court grand jury was told that the judicial part of the constitution should be preserved by the jury, "who are a fair and unexceptionable representative of the people and Country";[106] next year the same note was struck with "the Jury are the representatives of the People of England."[107] In Virginia, as Gwenda Morgan has shown, "great care was taken to achieve a balance between different sections of the county so that all precincts were represented."[108] By the 1760s, Richmond County grand juries were willing to castigate members of the upper gentry who were given to loose living and were neglecting their official duties.[109] The personal independence secured by freehold ownership of land gave Virginia's gentry a robust self-assurance very comparable to the sort found in England's largest county, Yorkshire; but the more so because the men of Virginia were not subject to visitations from judges holding their brief from Westminster. Nor did any of the colonies have within its own boundaries a powerful central government sending out judicial visitations to the counties. And the same diminished central spring applied to the colonies as a whole: they had no capital city, no seat of government, no archbishop, not even a bishop to call their own, no Whitehall, no Westminster, no Lambeth Palace. This absence of any authoritative center of judicial gravity within the colonial spectrum permitted centrifugal tendencies in the development of the judicial rules of individual colonies. The unprinted reports of colonial case law rarely came to the notice of the Privy Council, which would review them only on the rare instance of an appeal to London by a dissatisfied party.

When necessary, the grand jury, unlike the petty jury, was able to address itself to matters of policy. This function remained remarkably stable with the passage of centuries. John Morrill thus tells us of the Cheshire grand jury in the mid-seventeenth century: "They could be called upon to join the Justices in petitioning Parliament and the Crown as the authoritative voice of the County." In the next century, at the York assizes of 1764, the grand jury voted approval of the stand of their M.P.'s against General Warrants.[110] The principles were similar when the grand jury faced the chief justice in Middlesex County, New Jersey, at the traditional opening of the quarter sessions in April 1776. The difference was that the crown's authority in the person of the presiding judge, and that of the grand jurors as representatives of the people, were now on opposing sides in a constitutional crisis.

Chief Justice Smythe, who delivered his charge from a fully handwritten script, began with a strong warning against exceeding lawful bounds in protest against Parliament. The colonies rightly valued their liberties but should remember that all their liberties depended on law, which it was the grand jury's duty to enforce. The grand jury respectfully replied by noting that the chief justice had said that all their liberties depended on the law—by which he meant British law—but they begged to demur, preferring to affirm their belief that although liberty "was defined and protected by law, we nevertheless think that it is built on the rights of human nature."[111] This microcosmic replication of the great transatlantic debate reveals the grand jurors as standing in as representatives of the popular cause in a situation in which the ordinary channels of politics were closed. Although this expressly political intervention was provoked by the extraordinary character of the times, the political role of the grand jury was far from being a novel departure; for what the grand jury was doing was to represent the interests of a political constituency by pursuing, if perhaps enlarging on, the role which was already proper to it in normal domestic affairs.

When private economic enterprise threatened the well-being of other members of the community, the grand jury would be the agency to receive the grievance and if necessary to make a presentment. In 1770 certain residents of Hudson County, New York, complained to their grand jury that William Duane had built a mill, "the dam of which extends so far out that it seriously obstructs the communication of the inhabitants of Queens Bury and King Bury and above Fort Edward from rafting down timbers to Albany."[112] It does not appear that a presentment followed, however, or that Duane's political influence outweighed even the local grand jury.

VIII. The debates on ratification of the Constitution, which rumbled throughout the states from the autumn of 1787 until the following summer, were carried on in newspapers and pamphlets, in which they have generally been traced by historians. They were undoubtedly also carried on in taverns, meetinghouses, and markets. As a source of political direction, however, the judge's charge to the grand jury is a clue not to be overlooked; the deference owed to a judge and the hierarchical scale down through the petty jury to the people at large may help to explain the Federalist advantage in the great debate. The grand jury in Edenton, North Carolina, which met in November 1787 for the Michaelmas (the autumn) session, issued a long statement advocating ratification. One does not immediately think of this as Federalist territory; yet, after affirming the need for a firm and lasting union, they observed, "We admire in the new Constitution a proper jealousy of liberty mixed with a due regard for the necessity of a strong and authoritative government." The statement was drawn up with the assistance of the judge, James Iredell, soon to be a justice of the new Supreme Court.[113] When charging the federal grand jury in Savannah in 1792, Iredell expressed the conventional legalistic view of the fact and law question, which assigned the finding of fact to the jury while reserving law to the court.[114] In supporting the Constitution, and ten years later in explaining and defending the controversial Alien and Sedition Laws,[115] Iredell was taking a more interventionist part in constitutional realignment than even that of the English judiciary in connection with the Glorious Revolution.

The grand jury was a potent player in the judicial team. In the eighteenth century, its political role was so well understood that only men of considerable property were permitted to exercise so much political influence; but ever since the Middle Ages, the keynote of the assizes was participation.[116] Both the high public duties in which men of property were called to play their parts and the social aspects of the occasion must have intensified the integrative function of these sessions. They bound men into a sense of community and gave both men and women an opening in which they were free to speak with their own voices.[117] It was a remarkably economical and effective way of running local government while maintaining the bonds with the center which mixed discipline with allegiance. This same system of local participation did much of the practical governing in the American and West Indian colonies; it was not based on or derived from either theory or ideology, but it amounted to an active public engagement which yielded a considerable amount of control over their lives to local people. This is the state of affairs for which, as has been asserted elsewhere, the term "the sociology of consent"[118] seems both rhetorically and functionally appropriate.

But both in early modern England and in its colonies, community had its limits as well as its internal distinctions. Community to all intents and purposes was defined as much by exclusion as by membership; and a community was often defined by its own internal hierarchy.[119] The population of manual and agricultural laborers (whether slave, indentured, or free), the very extensive though poorly defined classes known as servants, and, so far as jury service was concerned, all women were excluded. So, in the colonies, in all probability, were Indians and African-descended persons (though it is doubtful that this exclusion was universal, not least because the definition of such categories was imprecise). Formal structural similarities between England and its colonies were evident, as were formal procedures. Differences, however, were significant. In England the system had a basic wholeness and unity which was lacking in the colonies. The English judges were "the eyes of the kingdom,"[120] who would return to Westminster after the courts had closed, leaving the county communities aware of the existence of an overarching authority. Throughout the centuries, the government in every era needed all the information it could get. England had emerged under the Tudors as in many respects a divided nation whose social order was frequently threatened by rural and regional unrest and by deep religious divisions; the introduction of the Reformation was an incomplete process. Policing the Reformation was one of the functions of the English judicial system.[121]

4

American Independence and the Crisis of Sovereignty

I. The issue of sovereignty links with other essays in this study because sovereignty is the legitimate use of superior power, and legitimacy, according to Anglo-American traditions, is conferred by some form of contract. When the British Empire split, it was along the seam which identified sovereignty as power joined to legitimacy. British sovereignty over the empire appeared from a parliamentary point of view to be a self-evident condition, almost a tautology, which reached its apogee in 1766 with the passage of the Declaratory Act, asserting that Parliament had the right to bind the colonies "in all cases whatsoever."[1] Was it not, after all, the *British* Empire? The problem was more than one of nomenclature. Certain American provinces of the empire had for some years been ceasing to identify themselves as exclusively British. There developed a creeping doubt as to how long national identity could be determined by the character of the governing institutions; and although they were reluctant to name it, or to address the problem of sovereignty directly, this fatal possibility began to emerge in the rhetoric of colonial pamphleteers such as, notably, James Otis and John Adams in Boston, and Patrick Henry in Virginia; in the subtle questionings of John Dickinson, the pseudonymous "Pennsylvania Farmer"; and in pamphlets or speeches by William Hicks and James Wilson in Pennsylvania—all except Hicks being lawyers, and it was of no small significance that Adams and Henry gained both inspiration and opportunity in law courts. The young John Adams claimed that American independence was inspired by James Otis's speech against writs of assistance in the Boston courthouse; the young Patrick Henry seized the opportunity to Americanize the local issue of the Parsons' Cause in Virginia.

In the same period, English common law, which colonists were proud to share with their English fellow subjects, was subtly morphing into an *American* common law or, more exactly, into regional varieties of American common law. There could hardly have been a more convincing demonstration of the power of the periphery in the governance of empire.[2] Yet the sovereignty of Parliament was confidently affirmed in this same period by William Blackstone, the first Vinerian Professor of Law at Oxford University, in whose *Commentaries on the Laws of England,* which exerted enormous influence on American legal thought, law was defined as the command of a superior to an inferior.[3] And Parliament knew no constitutional superior. The difference was logically irreconcilable. In the colonies, a hard and fast definition proved more elusive; political power was never absolute, and its underlying principles were in a continual state of challenge and negotiation.[4] Although only a few colonists showed much interest in theory, new assertions of parliamentary authority to act in areas which colonists habitually regarded as their own made it increasingly necessary to establish the primary conditions of legitimacy—how it was verified, where it came from.

During the 1760s, as controversy began to focus on a variety of particular issues, all of which involved the location of authority, colonial representatives recognized that the colonies were parts of a larger whole, which must be subject to some central power, at least where regulation served the interests of the colonies equally with the British at home.[5] But until they were unavoidably tangled in its toils, American spokesmen generally avoided the language of sovereignty, with its feudal undertones and absolutist resonance. John Dickinson, whose exposition of colonial interests was the most influential of its time, only allowed the colonies to be "as dependent on Great Britain as a perfectly free people can be."[6] This was audacious language fraught with quiet, understated menace; for on close examination, Dickinson's reasons for colonial submission to central direction were based on grounds of utility, not loyalty or obligation. If separation from the empire were perceived as serving the interests of the colonies, a shift toward some form of home rule, by implication, would follow. Sovereignty stood on shaky ground.

II.

The modern concept of sovereignty had emerged in sixteenth-century Europe as the defining characteristic of the nation-state. In this form, the doctrine had first been expounded at length in 1576, when Jean Bodin, who had narrowly survived the massacre of French Protestants on St. Bartholemew's Day, 1572, published the first full exposition of what became the classical European theory. But Bodin did not claim novelty for the concept of sovereignty; he derived the name from the "majesty" of the Roman Empire, asserted in AD 212 in a decree when the Emperor Caracalla, probably more in the interest of taxation than constitutional law, declared all Roman subjects to be Roman citizens. Charlemagne was a veritable embodiment of the idea of sovereignty, while the titanic investiture controversy between empire and papacy was nothing less than a struggle for sovereignty; and when Henry VIII's Parliament declared in 1533 that the realm of England was "an Empire" it was asserting English sovereignty in defiance of papal Rome. All these historical instances had contributed to defining the doctrine. According to Bodin, sovereign power had two essential characteristics: First, it was absolute; there could be no appeal to a superior power, although it has been a common mistake to regard it as merely arbitrary. "Princeps legibus solutus est": *absolved* of the laws of men, the monarch was always responsible to God. And second, it had in some approved sense to bear the hallmarks of legitimacy.[7] But Bodin's sovereign demanded allegiance to the ruler's person; the abstraction of "the state" ("lo stato") had earlier begun to develop in the city-states into which Italy fragmented, but took longer to form from the eventual coalescence of the provinces of the disintegrating empire.

The demands of sovereignty had to be backed up from time to time by assertions of a power which the old monarchies claimed but were not always able to enforce. It was also in 1766 that the French king Louis XV issued a decree of the most unremitting absolutism: "It is in my person that sovereign power rests; to me alone belongs the legislative power, independently and unshared, and it is on my authority alone that the officers of my courts proceed, not to the formulation, but to the recording and promulgation of my law. . . . The whole of public order emanates from me; my people is at one with me, and the rights and interests of the nation are . . . necessarily united with my own and rest solely in my own hands."[8]

These pronouncements, which represented the culmination of a shift toward absolutism undertaken by the Valois and Bourbon monarchs, did not call for validation of the monarchy by any form of consent or contract. They stood in a line of descent from the divine right of kings. In England they had been anticipated in *Hamlet,* some quarter of a century after Bodin, in the words of the threatened king Claudius:

> There's such divinity doth hedge a king
> That treason can but peep to what it would,
> Acts little of his will.[9]

From a king who had reached the throne by killing his brother, these words were baited with a treacherous irony; divine right might not after all be self-enforcing. In contrast to Louis's ministers, who had drafted his decree in language of unmistakable clarity, Jean-Jacques Rousseau had also recently proposed a view of the state which amounted (though he did not say so) to a justification of sovereignty. Rousseau's general will (*volonté générale*), which involved the whole population in a mutual contract,[10] is the most extreme form of popular sovereignty ever proposed, before or since. Rousseau had leaned heavily on the contractual theory of John Locke, who by the mid-eighteenth century was also exerting considerable influence on colonial expositors of the law. The work of adapting the law to comply with American—and republican—principles fell to legislatures or their committees, and to specially called conventions and courts. But in the mid-eighteenth century, as the colonists edged Parliament out of their domestic jurisdictions,[11] the common law, which confirmed their rights as British subjects, implied an equally valid claim to make their own laws and govern through their own institutions. One by one, the new states' claims to sovereignty came about as a *result* rather than a cause of independence. Having rejected Parliament, the colonists found themselves holding the residue of parliamentary sovereignty in their hands.

III. The struggle for American independence was to have deep unintended consequences but was never intended to bring about a revolution in law. No such overturn was conceived to be necessary. But once independence had been achieved, it represented two genuine, interrelated revolutions.

The first was simply geographical: the transfer of the formal claim to sovereign power from Britain to the united, if loosely connected, states of America. The other, by piecemeal and episodic processes, was a transfer of legitimate power of *domestic* sovereignty from the hands of traditional authority to those of the amorphous body euphemistically known as "the people." Nothing less than an appeal to the will of the people could justify the overthrow of the reigning monarchy. This formulation, however, failed to explain whether "the people" were now collectively the populations of all the states (as in the Declaration of Independence) or were the several peoples of the individual states. In the Articles of Confederation the claim became explicit: each individual state claimed to be the heir to the sovereignty formerly exercised by the crown over its colonial predecessor; legitimacy was held to be inherent in the succession. The semantic contest was the manifestation of a struggle for power which persisted throughout the debates on the Constitution and left its mark on the Constitution itself.

These momentous events gave an unprecedented prominence to the concept of sovereignty in American politics. In the war of words between Parliament and its opponents, sovereignty became, on the colonial side of the argument, a synonym for self-rule, and by the early summer of 1776, this meant independence. The leaders who ran the affairs of the states suddenly became the political authorities of independent powers.

The Articles of Confederation, adopted only on French insistence after years of wrangling, committed the Confederation to a guarantee of "state sovereignty" while entrusting to Congress the overarching powers and responsibilities essential to government. In fact, the Continental Congress had exercised these powers for some six years before the Articles could be ratified. The concept of state sovereignty, however, proved impossible to validate and became the source of infinite contradiction and confusion. The states, for all their protestations, were not nations. None of them alone could have maintained sovereign power. None of them, probably not even New York, could have built and maintained its own army and navy or conducted an independent foreign policy. The delegates' intellectual confusion was manifested in the second item of the Articles of Confederation's guarantee of sovereignty to each state. During the prolonged and tortuous debates on the Articles, Thomas Burke of North Carolina, who though a recent arrival threw himself into the cause of state sovereignty with such effect as to threaten the whole negotiation, even envisaged the possibility that the Congress might go to war without involving all of the states.[12] The consequences to say the least could have involved conflicts of loyalty and law. No single authority could have discharged the obligations incumbent on a sovereign power.

Since the forming of the early modern state, sovereignty had faced in two directions: inward, keeping peace and order in the realm; and outward, maintaining the state's autonomy in a potentially hostile world. But the meaning of sovereignty was confused by the state-sovereignty advocates with the people's right to rule themselves. Power, argued these advocates, could be known as legitimate only when it was exercised through known and lawful procedures. Thus, in the previous century, Oliver St. John, defending John Hampden against Charles I, had argued that the king could act lawfully only when he acted through prescribed channels, "for the Law of England, for the applying of the Supreme power which it hath settled in his majesty to the particular causes and occasions, hath set down a method and known rules, which are necessarily to be observed."[13] That was in the famous case of ship money, when Charles I's personal rule was reaching its limits. Transferred in the next century to America, the issue was formally but only partially resolved by the popular ratification of the Constitution. American government would contain—and still contains—many obstacles to the sovereignty of the people.

The key expression marking legitimacy was "the consent of the governed," which duly appeared in the Declaration of Independence. Consent has traditionally been expressed through institutions of representation; this book argues that judicial institutions made almost equally important contributions.

The Continental Congress, in proclaiming American rights, claimed the protection of the common law against Parliament's encroachments; willing to adapt the common law to their own style and claims, colonial leaders, as British subjects, were proud of it as their own possession and had no aim to undermine its rules, procedures, or, for the most part, principles. They had no comparable precedent-based body of domestic law to install in its place, no single source of unified authority, no apparent need to replace it, and no rival system waiting in the wings of revolution. Property and procedure were its foundations. Property, it was true, could be seized from landowners under wartime statutes, but only after they had renounced their rights of citizenship by remaining loyal to the crown; other arguments exhausted, the principle of property remained undisturbed.[14]

The upheaval that led to political independence, however, opened doors that were only loosely secured, and in turn led to numerous, though not always consistent, paths of reform. Much the most prominent was Virginia's commission to revise the laws, of which Thomas Jefferson was chairman. The strong strain of individualism which found expression in the propensity of Americans to seize every opportunity for self-advancement took shape in the widespread ambition to own and develop sustainable, family-size portions of land. Jefferson, who tried unsuccessfully to confer a fifty-acre farm, and with it a qualification for the suffrage, on every willing settler (providing always that he was male and white), recognized this social force in his passion for ownership in fee simple. Not without having to overcome conservative resistance, Jefferson succeeded in overturning the practices of primogeniture and entailing estates—reservation of the property to the eldest son (in cases of intestacy). But these almost revolutionary departures from British tradition responded to internal social pressures which already differentiated Virginia and many other colonies from the style and practices of England. A still more profound departure was made in 1786 with the passage of Jefferson's Statute for Religious Freedom. Jefferson himself was in Paris as congressional envoy, leaving to James Madison the task of leading the struggle and steering his bill through the state legislature. Jefferson with some justification had this recorded in the next edition of the *Encyclopedia*.[15]

If the Revolution achieved more than most of its authors had intended, colonial lawyers, who for half a century had been coming into their own as an independent and self-assured profession, had never sought to undermine the common law. In their confidence in the principles of English jurisprudence, they were reinforced by the absorption of civil law, or equity, a branch which had originated in the late Middle Ages when judges began to recognize that the recondite methods of the common law too often failed to yield substantial, or "natural," justice, and took their own steps to remedy these defects by resorting to law according to the chancellor's conscience.[16] The processes by which English law, which, imperceptibly, through the centuries, had been sipping from the Roman or civil cup, were encouraged in the second half of the eighteenth century by Lord Mansfield, chief justice of the King's Bench, who remarked that he never liked common law so much as when it was like equity.[17]

Chancery courts, through which equity was administered and which dealt with issues arising under admiralty law, dispensed with juries (which was why Americans saw them as a threat to their liberties); but in most respects, equity and common law in colonial practice converged along different routes to reach similar results. Advertisements placed by lawyers in colonial newspapers invariably claimed competence in the practice of "law and equity." Jefferson's reform program undoubtedly owed much of its rationale to the civil law, which he had studied along with the common law under George Wythe's tutorship at William and Mary. Subordination of procedures to outcomes must have appealed to Jefferson, who in any case was by no means averse to diminishing English influence. The influence is made all the more probable since Jefferson's interest in the civil law was shared by his senior, Judge Edmund Pendleton, also an influential member of the commission.[18] In general, however, law reform took place piecemeal, without commitment to imperative ideological principles. In the constitutions of most of the newly independent states, laws in existence in 1776 remained in force unless repealed.[19]

Neither in common law nor in equity, then, did colonial practice suggest any reason to expect a revolutionary project of adapting the law to American or republican principles. But certain reforms may to some degree be claimed as among its consequences, and some of them—notably, as has been noticed, in Virginia—represented the most humane of current Enlightenment principles of European origin. Of these, the primary source was the Italian aristocrat Cesare Beccaria's tract *Of Crimes and Punishments* (1763). Beccaria, who was widely read, advocated a relatively humane and basically utilitarian approach to penal policy; he deprecated the sanguinary punishments that were governments' preferred means of law enforcement and argued that punishments should be made appropriate to the crime. This approach marked a sharp contrast with the bloody code of English criminal law, but even this was already yielding in England to the humanizing pressures of John Howard and other reformers. American experiments in penology after the Revolution took shape in a context of utilitarian and Enlightenment thinking about public policy.

Colonial lawyers, from roughly the 1720s and 1730s, put more and more value on citing English sources and precedents. English common law formed the firm foundation, not only of colonial law, but of the American sense of justice. It came to be indistinguishable from natural law.

In sum, independence certainly freed the American policy-making classes to use both their legal and their legislative powers (which were now placed firmly in American hands) to enact their social and economic policies in many fields, and these were necessary consequences of American self-government. But it would be a mistake to take them as representing the fulfillment of a reformist, or still less a republican, program that originated before the Revolution and that the Revolution was intended to accomplish. Transformations, such as they were, in law were results, not causes, of independence.

If only because it came into existence to do in the common interest the things the states could not do on their own, the Continental Congress soon started to behave in important respects like the government of a sovereign state. The conflict of interests became a conflict of ideas which persisted throughout the Confederation's life—and beyond. But the concept of state sovereignty, whose proponents believed that liberty could only be preserved by the individual states, was subjected to a searching critique in the next century by Justice Joseph Story, the first Boylston Professor of Law at Harvard, a nationalistically inclined Supreme Court justice whose career partly spanned the eras of Marshall and Taney.

Story began by drawing on the colonial period, when the colonies were clearly *not* sovereign states; any sovereignty in existence belonged to Britain, and could not have passed from colony to state because the colonies had no sovereignty to confer. He then took up the Declaration of Independence, on which he was able to invoke a speech by Charles Cotesworth Pinckney in the South Carolina House of Representatives' debate on ratification. "This admirable manifesto," said Pinckney, "sufficiently refutes the doctrine of the individual sovereignty and independence of the several states. . . . In that declaration, the several states are not even enumerated. . . . The separate independence and individual sovereignty of the several states were not even thought of by the enlightened band of patriots who framed this declaration." As for the words "sovereign and independent" as protected by the Articles of Confederation, they could only have been intended in a subordinate sense, since a majority of the states could bind the minority. This provision alone was enough to deprive the states of their claimed sovereignty. Story then listed the exclusive powers conferred on Congress by the Constitution, which called for intervention in disputes, a power incompatible with state sovereignty. He concluded by invoking the external meaning of sovereignty. "To foreign governments we were known as the United States only."[20] This point was only too significant in 1776 and 1777. The Continental Congress could have had no hope of French assistance without a declaration, which it alone could make, that the states were not only independent but independent in their *collective* capacity. The French court had no interest in restoring Britain's empire. Facing outward, Congress could only confront the world with the attributes of national sovereignty.

Story then argued that claims of state sovereignty could no longer survive under the Constitution. When any state submits to a larger political body in which a majority vote has power to reach into the individual states, affecting their laws and directly touching their citizens, those states have given up their sovereignty. All of the original states acceded to this principle through their ratifying conventions when they adopted a federal constitution which contained procedures for its own amendment, since a constitutional amendment must control the states which dissented from it as well as those which agreed. The prospect of expansion into the as yet uncharted West would inevitably have raised the issue in a more acute form, for future territories could be established, as under the Ordinance of 1787, and future states admitted, only under the aegis of the Constitution.

Anti-Federalists, in opposing adoption of the Constitution, never disputed the validity of the classical doctrine of absolute sovereignty. That in fact was just what they feared. To have dismissed it as a myth which the Revolution itself had discredited would have been a fatal tactical error. They insistently denounced the consolidationist aims of their nationalist opponents precisely because, as they feared, consolidation would locate the old sovereignty in the new government. These tactics forced the Federalists onto seemingly democratic territory, in which they may have been more comfortable in rhetoric than in reality, from which basis they (perhaps uncharacteristically) maintained that all sovereignty lay in the people. Bits of it were then deputed to organs of government on loan, as it were, and to be returned after use.[21] The principle of legitimacy as action through recognized agencies did not play an instrumental role on either side of this somewhat tortuous debate.

The conceptual torment of the men who were struggling at one and the same time to perpetuate state sovereignty and to create a superior and perpetual union of those states reflects the contradiction inherent in their aims. No state in such a position can validate a claim to sovereignty in its classical form. If sovereignty were truly indivisible, the "people" of the United States must conform to that indivisibility, and if the one divided, then (as Abraham Lincoln was to warn them) so would the other. It was a contradiction which took its fatal toll in the years 1860 to 1865.

The dread of that calamity, or of a complete disintegration of the Union, provoked by intense and widespread hostility to the proposed Constitution, persuaded Hamilton, Madison, and Jay to combine their intellectual forces to write *The Federalist Papers,* which began to appear in the New York newspapers in October 1787. The stresses and strains to which classical sovereignty had been recently subjected had only served to convince them of the importance of demolishing the credibility of state sovereignty or of any form of shared or divided sovereignty. Anti-Federalist aspirations to preserve state sovereignty under the Constitution, they insisted again and again, were utterly incompatible with the sovereignty of the Union. The idea of a sovereign over sovereigns was "repugnant and irreconcilable," as Hamilton forcefully wrote in *Federalist* 15; it was an "*imperium in imperio*"—a "political monster," "a solecism in theory" and in practice "subversive of the order and ends of civil polity,"[22] as Madison and Hamilton jointly stated in No. 20. Publius had taken over wholesale the classical principles of sovereignty and applied them to the American situation.

This commitment to absolute sovereignty or no sovereignty appeared in *Federalist* 15 on December 1, and again, on December 11, 1787, in No. 20. But by January 2, in No. 32, by Hamilton, a subtle semantic change makes an appearance. While repeating the denunciation of the concept of divided sovereignty as "totally contradictory and repugnant," Hamilton now allows that under the plan of the convention, the state governments "would clearly retain all the rights of sovereignty which they had before and which are not *exclusively* delegated to the United States."[23] The compromise hinted at here depends on the separate functions of state and federal governments, leaving the states in possession of such "rights" of sovereignty as they need to conduct their own business. But if true sovereignty was indivisible it could not be subject to modification. These rights cannot be logically distinguished from the core of sovereignty itself. By No. 39, on January 16, "The Conformity of the Plan to Republican Principles," the states retain a "residual" sovereignty after the Union has assumed all it needs to perform its duties; but Publius now proposes a radically new definition of the character of the Union, which is to be neither wholly national nor wholly federal, but a novel composition of both. Sovereignty has, after all, been divided. On January 26, in No. 45, which is addressed to "the supposed Danger from the Powers of the Union, to the State Governments," Madison is even more reassuring to the states, which will retain "a very considerable portion of active sovereignty."[24]

This measured withdrawal from the mountain peaks of absolute sovereignty to the dusty plains of mundane utility cannot be explained as proceeding from the preconceived plan of the essays. It is clearly tactical. Anti-Federalists are mounting a serious challenge, and Publius is forced to respond to the charge that the Constitution will lead to consolidation under an all-powerful central government. The change of tone is intended, in a debate which the Federalists have not yet won, to reassure not only avowed opponents but uncommitted voters who are open to persuasion. This was a critical moment in which American political discourse spoke in a different voice from that of Europe. In all probability, Hamilton and Madison—who were both in New York—met to discuss their strategy; they were forced to recognize that adamantine adherence to the classical mold as the *only* legitimate model of constitutional authority had failed either to persuade or to intimidate the opposition and was damaging their cause by making the Constitution look more of a threat to the integrity of the states than the authors (Jay had dropped out through illness) had ever expected.

The change of tone was more than a matter of style: it represented a crisis of definition. Ideologically, it may have been less critical for Madison than for Hamilton. Examination of Madison's preparations for the Convention reveals him as less committed than his fiery colleague to the absolutist view. In April 1787 Madison had anticipated the crisis in a memorandum which he headed, "Vices of the Political System of the United States." In outlining his aims, Madison was both candid and clear. "The great desideratum in Government," he argued, "is such a modification of the sovereignty as will render it sufficiently neutral between different interests and factions, to control one part of the society from invading the rights of the other, and at the same time sufficiently controlled itself, from setting up an interest contrary to that of the whole Society."[25] Madison, who was meticulous in his choice of language, could hardly have specified the need for a "modification of the sovereignty" if he had been wholly committed to the conviction that sovereignty could not be modified. Both he and Hamilton took high ground in writing *The Federalist*, but it seems probable that Hamilton set Publius's tone for this central theme. Madison and those who thought like him had almost been reduced to explaining the Constitution by admitting that "divided sovereignty" was both a contradiction in terms and a new political principle.

When, after the purgation of civil war, American political scientists faced the new problems of order and stability brought on by mass immigration, urban expansion, industrial unrest and disorder, monetary instability, and other conditions that the complex structures of law and politics had not been designed to meet, they found in classical sovereignty little to assist them in analysis or action. As a political scientist holding a professorship at Princeton, Woodrow Wilson revealed in early writings the interest in practical investigation of what happens, who gains and loses, in the politics of process which increasingly caught the attention of intellectuals of the Progressive Era. This realism, brought to bear on the meaning of sovereignty, exposed the absurdity of using the same language to describe the people of the United States and the czar of Russia. But Wilson could not resist the temptation of attempting his own definition. Sovereignty, he said, was "the daily operative power of framing and giving effect to laws. It is the originative, directive, governing power. It lives, it plans, it executes. It is the organic origination by the State of its law and policy; and the Sovereign power is the highest originative organ of the state."[26] None of this overheated language explained precisely what sovereignty was, where it came from, how it was known. Yet in this same essay, Wilson derides "this mad pursuit of a sovereign amid the obvious phenomena of politics."[27] Wilson, who was later to embody the sovereignty of his country at Versailles in 1919, discovered the limitations on political power when the Senate rejected his treaty and denied America entry to the League of Nations.

The English political philosopher John Austin, lecturing at Oxford in the 1830s, echoing Blackstone, had emphasized that law was "command of a superior to an inferior," and Austin has generally been read as the epitome of the authoritarian view. But Austin begins his discussion of sovereignty with the observation—an observation, not a theory—that "the bulk of any given society are in the habit of obedience," and that the recipient of this obedience is *not* in the habit of deferring to anyone else. Yet Austin also observed, "In most societies political and independent, the constitution of the supreme power has grown."[28] If this comment does not astonish the modern reader it is because it is itself modern in tone, and represents a profoundly different viewpoint from that of earlier philosophers who deduced the need for sovereignty from human nature or derived it from the structure of the universe.

Wilson, with obvious reference to Austin, observed that "in a very profound sense, law originates in the community."[29] This looked back to Blackstone's respect for community-based law but offered little to play with in reconciling ideological, let alone political, differences. With all these observations, a sociological element was creeping into the Anglo-American comprehension of the issues. But the first American political scientist to develop a full-scale account of political society on observational principles was Arthur F. Bentley, who gave his book the very modern title *The Process of Government*,[30] an approach which represented a departure from past principles; the point was illustrated by the Italian commentator who observed that it would be almost impossible to translate Bentley's title into Latin.[31]

The increasing validity of the realist standpoint found explicit title in Bentley's contemporary John R. Commons, later to become the first historian of American labor. Not yet ready to dismiss sovereignty from the political vocabulary, he treated it as a sociological phenomenon, calling for sociological remedies.[32] But the truth is that this represented a modernization of issues that would not have been unfamiliar to earlier generations. Sovereignty had never been self-sustaining and had never been able to translate theoretical power directly into humbled obedience. Early modern government may have been theoretically supreme but it was often mercifully inefficient (even royal messengers were waylaid on remote passes); great monarchies like small republics had practical purposes to fulfill and limitations to contend with—a state of affairs which Bentley and his contemporaries would have recognized. The political vocabulary of federalism, pluralism, or localism might have seemed strange to early modern monarchs, but inefficiency, official corruption, the sale of public offices (or public honors), and various forms of devious noncompliance often mitigated royal power. Practices that sound strangely medieval could also be discerned in late nineteenth-century America. The truth was that sovereignty had always had sociological dimensions, taking different forms in different periods and circumstances. Bodin himself explained in numerous detailed chapters that sovereignty could never be comprehended as a mere juristic abstraction indifferent to the political context of time and condition. Having said which, it was far more important to Commons, Bentley, E. A. Ross, Woodrow Wilson, and their contemporaries to jettison high-sounding abstractions; general principles, for them, were to be built up from observations of events and process. Commons was modernizing an ancient theme when he explained the unity of sovereignty as the *machinery* of government, which itself depended on "the organized participation of the political classes." Sovereignty's keynotes, for Commons, were coercion, order, right. While Bentley could not have been impressed by this vocabulary, of which in fact he was inclined to be contemptuous, there remained a significant similarity, since both Bentley and Commons used distinctly similar key words: For Commons the keynote was "flow," for Bentley, "process." It was characteristic of the new political science that it never sought for a higher political authority than was to be found in the political process itself. And Wilson, though he may have retained a slightly more conventional respect for structures, also wanted to know how things actually worked and was concerned with the subtle ways in which social pressures, personal ambitions, and rivalries were converted into political events.[33]

As with Bodin's nine "marks" of sovereignty—one of which was the power to enforce a uniform language on his subjects, a prescription for rebellion if ever there was one!—so with the formal procedure indicated in the ship money trial, in which a subject challenged a king in a court of law. These were procedure in practice. Earlier thinkers attributed to sovereignty a fairly specific location either in an assembly or, more probably, in a monarch (the giant figure with arguably Stuart features as the frontispiece of Hobbes's *Leviathan* is paradigmatic). Modern jurisprudence displaced this principle of location in favor of a series of specified procedures. It was the power of the millstream which turned the wheels whose action ground the corn; intention was converted into action by the operation of various pieces of regulated and interlocking machinery. "The waters of democracy are useless in their reservoirs unless they may be used to drive the wheels of policy and administration," according to Professor Woodrow Wilson of Princeton University; and the metaphor had evidently been suggested by Sir Henry Maine, whom he quotes to similar effect: "It would seem that, by a wise constitution, democracy may be made nearly as calm as water in a great artificial reservoir."[34]

In more recent years, the nations of Europe have merged their several sovereignties in the European Union, a Court of Human Rights, even, in most cases, a common currency. Whether the sovereignty of the United States will survive unalloyed by the events of the eleventh of September 2001 will be tested by that old, common arbitrator Time.

5

Inferences and Continuities

Ever since Alexis de Tocqueville published *Democracy in America*, it has been a familiar observation that England's settlers brought no aristocracy to American shores. Tocqueville himself, visiting the United States in the early 1830s, found the closest resemblance to an aristocracy in the legal profession.[1] His list of attributes absent from the colonial and early national scene could be extended in the manner of Henry James: no great houses, no Gothic cathedrals, no little Norman churches, no bishop, no royal court, no Houses of Parliament, no capital city, no Eton nor Harrow . . .

This absence of a hereditary and legally privileged aristocratic class carried—if absence can be said to carry—the absence of feudal land law. Or very little of it: as early as 1641, the Massachusetts Body of Liberties, to be consolidated by the Code of 1648, swept away the bulk of surviving privileges, restrictions, and legal technicalities of feudal origin.[2] Long before the seventeenth century, when the earliest settlements took root, England's land laws had become a morass of diverse tenures, entitlements, privileges, exemptions, all reeking of feudal ancestry and hereditary rights ultimately determined by status, and recorded in books to which only years of training could give access. From these complexities the colonies, though differing among themselves, were all largely free. Though land itself was never literally "free," the relative absence of these encumbrances generally facilitated both original settlement and agricultural productivity. As colonial economies matured, farm produce sustained and led an internal market. Agricultural exports stimulated internal investment.

Colonists took with them, or ordered from "home," such records of the common law as suited their circumstances. Using these and the legislative powers conferred by their charters, they shaped their legal systems according to the customs, needs, and preferences of their own more elite classes. In England, as we have seen, for many centuries much formative law flowed from the courts; most colonial law, by contrast, emanated from the elective assemblies—though appropriate exceptions have to be observed—and town meetings in New England, but in Virginia appointed county courts, ruled those localities.

Legislative bodies, whether elected, appointed, or hereditary, dominated political and economic life. In England, the creative powers of Parliament had begun to manifest themselves in the mid- to late seventeenth-century navigation acts, and began to enter more fully into the national economic calculus around the turn of the eighteenth century, when, prompted by various economic initiatives, Parliament created the Bank of England in 1694, established the Board of Trade in 1696, and passed the first Copyright Act in 1709.[3] (Some thirty years earlier there had in fact been a court decision in connection with a right to the sale of *The Pilgrim's Progress*.)[4] Patent law, which derived from royal grants of monopolistic privileges, modified by the Monopolies Act of 1624, was adjudicated by the Privy Council until 1753, when a particularly complex case persuaded that august body to yield these powers to the common law courts.[5] By the time Lord Mansfield was on the bench, from 1756, these laws were generating many disputes involving claims and counterclaims to intellectual property. A, for example, patents an invention but B improves on it; has B a right to patent the improvement? But has A the right to the benefit of the improvement on his original invention? Mansfield was strongly protective of authors' rights, but a great legal debate took place in the 1770s as to whether a common law right existed independently of statute. Camden, Lord Chancellor, held that a published book became common property and in 1774 his view prevailed.[6]

In 1712 Parliament introduced the Post Office, with a clause extending it to the colonies.[7] (This parliamentary intervention would have been beyond the powers of the colonies.) Then in 1714 Parliament sought to strengthen Britain's position on the high seas, both naval and commercial, by offering a great prize for the invention of a maritime chronometer by which a captain could establish his longitude at sea.[8]

It took the great self-taught inventor John Harrison nearly half a century to complete the task, and even then he gained his award through the personal intervention of George III. ("I'll see you righted, Harrison!") But the cost of the instrument put it beyond the resources of ordinary sea captains; it did not become standard naval issue until 1840.[9] It would be very hard to determine when the marine chronometer began to make a real difference to Britain's maritime power and wealth. It was the intention rather than the effect that has to be sought in these initiatives.

Legal decisions such as Mansfield's may be said to have nudged rather than propelled the law in ways which facilitated economic mobility. In the important area of marine insurance, Mansfield's work in clarifying and rationalizing the law has been claimed by his editor as among his greatest achievements.[10] But, once more, it would be extremely hard to demonstrate to what degree common law or chancery decisions materially assisted capital accumulation or marine insurance and other needs of investment and development. From the point of view of the inventor seeking redress against violation of patent, litigation was discouragingly expensive, tedious, and uncertain in the outcome. Uncertainty was compounded by the thin paper trail of precedent on which the courts could draw. But if commerce was to flourish at all, disputes between merchants and their clients and others had to be resolved in ways that had the force of law, and gave credible certainty for future guidance. The common law gave this kind of assurance through its reliance on precedent. But Parliament, consisting largely of landlords, cleared away traditional rights which stood as obstacles to capitalist agriculture.

Law in Britain operated in a geographically open economy: the law was in force throughout the country; there were no internal barriers to the passage of goods. Continental Europe, by contrast, was a mosaic of great and small jurisdictions, imposing their own fees and taxes even within a kingdom like France.[11] A carrier taking a wagonload of goods from Marseilles to Bordeaux would be relieved of much of his gains by fees for the privilege of entering and leaving the cities on his route. Replicated all over the kingdom, this situation did not conduce to adventurous investments or entrepreneurial enterprise. A few specialized industries such as weaving and ceramics did, however, benefit from official patronage. The German Empire was little more than a name for a sort of mélange of authorities, made up of ten nominal *Kreise* or circles (which were not circular), themselves consisting of electorates, margravates, duchies, archbishoprics, principalities, and other denominations, each of the circles being represented at the Aulic Council in Vienna. Many of these authorities issued their own currencies, which greatly multiplied the expense and time of internal movements and transactions. Transactions were affected by local rules; imperial decrees were often ignored. Significantly, James Madison drew attention to these problems in No. 42 of *The Federalist,* when warning Americans of the dangers of multiple jurisdictions.[12] The computations necessary to working out the relative costs and consequences of all these considerations would be speculative and their results imprecise; no such attempt is here intended. But it would be hard not to attribute to the common and nationwide statutory laws of Great Britain some credit for the nation's commercial and industrial progress in the eighteenth and nineteenth centuries. And on an even larger scale, American colonists were able to develop their economy in relative freedom from such internal impediments.

Britain's colonies enjoyed a double advantage. Not only did their trade prosper under the common law's protection, but they also found ways of varying the rules as they went along. Imports and exports accounted for a segment of the economic growth which, by the eve of revolution, had distributed relatively high standards of living together with hopes of improvement among more of the population than was common in Europe. Contributing incrementally to rising internal prosperity, colonial merchants crisscrossed the Atlantic and the Caribbean waters in complex trading patterns; every surviving print of an American seaport shows its harbor thronged with masts. But these masts were also engaged in intercolonial voyages. North America's coastal waters were hosts to the exchanges between the ports of New England, New York, South Carolina, and numerous lesser stages, jetties, and landing points.[13] Accompanying the frequently reported intercolonial commerce of the mid-eighteenth century was the less frequently observed adaptability of the legal system to the needs of merchants.

The primary agency of this sort of adaptation was the court, acting in its equity capacity. In a manner consistent with older New England ideas of community, the courts applied principles of fairness where a weaker party felt hard done by. The Connecticut judge Zepheniah Swift, writing the first American legal treatise in 1795, observed that the court would not sustain an unreasonable contract; courts of equity, he added, would set aside "all catching bargains, or contracts made with heirs or expectants for the disposal of their expectancies, considering them as intrinsically corrupt, fraudulent and unreasonable."[14] American courts were often guided as much by values as by rules. And values were likely to prevail when in conflict with the strict rules of the common law—which was the reason for equity. This principle was strikingly illustrated by the case of *Rich and Richards v. Bradfield*,[15] heard in the superior court in Philadelphia in 1768, in which several of the threads of these studies come together.

A factor in New York had submitted an invoice for goods dispatched on an order from Philadelphia. But the assignment had gone astray and the intended recipient protested that he was not obliged to pay for goods not received. The defendant objected "that the factor himself ought to have been brought to give evidence viva voce or at least the Account ought to have been proved under the City seal of New York agreeable to the Act of Parliament with regard to proving Colony debts in England." This act had been passed in 1732 to facilitate the collection of colonial debts claimed by merchants in Great Britain, who might attest their signatures before the mayor of their own city.[16] Its terms did not expressly extend to internal affairs in the colonies; in the absence of explicit disclaimer, however, it could have been so construed if the court had wished. For the plaintiff, Mr. Chew, a prominent Philadelphia lawyer, "answered that this being a mercantile transaction such evidence as merchants usually submit as proofs of a foreign transaction should be received here." Mercantile custom responded to practical considerations: "If the Law of Evidence was to be urged with all its Rigor, the course of trade would be totally obstructed." Further,

> An Affidavit is as acceptable in the Eye of the Law as a simple act of sales. Viva voce testimony from the nature of trade can never be procured. A man may on one and the same joint concern have shipped ten different cargoes to different Factors in different parts of the world, to satisfy the demands of such testimony as is required by the rigid Law of Evidence these ten different actors must attend this Court, though they are not within our reach, we can issue no process to compel them, and indeed no cause under such severe circumstances could be prosecuted for anything less than £10,000.

Chew's case also relied on the claim that "Custom of Merchants" was "an essential part of the Law" and would not be strengthened by an affidavit. "Nothing more is required than proof of the factors hand writing." The plaintiff here seems to have introduced a redoubling argument by way of forensic tactics. The court agreed, ruling that the custom of merchants trumped the "strict rules of Law with regard to Evidence." It followed that, "On proving the hand writing of the factor let the account of sales be given in Evidence, which was accordingly done"—with judgment for the plaintiff and damages of £57.

In 1767, only a few months earlier, John Dickinson had declared in his persona as the Pennsylvania Farmer that the Americans were "a perfectly free people," whose ability to determine what parts of the common law applied to them was a proof of their sovereignty.[17] Pennsylvania's superior court had now set aside an act of Parliament and had determined that the custom of merchants, in effect the practices of their community, were protected as having the force of common law. Twenty years later, these principles were also protected by the cover given by the Constitution to the sanctity of contracts, which shone forth as an expression of the freedom which Americans had fought for. But freedom, a term used interchangeably with liberty, was a variable concept.

One conclusion which must by now have emerged from the foregoing reflections is that the concept of "Americanization" is inadequate, even misleading, and should be used only with many qualifications. Different colonies, or clusters of colonies such as those of New England, differed from each other as steeply as any of them differed from old England. Virginia was in certain respects more like Yorkshire than it was like any of the New England colonies; New York bore certain similarities to Virginia, South Carolina to the British West Indies; examples could be multiplied. These steep regional distinctions were particularly marked in matters of religion but also in social structure–but correspondingly, in law. Common law derived much of its authority from its respect for custom, a convention which gained strength after the importation of Blackstone's *Commentaries on the Laws of England* published between 1765 and 1769; it appears from student notebooks that Judge Gould virtually transcribed Blackstone in his lectures at the Tapping Reeve law school in Connecticut. A good, legally valid custom must be "immemorial" and uninterrupted, must not be "unreasonable," must be peaceably acquiesced in, certain and intelligible, not vague; compulsive, not optional; and customs must be consistent with each other. Gould added, "It is clear that courts ought not to reject common law unless it is either unjust, absurd or inapplicable." Every country, he maintained, must have some form of unwritten law, without which there could be no administration of justice; this statement answers a question as to whether the common law could subsist after America's separation from England, which, after all, was the source of the common law, and implies that the common law remained the unwritten law of America.[18] In an increasingly competitive society, and with transactions extending over longer distances, custom could not be relied on to determine behavior. In the end the courts would decide which custom to enforce.

In one major respect, however, the colonies bent the common law out of its original shape. While the British economy flourished by the slave trade, and racial slavery and even slave markets existed in England, it never gained the official protection of English common law. When slavery's crisis of legitimacy came, with the Somerset case in 1772, it was slavery that failed the test, and ultimately withered away. In America, by contrast, slavery was defined by race as early as the mid-seventeenth century; indications that Africans were treated as different from whites first appeared in Virginia in 1640, in the 1660s Virginia and Maryland banned interracial sexual relations, and in the last quarter of the seventeenth century, says Winthrop Jordan, "the trend was to treat Negroes more like property and less like men."[19] By the close of the seventeenth century all the indications for the future were that the condition of slaves of African descent in America's southern states was that of chattels. In law, African slaves were things, not persons. This designation was already in effect in Virginia in 1705 when slaves were made susceptible to attachment to land, with which they could be transferred and inherited. And in the long aftermath of racially defined slavery, the land and society that exulted in liberty had been endowed with a seemingly impermeable caste system, spelled out in meticulous detail, enforced and maintained by law. Not from every point of view was the liberty conferred by independence an unmitigated blessing.

Liberty: that was one consideration. But liberty had proved to be one variable among others and was measured out or protected by law in widely differing proportions among different sectors of both the domestic and colonial (and, now, postcolonial) populations. In America as in India, caste had all the force of communal custom and still marks out limitations to human freedom. But custom is not the only source of law and not the best excuse for inertia; custom may yield to policy, as has happened in both Britain and America through legislation prescribing equality of rights. One achievement of the common law was to convert *interests* into *rights*.

When Alexis de Tocqueville visited America in 1831 he was so impressed by the integrative functions of the jury that he described it as the binding force to which the American experiment in democracy owed its prospects of success.[20] This observation may be considered a tribute to the moral agency of the American jury system. Tocqueville had not yet visited England, but it is a pity that he didn't have the opportunity to compare English and American juries. He might have reflected that American society, or rather the federation of societies that made up the Union, was subject to so many fracturing forces, from the religious and ethnic to the social, geographical, and economic, as to need such binding every bit as much as did the more class-bound state of England, which was experiencing its own contemporaneous upheavals.

English working-class radicals were still being transported to Australia. In America, however, the form and spirit of republican government did not so permeate the system as to restrain elected authority from persecuting its critics, against which the First Amendment's teeth seemed surprisingly blunt. The issue of seditious libel, with all its authoritarian and monarchical implications, was reopened under the aegis of Jefferson's presidency and at that popular democrat's instigation. *The People v. Crosswell* was the administration's response to a journalistic criticism of the president, which was held to be libel of exactly the same kind as had brought scandal and contempt onto earlier and more regal governments; and the trial judge restricted the jury to finding the fact of publication, as British governments had tried to do with Woodfall and the dean of St. Asaph. This left the judge free to find the libel. On appeal, Alexander Hamilton, now returned to his law practice and briefed for the defense, argued that it was *intent* that constituted the crime, and intent was itself one of the *facts* of the case—a position identical to that of Hawle's oft-reprinted tract of the 1680s and heard recently in Britain in Erskine's powerful defense of the dean of St. Asaph. "Texts taken from the holy scriptures, and scattered among the people," Hamilton argued, "may, in certain times . . . become libellous, nay, treasonable . . . surely the time, manner, and intent are matters of fact for a jury." He agreed that the jury ought to pay respectful regard to the opinion of the court, but the jury might conclude from their own reading and on their own judgment that "the law arising from the case is different from that which the court advances."[21] Chancellor James Kent concurred and, giving judgment for the appellant, observed that the Sedition Act itself had specifically decreed that the jury who tried the case should have the right to determine the law and the fact under the direction of the court; the Supreme Court, indeed, had set similar precedents.[22] Alexander Hamilton declared in this last public pronouncement that a people could be called free only when they had a share in the representation and the right of trial by jury.[23] His speech in all probability influenced the passage in 1805 of a state law permitting the defendant to plead truth in libel prosecutions, provided that the writer could show that his publication was influenced by honest motives to serve justifiable ends.[24] Hamilton had made his last contribution to American public life, and one that may be said to have matched his better known achievements, a contribution which may not ineptly be considered a late step in the anglicization of American law. The old legal convention could not withstand the seeping tide of popular sentiment. When the state of New York in convention revised its constitution in 1821, Hamilton's position was given constitutional status.[25]

Government has been reluctant to yield the prerogative of censorship. The issue was fought through on several further occasions, in each of which the same precedents were cited.[26] State legislation or constitutional revisions eventually if gradually tidied up the question in the jury's favor, an almost unnoticed step in the passage to more democratic government in the United States usually—though very loosely—associated under the umbrella of Jacksonian Democracy.[27]

The authority of the courts was not surrendered lightly. In 1794 the recently constituted Supreme Court had sought to settle the law-and-fact issue in a conservative sense by a formal pronouncement which omitted to take account of Fox's Act in England;[28] on this construction, English common law principles which had not been repealed by state action remained in operation in America, unaffected by subsequent British acts of Parliament.

On the issue of fact and law, and on the related issue of the relations between judges and juries, no single rule can be said to have predominated. A strong inference, however, can reconcile the contradictions in the evidence. Eighteenth-century American jurors, as William Nelson argued some years ago, were quite capable of being robust in asserting their power to give the law; and by the same token, early American judges were generally reticent about overriding or directing the views of the jury. In South Carolina, one jury in the 1780s was instructed "to find a general verdict, or a special one, . . . as they thought proper," while another jury was told "to give what they thought reasonable in damages." There were other cases in which it was noted the judge refrained from giving any instruction; in numerous cases in Virginia the judge permitted the jury to retire without offering comments on the merit of the case. Instructions, when given, were often contradictory.[29] An explanation which suggests itself is that early American judges, very nearly down to the end of the eighteenth century, were far less imposing or authoritative figures than their English counterparts, and frequently lacked the technical knowledge or self-confidence to instruct a jury, but the more conservative views which have been cited in the text came from professionally trained lawyers occupying official positions or senior judgeships. It was this tranche of legal minds who began to develop an agenda of judicial authority in the 1790s. These men began to assert the authority on the bench from a standpoint stiffened by professional training, experience, and self-confidence.

Coming some sixty years after Zenger's case, this conservative orthodoxy in the judiciary appears out of keeping with the tone and tendency of American society. But the Supreme Court was setting the tone for a conservative thrust on the part of the judiciary to rein in the power of the American jury; if anyone was to make law in the American system, it was to be the judges, not the people's representatives.

The judiciary could not dominate the scene, much as they preferred to exert the balance of power in their own courts. But the argument rumbled on. In 1831 the *Westminster Review,* a leading British journal of opinion, published an article asserting the right of the jury to determine questions of law as well as fact in constitutional questions, which was reprinted by the *Carolina Law Journal.* This was a further step by which the powers of the jury were being subtly but effectively reinforced by the social temper of a self-assertively democratic society. In its representative character, the American jury increasingly followed the greater openness of American society. But that broad statement can hardly explain the extent of the differences which have opened between the American and English systems, though both would still subscribe to the guiding principle of moral agency. With the rapid development of industrial production and industrialized means of transport and communication, American judges increasingly showed themselves content to pass to the jury the determination of responsibility in cases which allowed them to respect the language of the fact/law taxonomy. What behavior constituted culpable negligence, what precautions might be expected of a "reasonable man," but what differences of opinion might arise among "fair-minded men," what time was "timely"—these problems required a fusion of judgment and sentiment. But no essential purpose was served by squeezing modern judgments into the straitjacket of ancient categories. A more pragmatic and commonsense approach was suggested in 1873 by the paradigmatic case of a small boy injured while playing on an insecure railway turntable. The Supreme Court upheld the trial judge's decision to let the jury determine the question of contributory negligence.[30] The Court deftly avoided the fact/law issue and opined that it was for the jury to decide, because a jury of twelve experienced men from different walks of life was better qualified than a judge sitting alone. But, as the historian who retrieved this case pointed out, the Court later returned to these categories in deciding a case involving the question of reasonable care to be taken at a railroad crossing. The principle guiding a "reasonable man's" precautions, as handed down by Mr. Justice Holmes, now became the law, a precedent became a rule of law for the future.[31] This judgment respected the principle of the jury's right to determine law as well as fact. But it soon proved impossible to specify legality in step-by-step conduct. Seven years later, the Court adverted to "the need for caution in framing standards of behavior that amount to rules of law." Even agreement among successive juries on similar problems, though they might provide guidance, could not lay down law. "Standards of behavior," the Court declared in 1950, "should not be set down as matters of law, but should be matters for juries."[32] By the same token, English court rules protected the privacy of the jury. On the other hand, however, the American Supreme Court's relentless application of the somewhat abstract theory of judicial review, especially after the Civil War, encroached steadily and deeply into law-making territory.

Judicial deference to the jury, particularly at the state level, averts unpopular decisions by judges aware of the politics of reelection. It subscribes (perhaps yields) to the principle that the jury has representative responsibilities, which we have traced to ancient times. American jurors can and do explain their reasons to the press, helping to convert the court and trial into a sort of gladiatorial contest in the public arena. Under the aegis of the First Amendment, the right to know verges on a right to participate.

In England it is still difficult to pursue systematic journalistic or academic inquiries into jury proceedings without risk of being held in contempt of court. Substantial reasons can be adduced for both sides. The occasional oddities and irrationalities of English jury deliberations have to be gathered from anecdotal evidence. There are enough of these on the record to raise serious doubts as to whether the system may not have outlived the reputation for which it is so famous. Other countries do not hurry to imitate either England or, for that matter, America.[33] It may not be going too far to suggest that the concept of moral agency is itself an issue to be refined in the process of legal argument.

The word "jury" has not proved historically to be synonymous with the best that can be said for the principle of justice. The concept of community (from which the jury is drawn) usually suggests a certain kinship in shared affections and values. But a community's sense of justice is likely to be organically rooted in its habits and is not invariably derived either from instincts of fairness or from an ability to weigh evidence or a disposition to appreciate scientific advances. Much historical evidence could be adduced to demonstrate that a jury called together from the locality of an alleged crime could be fallible, prejudiced, and ignorant. This danger had in fact been observed by Blackstone in the 1760s when writing of the medieval jury. The advantages of jurors who brought their local knowledge to court could be and often were offset by the pronounced disadvantages of jurors who brought their local prejudices. The immediate vicinity of jurors' qualifications was still known as the medieval "hundred" and its inhabitants were "hundredors." Blackstone traced changes in the number of hundredors who were required to take their places in a full jury drawn from the whole county; their numbers varied from six to four, back to six under Elizabeth, then down to two, to be abolished under Anne in civil cases, and under George II in penal cases. The jury was now to be drawn "de corpore comitatus"—that is, "from the body of the county at large, and not de vicineto, or from the particular neighbourhood."[34] It is not likely that American colonists had such fine distinctions in mind in their claims for local juries. But the differences could have serious consequences. Jurors drawn from over the whole of a large county would not in fact necessarily have the local knowledge that had been attributed to medieval juries. Local character and environment, moreover, could sustain stubborn prejudices; English country juries who persisted in believing in witchcraft resented the intrusions of enlightened justices from London who dismissed such country folklore as superstition. Similar forces were at work in America when white Southern juries went on fighting the Civil War through the years of reconstruction and deep into the twentieth century. And deep into the twentieth century, in ex-Confederate states, any black man tried by a white jury for an alleged offense against a white woman was likely to become a victim, not a beneficiary, of the trial process. This consideration puts a new gloss on the ancient concept of trial by one's peers, which in the American environment needed amendment to mean trial by a jury of one's own color or race; failing which, the medieval mixed jury might be revived to accommodate representatives of each race. The locality principle was much in evidence with the acquittal by a largely white Los Angeles jury in 1992 of white police officers who had been seen on videotape beating and kicking an arrested suspect. The incident drew presidential condemnation and international attention to the difficulties that could arise in reconciling dominant local sentiment with the rule of law and the protection of civil rights.

At the present time, in American civil cases involving corporate suitors with high interests at risk, the right of challenge reflects another subtle but deep transformation. Deriving the practice from the right of either party to challenge members of the jury panel, major law firms will now spend millions of dollars of their clients' money in elaborate "simulation" exercises directed not merely at eliminating potentially hostile jurors but at constituting a *favorably* disposed jury; the right of challenge will then be selectively used to place as many as possible of those members on the actual trial jury.[35] It seems far from clear that this practice conforms to the ruling of the Supreme Court that the right of challenge does not confer a right to have *friends* on the jury.[36] The random character of jury composition, an important original element in its presumed impartiality, is further eroded by consultations with specialists in that arcane refinement of the judicial process. The transition to the search for positively friendly jurors from the older aim of eliminating potentially hostile ones may be explained as a logical extension of the adversarial system, but can hardly be considered an advance on the simpler medieval concept of the jury as moral agent in the disinterested search for truth or justice. The challenge, originally a means of ensuring fairness, has become a subtle instrument of the art of jury packing.

Nor is this all. Tocqueville today would not be able to repeat his observation on the democratic effects of the jury system, for the simple reason that jury trial has ceased to represent the prevalent method of arriving at verdicts in criminal trials. The publicity attracted by trials involving celebrities or surrounded by scandal has obscured the effects of plea bargaining, which has evolved as the dominant method of settling more routine cases. By 2001 no fewer than 94 percent of criminal cases in district courts were concluded by plea bargains conducted between counsel on either side. Analysis of trials in state courts resulted in a similar figure.[37] In the background there hovers a jury ostensibly ready to deliver a verdict based on the evidence and the arguments in court; and the bargain arrived at between prosecutor and defense is based on a presumption that the jury would have an opinion if asked, and inferences of the judge's probable sentence, but not on the jury's participation in the trial. The judge herself has receded into the background, becoming more an umpire or mediator.[38]

Nevertheless, the right to trial by jury, enshrined in the Constitution, is a landmark principle of America's claim to republican government. In England, where the right has been whittled down by successive court rulings based on a general statute of 1854, jury trial in civil actions now seems to be restricted to libel.[39] Whether the jury, whether responding to the subtle ramifications of interest representation, or agitated to collective indignation by stirring rhetoric from the floor, or merely sharing in local customs or prejudices, gave impartial justice or better government would remain a fundamental question for republican government, which perhaps could never be conclusively settled by popular consent. It would continue to depend, not only on the combination of the heart and eye, but on whether the eye was asking the right questions and, ultimately, on whether the heart was in the right place.

II

Occasional Essays

6

Some Problems of a Colonial Attorney General in a Multicultural Society

Even the wide variety of personalities, with their different backgrounds, grievances, and disputes encountered by William Kempe in both his private and official practices as attorney general of the province of New York in the mid-eighteenth century can hardly have prepared him for the appearance, on some unspecified date apparently in or around 1754, of the disconsolate figure of Juan Miranda. For not only was Miranda a mulatto and Spanish-speaking, but he was a slave. And it was extraordinary, probably unknown, for a person of color, let alone a slave, to present himself in his own person to such an eminence as the attorney general; in fact, in all probability, the same applies to any lawyer of the city. Yet Miranda had a story to tell which compelled William Kempe's attention, and deserves ours.[1]

This essay will examine two very different instances of complex legal problems, each reflecting the multinational character of the population of the province of New York, which had to be resolved through the legal system—and the records which have been recovered from the legal records. They throw light on the society to which that system ministered, and thus help to establish legal history as a component element in what is generally recognized as "general" history.

It seems that Miranda had the company of friends. It is also likely either that the petition which survives in his name had been drawn up by his supporters, or that it was drafted in the attorney general's office from his verbal statement—which seems the most likely procedure. What mattered to the crown's chief law officer and what matters to us is the story itself, as reconstructed from a cluster of depositions taken over a period of years and now reposing in one folder, and the response of the provincial authorities, much of which is in the same collection; the rest is in bound volumes of judicial records held by the Division of Old Records in downtown Manhattan.

The story begins about twenty years earlier, before the outbreak of war between Britain and Spain in 1739, when the sixteen-year-old Juan Miranda, a native of Cartagena, Colombia, then a possession of the Spanish Empire, was making a voyage from the city in a *guarda costa* (a coast guard vessel). Despite the fact that peace formally prevailed between Britain and Spain, a British naval vessel attacked the Spanish *guarda* and seized Miranda by force; eventually, after a sojourn in Trinidad, he was put on a vessel bound for New York. The ship's master, Captain Axton, not knowing what to do with Miranda, one of the passengers offered to take him. An offer was now made to Miranda that if he agreed to go ashore to a Mr. Winclere's house he would be taught a trade, would serve Winclere's family, and would be given his liberty after seven years. It is very unlikely that Miranda was given to understand that he would be classed as a slave and would be deprived of civil rights, but in any case he was virtually powerless and his choices were severely limited. Miranda appears to have agreed, so there is an implied contractual element in his subsequent position. The ability to enter into a contract, incidentally, implies the right to refuse, which would, if formally recognized, be incompatible with slave status, though his statement does not make this point. In any case the promise was not kept. Miranda served the family faithfully and is sometimes described as a servant; but Mr. Winclere died, and Miranda was taken in by the Van Rants or Van Rantz family, where he was taught the trade of a sailmaker. (The depositions are not entirely consistent as to the sequence of events.) Miranda might at this stage have reflected that there were worse fates than a free ride to New York and the offer of apprenticeship in a valuable trade, but Mr. Van Rantz also died before the term expired; and when that time came, his widow, Sarah Van Rantz, refused to recognize Miranda's freedom and claimed him as her slave. Miranda's color can have been the only grounds on which this claim was made: he was a mulatto, with no proof of his own claim to freedom. His status had never been defined in law, and he passed from servant to slave without any apparent formal sanction. He had nowhere to turn for help, no legal standing.

The case raises the broader, though secondary, question of how slave status was acquired, or certified. Many wartime captives were sold into slavery; mere powerlessness was a cogent persuader. More normally, a slave was known through his parentage. But Miranda and his supporters claimed that his parents were free, and no evidence was produced that he had ever been sold, either to Winclere or Van Rantz; his condition thus seems to have rested on a presumption from his color. It could not have rested on his original agreement to serve the Van Rantz family because that admission would have implied that he was free at the time he entered into it—which was the very basis of his claim to freedom!

Thus Miranda the sailmaker passed some twenty years. Then, in October 1754, wandering, one imagines, disconsolately in the dock area, he amazingly recognized Lucas Farfan, a mariner, and a former playmate from his boyhood in Cartagena.[2] Farfan signed a deposition that Miranda was the son of a free white man and a free Negro mother. At the time of his capture he was—and this was to be crucial—a free subject of the king of Spain. Mary Pinhorn, spinster, supported by Mrs. Gouverneur, testified to remembering the circumstances of Miranda's arrival in New York, confirming the story as told by Miranda and Farfan. Another of Miranda's boyhood friends turned up in New York in 1755 and gave similar testimony. There is also a second deposition from a New York lady, Gertrud, wife of John Pinhorn, supporting Miranda's version of events. A case was building up, but how it may have affected Miranda's relation with the Van Rantz family remains unclear.

Why no record survives of any further development for three years is unexplained. The Van Rantz family did not acknowledge his freedom, whether or not he was still serving them. But by early 1758 the case is making headway, and events take a turn for which histories of slavery have not prepared us: for on March 18 the provincial council orders the attorney general to commence an action in the Supreme Court of Judicature to try the matter of Miranda's freedom. Then on November 3, William Kempe, Esq., attorney general of New York, writes to Lieutenant Governor James De Lancey in Council to report that Cornelius Van Rantz has seized Miranda and confined him in the workhouse, intending to send him away and sell him as a slave; the attorney general now requests an injunction to restrain Van Rantz, that he be ordered to give sureties for his peaceable behavior toward Miranda, and, in view of Miranda's poverty, applies to represent him *in forma pauperis*. Soon afterward, a draft letter unsigned and undated, but probably at Kempe's dictation, and addressed to Lieutenant Governor Sir Charles Hardy (therefore in either 1757 or 1758) points out that as the *guarda costa* was taken in time of peace as an act of retaliation, even a slave on board would not have become the property of the British captain. No steps were taken at the time to have Miranda condemned as contraband. (Such a procedure would presumably have revealed the illegality of the kidnapping.) There are rudiments of international law in the situation. Objections entered in a lengthy submission by Van Rantz are refuted by the attorney general point by point. The trial was now in progress, and these papers were probably presented to the court. But it is also reported here that Van Rantz *sold* Miranda to one Peter Brower, who attempted to seize him but was prevented by the intervention of a member of the Common Council, the city's governing body, called (gratifyingly) Mr. Roosevelt. It seems from this document that the mayor of New York had encouraged Van Rantz to sell Miranda, even with the trial in progress, claiming that judgment would go against him.

We seem, through the investigation of legal records, to have stumbled on a forgotten cause célèbre. The dispute between Miranda and the Van Rantz family has acquired reverberations between the city and the province; the mayor is contradicting the attorney general, who has made Miranda's cause his own and is clearly taking steps to protect Miranda's interests. On November 3, 1758, Juan Miranda, an alleged slave, makes legal history by seeking permission to sue Cornelius Van Rantz, who claims to be his owner, for assault, illegal detention, and trespass; the plea is agreed by the Honorable John Chambers, a judge of the superior court. William Kempe is duly assigned to represent Miranda *in forma pauperis*. The New York slave code, developed through a series of early eighteenth-century statutes, gave a master a free hand in the chastisement of his slaves: in 1735 a master had gone unpunished after beating his slave to death.[3] The permission to sue granted to Miranda is difficult to reconcile with the status of a slave, which seems by implication to have been suspended. Miranda may be in judicial limbo, but he is in physical danger: John Tabor Kempe, William's son, who works in his father's office, has deposed on November 2 that he personally went to the workhouse to tell the keeper not to let Miranda go into the hands of Van Rantz, suspecting that he intended to sell him, as he has done (or tried to do) before. The sale to Brower must have been canceled or incomplete, because it is now Van Rantz, not Brower, who claims him. What is all too clear is Van Rantz's virulent determination: he has defied and insulted John Tabor Kempe, telling him that he would take Juan Miranda in spite of him. Since John Tabor was representing his father, the attorney general, Van Rantz's attitude shows a remarkable degree of contempt for the authority of the crown, his confidence probably stiffened by the feeling that he has the backing of the alternative authority of the city's mayor. But Miranda proceeds to sue Van Rantz for a hundred pounds in damages.

A significant transition has quietly taken place in the attorney general's role. Much of his work, probably accounting for most of his income, continues to be that of a professional lawyer representing private clients; there are many land cases in the files, often resulting from writs of ejectment, which are conllusive actions by neighbors trying to establish their boundaries; and Kempe is responsible for such government business as periodically occurs. But he did not make a very prosperous living, and early in his tenure of office he complained to the Board of Trade that he could barely support his family.[4] When Juan Miranda first came to his office there is no way of knowing whether he was seeking Kempe's help as a private lawyer or in his public role. But Miranda had probably been advised to bring his complaint to the colony's chief law officer. In any case, the nature of Miranda's story, particularly his claim to be not only a free man but a foreign subject, immediately brought an element of public interest into the question, and Kempe could have had no doubt, from a very early stage, that he would be dealing with a delicate mixture of personal business in Miranda's claim against the Van Rantzes, and official business in the matter of Miranda's allegiance with its possible international repercussions.

When Attorney General William Kempe appears before the Supreme Court of Judicature—which is the high court of the province, not the Mayor's Court of the City—representing Miranda *in forma pauperis,* he does so on the instructions of the provincial council (these instructions he may well have drawn up himself in his own office). Benjamin Nicoll appears for Cornelius Van Ranst [*sic*]. The record now passes to the court's *Minutes,* where the case appears as *Van Ranst v Juan Miranda,* so it seems that, by an obscure legal technicality, the opponents have changed roles and Van Rantz has become the plaintiff, Miranda the defendant.[5]

There ought in principle to be two trials: the council's investigation, apparently to be pursued in the supreme court, into Miranda's claim to freedom; and Miranda's private action for damages. Unfortunately, the notation naming the action is merely nominal and does not identify the type of case. It would be satisfactory to have an express declaration, but the inference is that Miranda's freedom has become a premise of his action against Van Rantz, since the laws would not have permitted a slave to recover damages from his master for assault, and false imprisonment would have been a contradiction in terms. But on October 25, 1759, Miranda is given permission to proceed, "by proviso." Under this procedure the case is brought on by the defendant where the plaintiff, issue joined, neglects to proceed to trial.[6]

Frustration follows. Successive deferments from session to session throughout 1759–60 make clear only that neither party had secured a judgment, and the record eventually dries up. The operative volume runs to August 1760, without recording a decision. The following volume is missing from the shelves, but if the Van Rantz family had still been pursuing their claim against Miranda, it is unlikely that, after failing to prove it for more than a year, they could have revived it in October 1760, when the court would convene again. But this is probably to put the case the wrong way round. The action to try Miranda's claim to freedom was instigated by the council; the civil action was that of Miranda against Van Rantz: in neither case does the Van Rantz family institute a court action *against* Miranda. And after the case had been kept before the court by successive adjournments for a year, it also seems unlikely that the family could have carried out Van Rantz's threat of kidnap and sale: such an act would have been an extreme contempt of court, of which there is no sign in the records.

What, then, became of Juan Miranda? He might, just possibly, have made his way back to his native Cartagena. The archives of Colombia have no trace of him, which is hardly surprising.[7] He was an experienced sailmaker in a prosperous port and could no doubt support himself. And he would now have been clear of the legislative restrictions on slaves pursuing skilled trades. But he may well have left New York to avoid any renewed attention from the Van Rantz family, and to ply his trade and enjoy his freedom elsewhere; at any rate the extraordinarily detailed list of inhabitants of New York compiled by E. B. O'Callaghan does not mention Juan Miranda.[8] The "New York and Brooklyn Directory" reports the death, intestate, of Catherine Van Rantz in 1794. (The unlovable Cornelius had died in 1762.) And so the story dwindles to an inconclusive end; it would be satisfying to find in the books a definitive judgment in Miranda's favor, a hint looking forward to Lord Mansfield's famous judgment on Somerset in 1772: "The man must be discharged."[9] But the researcher in judicial records has to get used to the disappointment of innumerable cases which, after repeated deferments, are abandoned by one party or another, or settled out of court, without leaving a trace in the records. Miranda might have been persuaded to drop his action for damages, but he would never have compromised his liberty. After a year of deferments, it is possible that Miranda had failed to win his damages, but there is no sign that Van Rantz recovered Miranda's person. Miranda himself had probably had as much drama as would last one lifetime.

How are we to account for the extraordinary spectacle we have witnessed of the trial afforded to a mulatto slave against his master by the lieutenant governor and council of the province of New York, who have instructed the attorney general to represent the impoverished plaintiff without charge? Undoubtedly Miranda had a convincing case, once he was able to enlist his friends of boyhood years, and particularly in view of the witness of city ladies who recalled the circumstances of his arrival. But convincing cases do not always prevail when made by colored slaves against their masters in a racist environment. A clue of another character is contained in the council minute of March 18, 1758, ordering the attorney general to commence an action in the supreme court to try the issue of Miranda's freedom.

This document notes that "Juan Miranda's name does not appear among the number of Spanish Negroes or Mulattoes claimed as freemen some time since by the Spanish Governors of the West Indies." This remark has an important bearing on the case, since it indicates that Spanish royal officers were attempting to reclaim free (though colored) Spanish subjects who had fallen into British hands. This was probably a tidying up operation following the involvement of Spain in maritime war with Britain. The absence of Miranda's name is only to be expected; the *guarda costa* was a government vessel (which made the attack all the more provocative), but Miranda had been taken in peacetime some twenty years earlier, so he would not have been listed among prisoners of war. Miranda's declaration amounted to a claim to a right of protection by the Spanish crown, and though one can hardly imagine Spain going to war to reclaim an anonymous mulatto whose disappearance had never been noticed, one can more easily suppose that a British colonial governor would wish to avoid a diplomatic incident, which should have happened if Spanish complaints had been pursued in London.

Life on the Caribbean seas was a risky business throughout much of the eighteenth century, piracy and kidnapping were events that struck with the random character of storms at sea, and Miranda was far from being the first victim. In 1708 the petition of Manuel Jalla[10] to the governor of Massachusetts told how, a freeborn native of Spain, baptized and educated in Christianity, he had gone to sea leaving a wife and two children at home. Out on the high seas, a Jamaican privateer seized him, brought him to New York, and sold him as a slave. The governor, Lord Cornbury, heard his story and declared him free but also bound him to five years' service to enable him to compensate his purchaser, who had not known of Jalla's original status. Jalla's troubles followed year after year with successive captures, sales, and recaptures; his petition of 1708 played the card of educational status by invoking classical authorities on the immorality of slavery.[11] The eventual outcome was probably favorable.

Much closer to our immediate interest in both period and character was the case of Captain William Dennis of Rhode Island, who in 1746 sold twenty-two Spanish prisoners of war into slavery on no better ground than their dark skin pigmentation. When Dennis imprudently docked in Havana, however, the Spanish royal governor protested indignantly, demanding the mens' restoration as freeborn subjects of the Spanish king (exactly Miranda's claim a few years later); but he went further, and took nineteen of Dennis's sailors hostage. This precipitated an intercolonial problem of crisis proportions. Governor Greene of Rhode Island wrote urgently to his counterparts in New York and Philadelphia in an attempt to trace and reclaim the Spanish prisoners. Many of the men had been sold, and their new owners showed not the slightest concern over their freeborn status. The governor's efforts, endorsed by the general assembly, seem to have recovered only eight of the men, whom he sent back to Havana (one had died).[12]

This episode can hardly have been forgotten when Juan Miranda walked into the attorney general's office and told his own story of kidnapping at sea and condemnation to slavery. William Kempe, who became attorney general in 1752, must have been practicing in New York; James DeLancey, who had been chief justice at the time of Miranda's arrival in the mid-1730s, was still in that office throughout the Dennis affair, and served as lieutenant governor from 1753 to his death in 1760.[13] The correspondence from Governor Greene of Rhode Island was presumably in the files, the episode in people's memories.

The documentation and record of Miranda's claim suggest that his cause had gained influential friends, who would have put up a good fight for him. He might have won on the merits of his case. But a private action would certainly not have attracted orders from the council to the attorney general to represent him without fee—indeed the case might have gone to the Mayor's Court rather than the Supreme Court of Judicature. In order to hire representation at all, Miranda would have had to raise funds which he clearly did not possess; he also had influential enemies. Right was on his side, but his adversaries denied him the credit of rights, and there are good reasons to think that it was the possibility of diplomatic repercussions from the claim that he had been and remained a Spanish subject, stimulated by the memory of the Dennis affair, that defeated the Van Rantz family and explains the remarkable spectacle of the trial for Miranda's freedom in which royal New York was banked on his side, and which all the indications suggest that he won.

During the Juan Miranda trial, John Tabor Kempe was working in his father's office and, although he was only admitted to the bar in 1758, was no doubt being groomed to succeed his father as attorney general. After reporting William's death in July 1759, James DeLancey, who was now lieutenant governor, recommended that the Privy Council in London appoint John Tabor to that office, with which the council duly complied.[14] But not without controversy. Five days before DeLancey wrote his official letter, William Smith, who claimed recognition as the senior member of the New York bar, had set out his claim (the two letters probably went on the same ship); he had, Smith complained, been passed over in 1752; he cited a statute of Henry VIII (8 c. 15) against the method of the younger man's appointment.[15] In 1752, immediately after William Kempe had been made attorney general, the Privy Council, on the recommendation of the Commissioners of Trade and Plantations, had appointed Smith to the council, perhaps as a gesture of mollification.[16] But his protest again went unanswered the second time around. The Kempe family seems to have had influence with the ageing DeLancey, now in his own last year of life.

To judge by the immense volume of business in the records preserved in the New-York Historical Society, John Tabor Kempe proved a very active force in the legal system. In private law, he handled many cases involving landed property, and himself became a big landowner. In the crisis of independence, as the province's senior law officer, he remained loyal to the crown and emigrated to Great Britain; his property was confiscated in 1777. He was still living in Hertfordshire in 1791.[17]

As attorney general he had to handle a greater variety of cases, some of them of more complex political and legal implications, than had crossed his father's desk in the 1750s. British New York had always been multicultural, multilinguistic, and multireligious. It is not surprising, but is nonetheless illuminating, when these aspects occasionally reach the courts. A few years after the Miranda case, the multicultural aspect of New York society again impinged on its judicial system. The long-drawn-out case of *Domine Hermanus Meyer v. Paulus Ploeg et al., Elders and Deacons of the Reformed Protestant Dutch Church of Ulster County, New York,* which involved much correspondence with the classis of Amsterdam, was literally multinational. As a case for the province's jurisprudence, it began when Domine Meyer, minister of that church, breached the privacy of his own community and outraged many of his congregation by seeking relief in Chancery to the amount of £150 against the corporation for the nonpayment of his salary, which was due to him under the contract which had brought him from Groningen in the United Provinces of the Netherlands to the service of the Dutch community in the province.[18] (What the minister and his family lived on throughout these years is not entirely clear.)

Although Domine Meyer had been selected by the Theological Faculty of Groningen subject to the general supervision of the classis of Amsterdam, which superintended appointments in the Dutch Protestant Church, he did not please the elders of his Kingston consistory. His style of preaching was too robust, perhaps too accusatory. Issues of personality became inextricably entangled with ecclesiastical authority and even political allegiance. Behind the formal arguments it is possible to detect rumblings of dissidence within the congregation. Much of the case, however, was taken up in arguments involving the laws of contract. The elders had signed a contract which they could no longer produce because, they said, it had been sent to Amsterdam and could not be found. They were fearful, if they lost, of being held individually chargeable for the minister's salary and damages.

Communities which would now be called "ethnic," whether formed primarily for communal, linguistic, or religious reasons, had their own ways of resolving domestic disputes; much the same was true of the Congregational churches of New England, which preferred to settle difficulties by arbitration, and regarded resort to the courts as a sort of moral failure. The Dutch Church certainly made every effort to keep this increasingly bitter dispute within its own doors; exchanges of varying levels of acrimony had been going on for at least three years before the Kingston church called a convention of elders from the three most adjacent consistories, which met in February 1766—though not without some dispute as to the actual proximity of these parishes. The handwritten account of the proceedings, which notes that all these consistories acknowledge subordination to the reverend classis of Amsterdam, record a judgment that Dr. Hermanus Meyer had been guilty of "public schism."

There is no charge of heresy. Nowhere in these voluminous, aggrieved, and acrimonious documents is Domine Meyer accused of *doctrinal* error, except in the sense that acceptance of a proper subordination to established authority may itself be considered a matter of orthodoxy. But the charge is serious enough: "Domine Meyer's obstinate refusal to subordinate himself as he ought to under that Classis, is nothing but rejection of said Church orders, an absolute separation from the Church of Holland, and a desire to introduce Independentism." His behavior threatened the destruction of a flourishing community, and besides—but perhaps this was the core of the matter—"his offensive manner of preaching has made himself unprofitable to the Congregation." God, they said, invoking theology in support of terrestrial authority, was a God of order, not of confusion. Meyer is forbidden to administer or receive the sacraments for six weeks, but is to come to church; after which time it is hoped that he will see the error of his ways and will repent. A letter from the classis of Amsterdam dated January 11, 1763, copied into a letterbook, has already given support to the stand of the elders by asserting the exclusive right to examine candidates for the churches of the Netherlands, a right which it cannot concede to the churches of the New Netherlands, which must remain subordinate; and now a letter dated October 6, 1766, confirms the sentence.[19]

This year, we recall, is 1766; the storm over the Stamp Act has hardly had time to settle, talk of "Independentism" is by any standards provocative. But by an ironic twist of the dialectic, the threatened independence is from Holland, not from Britain. To all this Domine Meyer has an answer which he has already given in a statement (translated from the Dutch) on August 23, 1764, and which ought to have been of considerable interest to the British authorities: he has taken the oath of allegiance and supremacy which obliges him to abjure all foreign power over ecclesiastical matters. The minister is appealing to his British allegiance to protect him from the claims both of his consistory and of the Dutch classis which looms behind it. Neither party could have been ignorant that the oath of allegiance was designed to prevent Catholics from subordinating their allegiance to the crown to the superior authority of Rome; but Meyer was probably the first minister of any denomination to invoke it for any other ecclesiastical jurisdiction.

His statement goes on to indicate the substantive issue involved in the dispute. What the classis claimed was the right of ordaining ministers—which was in consequence denied to the ministers and congregations here, in New York. This claim Domine Meyer disputed. He was not the first to have done so; at the beginning of the eighteenth century, Dutch Reformed churches in New York had been divided over the question of subordination to the Amsterdam Classis.[20] And he also rejected their claim "to give sentences and judgment relating to the Government of the church here." So this was indeed an issue involving independence; the freedom of a *Protestant* church in the colonies to run its own affairs, make its own appointments, and in effect to take responsibility for its own principles, which might eventually extend to its own doctrine. All this was implied in Domine Meyer's statement of his grievances: yet this claim, ambitious as it was, lay coiled within a formal act of submission to the crown of Great Britain! The British monarch was head of the Church of England, but English law, since 1689, tolerated dissent, and extended this policy to the colonies; so Domine Meyer could be exempted from logical inconsistency. In any case, no one chose to challenge him on this point; but it was, at the least, a shrewd if distinctively provocative tactical blow. Nor was Meyer without support in his own community: a letter to John Tabor Kempe dated March 21, 1766, from one Colonel Hansbrook informed him of popular support for Meyer and alleged that, since he had denied the authority of the consistory meeting and had refused to appear before it, he has been condemned unheard. They had proceeded without hearing any defense on the issue of nonsubordination to the classis "and other frivolous charges." When Meyer, whom Hansbrook calls "our minister," went to church, two of the elders stopped him from going to the pulpit to preach, and told him they held the censure to be legal.[21] There is still—and unusually for a religious schism—no report on either side of differences on matters of theology; Dr. Meyer's views could have been and probably were doctrinally orthodox. Nor do the waves produced by the Great Awakening seem to have lapped over the Dutch congregations. But Meyer wanted to shift the locus of control to the colony, and that shift would have inevitably involved an awakening of a more social and political kind of self-consciousness in the Dutch community. It hardly seems fanciful to suppose a connection between the preoccupation of the elders with the authority of the Amsterdam Classis, and the maintenance of their own control of their congregation in alliance with a God of order.

The consistory was represented by James Duane, a prominent lawyer who was later to play a considerable part in New York politics during the Revolution. Notes of Duane's argument survive (perhaps taken down in court by Kempe) but contain no reference to the issue of allegiance. For the consistory, it was sufficient that the minister appointed to replace Meyer had taken the oath of allegiance without feeling any inconsistency with his subordination to Amsterdam; and there it seems that this potentially provocative question was allowed by both sides to rest. Kempe's notes of his own arguments nowhere mention the point.

Domine Meyer, it will be recalled, was appealing to the Court of Chancery. The Judiciary Act of 1691, which had established the judicial system, had made the Supreme Court of Judicature the province's senior court, and no addition had been made to that structure; so it would seem that the same supreme court was sitting in a chancery capacity. It would have been more usual to pursue a contract case through the common law rather than through equity, but the reason for Domine Meyer's procedure was given in his initial statement: he was obliged to admit that he was "remedyless by the strict rules of the common law, being unable to prove the instrument and contract, so that your orator can only be relieved in this honourable Court." (This ritual language was no doubt supplied by the attorney general.) Chancery had developed in medieval England as a court armed with a commission to mitigate the rigors and formalities of the common law, which would have ruled Meyer's case inadmissible. One of the superior powers of Chancery was that of enforcing the fulfillment of an unfulfilled obligation, which a common law court could not do. This choice of action must have been adopted on Kempe's expert advice.

The defense replied to the plaintiff's charges by entering a demurrer, a form of legal counter-challenge alleging that the facts disclosed and accepted by both sides did not require a response. This plea claimed that the missing contract could only be assumed to have been the act of the consistory *in its capacity as a corporation*. "It is insisted on the other side," notes Kempe, "that they [i.e., Paulus Ploeg et al.] are not obliged to make good their Contract, but the Corporation ought to be sued." In other words, the elders were not responsible *as individuals*, but only if they could be proved to have acted as the corporation. But could the corporation be sued? The case could turn on this legalistic question. Domine Meyer's attorney understood the problem: that was why his client was suing not the corporation but the elders and deacons as individuals. The object of the defense's strategy was to deflect this suit by arguing, first that it was the corporation and not its individual members who ought to be the objects of the action, but that second, since this could not be done in the present case, the minister's suit must fail. Duane maintained that only a corporate act, duly sealed, could authenticate a valid appointment; and if the corporation were liable, then the defendants could not be. He is arguing that the only legally identifiable object of the action is the corporation, but that in the absence of proofs, the corporation cannot be made the object of the action. But likewise there is no proof of individual liability. The things a corporation is and is not, and what it can and cannot do, were now dredged up from Blackstone, Bacon, and other English authorities.[22] The thesis was that a corporation was an invisible being which existed "only by the Intendment of the Law." Having neither body nor personality, "a corporation can neither act do or suffer as a natural Person." To incur liability at law, with proper formalities as a corporation, its acts must be done: "1. In the Name and Stile of the Corporation; 2. Under its Common Seal." Domine Meyer might as well have been brandishing a sword at shadows. Blackstone, incidentally, had only just been published; Duane, authenticating his brief with English authority, was proving a highly professional lawyer.

The essence of Kempe's case was to admit that the corporation was not liable, but to maintain that the *contract* was authentic and valid in law, and that since it had been signed individually by the elders and deacons, the full legal responsibility was theirs. The contractual instrument—presumably a copy—which in the absence of the original had to stand as evidence of the agreement must have been available to the court, for Kempe examines it in detail. *They* had signed their names to the contract. *They* had described themselves as "The Elders & Deacons of the Reformed Protestant Dutch Church in Kingston in the County of Ulster." As an act of a corporation this unsealed document was full of defects: "It is conceived Chancery can't make it an Act of the Corporation if it is not so in itself." But clearly it was indented by its authors as a contract. Meyer, a foreigner with no knowledge of English law, had accepted their good faith; *and therefore,* not having bound the corporation, they had bound themselves as individuals. If no charter existed, Meyer might have had relief in equity against all the voters for the elders and deacons.

Appeals to fairness flew from both sides. It was hard, Duane argued, that the defendants should be bound when they did not intend to bind themselves in their natural capacity: "Intention ought to govern." To which Kempe replied that if it was hard, that was their own fault. They might have bound the corporation if they had pleased; they that had committed the blunder should answer for it, not an innocent stranger ignorant of our laws and formalities, who had been imposed upon by his confidence in them as to the goodness of the contract. If they were not answerable he was clearly without remedy, but, "This is against all Equity & Conscience." On the matter of intent, he urged, "If they have not made it as they *intended*, they must abide by it *such as it is.*"

None of these arguments appears in the printed version of *Ecclesiastical Records*. The church would have preferred to suppress any report of Meyer's appeal to the English legal system. There is also, and for the same reason, no report of the arguments about contract, which, of course, related entirely to English law. The consistory appears to have been ignorant of the legal situation and to have lacked legal advice. Their proceedings were sloppy; but they had probably never contemplated the possibility of such a schism with their minister, and were painfully learning the importance of English legal forms and procedures. But in falling back on the argument of intent, Duane raised an issue that was becoming prominent in England. As recently as 1765, Lord Mansfield, chief justice of the King's Bench, had ruled in *Pillans v. Van Mierop* that the intention of the parties, not the accidental influence of the forms of action, ought to determine the scope of the contract.[23] But this doctrine assumed that the parties had shared a discoverable common intent; the "will theory," as it is sometimes called, depended on a demonstrable agreement. That is why it is more commonly known as the "consensual theory." The difficulty in the Dutch Church case was that the existence of such a consensus could not be proved.

Each side agreed there was a contract. The elders had no doubt considered themselves as acting in their corporate capacity, and there seems little doubt that the consistory would have been liable at law in its capacity as corporation if the original instrument had been brought into the court. It was plainly their intention to act as a corporate body representing the church.

That they totally failed to foresee or provide for the course that events later took in no way affected their responsibility. Domine Meyer simply accepted the good faith of the commitment which they offered. Another way of putting the elders' position would have been to say that the new minister abrogated his contractual obligation when he refused to subordinate himself to the classis of Amsterdam. But their primary concern was to avert the catastrophe of personal liability for an obligation collectively undertaken.

An undated decree, either 1769 or 1770, records that the lieutenant governor finds for the plaintiff. But this is later reversed when a decree for the defendants is signed by Lieutenant Governor Cadwallader Colden and enrolled on March 5, 1770.[24] It is hard to say whether the court, presided over by the royal governor, was decisively influenced by the legal arguments; on the face of the matter, the elders seem more concerned to avoid paying damages than to uphold the strict terms of the contract they had offered. The allegedly schismatic deviations of Domine Meyer may have seemed adequate justification for the elders' course, which, after all, aimed at preserving the general unity and authority of the church to which they all belonged. In the tense atmosphere of current imperial politics, royal authorities may have preferred to avoid antagonizing the governing authorities of an element of the Dutch community. The Dutch, aided by a forgiving disposition in Amsterdam, eventually succeeded in bringing about a resolution. Meyer was offered and accepted another ministry, while the Kingston consistory agreed to pay him "a sum of money." In 1784 he was appointed instructor in Hebrew and Greek, and died in 1791.[25]

The first and most obvious lesson from this excursion into legal case records is not that the two cases we have examined either draw on or contribute a body of case law; they are altogether too exceptional for that. It is, rather, that legal history, notwithstanding its forbidding barrier of forms and technicalities, leads into the history of society in its deepest and most unexpected ramifications. Although the cases of Juan Miranda and Hermanus Meyer have little in common, both involve non-British parties in the judicial system of a multinational British province. In neither case was English the first language of the plaintiffs. In Miranda's case, which begins as an appeal against unlawful enslavement, the judiciary, in using their discretion in the interests of justice, may also be said to have acted as an agency of foreign policy. Domine Meyer's case raised more familiar problems. New York had a large Dutch community, some of whom were merchants, and their names appear in ordinary common law actions. In 1765 the Dutch Church sued Colonel Bradstreet, an officer of the crown, on a writ of trespass. Bradstreet was accused of building on church land.[26] The difference in Meyer's case lay in his taking an internal complaint to the provincial court and subjecting the consistory to Chancery jurisdiction. Meyer was undoubtedly felt to be taking his schismatic propensities too far by a course which exposed a deep division in his own community.

The British system, however, was constitutionally superior to the systems of internal conciliation operated by the Dutch and other settlements such as the Germans in Pennsylvania. Neither case was decided under common law, which was the prevalent jurisprudence in the colonies as they assimilated their legal systems to England. But Meyer's case was an example of the way in which equity could take over from the common law in difficult circumstances—which is what equity was designed to do. Both cases illustrated the flexibility of this colony's legal institutions in dealing with the realities of the situation without being hedged in by formal writs and pleadings. *Meyer v. Ploeg* was an episode—a particularly contentious one, and therefore the more instructive to all concerned—in the gradual assimilation of the early minority communities into the dominant British system of law and government: a moment in the process of Anglicization. It is nonetheless significant for the fact that important features and principles of that system were soon afterward absorbed without much change into the independent state of New York.

7

Bicameralism and Republican Government in the British American Colonies and in the United States

At the time of the early English settlements in North America and the Caribbean islands, the bicameral structure of parliaments would not have seemed to need either explanation or justification. From the political point of view, the kingdom was made up of its estates. The Church of England, ecclesiastically self-governing, was represented in the House of Lords by the bench of bishops, the peers spiritual; the peers temporal, each of whom would be summoned to a parliament by a writ from the crown, sat there in their own right. The House of Commons—etymologically related to "communes"—consisted of representatives elected by the shires and boroughs. This state of affairs did not result from any previously existing theory of representation; it was the historical result of the needs of the crown, operating in a complex postfeudal kingdom. Sir Thomas Smith's treatise *De Republica Anglorum*, written in the 1560s and first published in 1583, wrote of "The Parliament" that "everie Englishman is entended to bee there present, either by procuration or attornies";[1] but treatises purporting to expound the general character of the realm, or what would later be called the structure of politics, were notable for their rarity. The theoretical foundations of English politics had to be sought in the interstices of English institutions.

This statement has some bearing on one of the themes that I hope to develop in this essay. A very powerful and convincing case has been made in our time for the explanation of American political development in terms of an ideology derived from England, though nurtured in the colonies;[2] and in the earlier years of this century, a case which contemporaries found equally convincing was urged for explaining American politics in terms of the dynamics of economic motives. It is no part of my purpose to detract from the force of these arguments, because I do not believe that the subject can be properly understood if either of them is neglected. I shall do no more than suggest that it is also true that neither American political development nor the institutional structures in which it was framed can be fully understood without taking account of another kind of dynamic, that of the accumulated effects of institutional memories and habits. Bicameral institutions, along with the electoral basis of the lower house, committees to deal with special problems, and parliamentary procedures, together with the informal understandings that grow up in the course of time, all formed elements of these institutional memories; they were seasoned by usage and members knew how to apply them to the needs of an immediate situation. They would not have seen much need to explain that their aims included the preservation of the institutions themselves. Although an interpretation on these lines can be inferred from some of the works of our own time,[3] and indeed of earlier times, it has not been developed as a specific explanatory thesis in its own right, it suffers the disadvantage of being less exciting than the theories I have mentioned, and has not enjoyed their literary prominence. The study of bicameralism provides one field in which the concrete meaning and value of political institutions to the persons who ran them can be given a hearing.[4]

Before attempting an account of the rather curious story of bicameral development in America, it will be helpful to glance forward, in a somewhat cursory way, at the realities rather than the theory of representative institutions in Britain. The firm but placid basis of the landed interest, which showed impressive powers of surviving its feudal origins and giving values as well as political power to succeeding ages, gradually ceased to correspond to the facts of British economic and demographic life. By the middle of the seventeenth century England's interest in commerce was already sending the nation to war against the Dutch; before the end of the century, a wealth of pamphlet literature testified to a serious and inquiring concern with the national interest in commerce and finance.[5] It took a long time for these matters to find any adequate reflection in political institutions. Moreover, from the ascendancy of Walpole, opposition critics of the operations of political power were more concerned with corruption emanating from the crown and its functionaries than with realistic analysis of the relationships between power and interest within the nation. David Hume may be said to have anticipated some of the arguments for the merits of interest politics, but Edmund Burke was the first to defend the existing structure of the House of Commons on the ground that it actually accommodated the great interests, landed, commercial, military, and legal, that had gradually formed in the nation.[6] This was the first explicit exposition of a theory of interest representation.[7] The theory that British parliaments in some way embodied the great estates of the realm, though not completely discarded, had become archaic; it failed to describe the facts that men needed to understand in order to work within the system. Although the House of Lords was still a major center of power throughout the eighteenth century, it no longer reflected, or represented, a distinctively different cluster of interests. Land was and had always been heavily represented in the Commons, and landlords who developed commercial, mining, or industrial enterprises had in the nature of the case an interest in those activities whether they sat in the Commons or the Lords. The one thing that distinctively characterized the Lords was the fact that its members *were* lords, representing nobody but themselves. A hereditary aristocracy was still an estate of the realm, and in this sense the system of representation worked to maintain the concept of estates after the concept had ceased to serve a valid political purpose. It would have been nearer to the realities of political power to call this a special case of interest representation. An estate is grander than an interest, and the people who inhabit it perhaps feel greater for that fact, especially when they are an aristocracy; no doubt that explains why men in public life were so slow and reluctant to acknowledge the changes that were coming, gradually enough, to characterize the system.

At no period did Britain's colonial governments ever fully replicate the English system. Colonial wealth was primarily held in land, though in both the West Indies and, during the eighteenth century, the southern mainland colonies it was also held in the slaves who made the land profitable, but landed property never constituted or was thought of as an "estate." The small circle of great men who constituted the governor's council in each colony were certainly drawn from the class who would have formed an aristocracy in the ordinary sense of the word, but in no sense did they represent that class. Nor could more than a fraction of the landowners find seats on the council. Those who were politically ambitious would find their way easily enough into the assembly of their province. Councils had important functions, many of which were judicial and advisory, but they were also genuine upper houses in the exercise of a share of legislative power; but in respect of some of their duties, and of their political base in the country, they are in some ways better compared to the British crown's privy councils than to the House of Lords.

According to legend, the American version of bicameral government originated in Massachusetts over the case of the widow Sherman's sow. Until the case of *Sherman v. Keayne* in 1642, the group of assistants who advised the governor but also sat in the General Court, and who like the ordinary representatives or deputies were elected by the freemen of the towns, shared a single chamber with the deputies. In 1640 an unpopular merchant called Robert Keayne was convicted in the county court of stealing and killing a sow belonging to one Sherman, but later, after Sherman's death, this verdict was appealed to the General Court. There, the assistants voted to reverse, while the representatives voted to uphold. At that time the assistants and the representatives sat together in one chamber, but the rules gave the assistants a "negative vote" over the more numerous representatives, which meant that their verdict prevailed, Keayne was acquitted, and a poor widow lost her claim to compensation. A bitter constitutional wrangle—in which it must be said that members of the General Court were not unaware of the faintly absurd origins of the issue—led to formal separation of assistants and deputies into separate chambers, the concurrence of both being required for the passage of any measure.[8]

Two points deserve attention. The first is that although the assistants were in effect a class of magistrates, they did not owe their position to a distinctive base in society; they were not an aristocracy in the landed—or mercantile—sense, and they did not remotely resemble an "estate." When in 1691 the crown imposed a new charter on the province of Massachusetts-Bay, it contained the unusual provision that the upper house—now a council—was to be elected annually by the outgoing House of Representatives.[9] Although the house habitually elected men of considerable prominence, they were obviously susceptible to the state of opinion in the lower house. In the turbulence of the 1760s, royal governors found them hopelessly subject to popular will. The second point is that what happened in Massachusetts did not give laws to other colonies. Bicameral arrangements unfolded elsewhere from royal or proprietary charters. (In Pennsylvania, William Penn himself conceded a new charter in 1701, with a much emasculated council; Pennsylvania is often said to have had a unicameral legislature.) They conformed to the needs of government, as perceived in Britain, and did not arise spontaneously from the history of the structure of colonial society. This is not to say that the colonial society was without structure; powerful landed and mercantile interests behaved in ways not unlike those of their European counterparts; but they did not find corresponding institutional forms to represent them. It is also not to say that the council should be discounted. From 1706 to 1710 the Council of Virginia ruled the entire province, during an intermission between royal governors, without the presence of an assembly.[10] It would have required some courage in that period to have predicted the rise of an assembly and the decline of the council.

But in the longer run there could be no other course. If the council was not wholly dependent on the crown it would have to depend on the people. In the former case, it was likely in times of controversy to be opposed to the popular interests represented in the lower house; in the latter case, it was too assimilated to the views of the lower house to have any particularly cogent reason for independent existence. With the onset of the crisis leading to the American Revolution, colonial councils had not the power, even in the rare cases where they had the will, to check the aggrandizement of the lower houses or assemblies.[11]

One immediate consequence of the Revolution was the Americans had to make decisions about their forms of government.

The students of bicameral institutions will find them, naturally enough, in the context in which the Americans remade their political systems in the new republican air of the American Revolution. Three specific phases, moments of republican creation, stand out for our immediate purpose. The first of these was the making of the new constitutions: during the first years of independence, this was undertaken in all states except Connecticut and Rhode Island, which had always claimed to be satisfied with the terms of their charters and made no changes in them. The second of these creative moments was the making of the federal Constitution at the great Convention in Philadelphia in 1787. The third reverted to a single state, Pennsylvania, which held its own convention in 1790 and there adopted a bicameral constitution to replace the unicameral instrument that had been forged in the heat of the Revolution.

Republican theory, as understood in the colonies and new states, called for certain conditions which, on the whole, corresponded to most of what colonists had been accustomed to regard as the better parts of the governments under which they had grown up—and the genuinely representative part of the British government. The concept of consent became more concrete; legislatures ought to be based on free and frequent elections, in which the propertied part of the male inhabitants would take part. But republican theory did not have very much to say about the precise forms to be taken by republican institutions. It was history, not theory, that had handed down bicameral legislatures.

Yet the idea of an upper house did not seem to have emerged from the colonial experience with very much credit. It had been a much weaker branch of the government than either the governor or the assembly; it had not established any very distinct legitimation for its existence in a society formally lacking in social differentiation. Richard Henry Lee criticized the constitutional structure of Virginia in a letter to his brother Arthur in 1766, drawing a contrast with that of Britain. Whereas in Britain the forms of monarchy, aristocracy, and democracy were nicely balanced, and the House of Lords played the essential role of maintaining the independence of the aristocratic element, in Virginia the crown controlled both the governor and council.[12] Lee did not here dissociate himself from the idea that the aristocracy might have an "interest" of its own to protect; to make this case, it was first necessary to find an aristocracy, then find a justification for preserving its privileged status, and then find some institutional way of doing so. Even Virginia gentry were hard-pressed to do all this, and Lee's principal point was that a stronger upper house would have acted as a restraint on the crown interest in the province. Claims to privileged status were already unpopular, and in the next few years things moved so fast that in 1775 the Virginia Council found it necessary to disclaim any intention of acting in an independent interest from that of the people.[13] But if the councils had strengthened such suspicious tendencies, that alone might have been expected to weaken their claims on the ideology of the new republics. The lower houses of legislature, which had made all the running for half a century or so, in some cases considerably longer, became the real centers of political power in the several states. In most cases they soon became somewhat more accessible than their colonial predecessors, and new constitutions carefully provided for public access to galleries and the printing of records. On the whole, though, the keynote was continuity; the Revolution was not a revolution in institutional forms. In these circumstances, it is the retention, and not only the retention but the strengthening, of the upper houses by the constitution-making bodies of the new states that seems to call for some explanation.

The explanation should begin with the institutional habits to which I referred at the beginning. Colonists had been running their own affairs through their own institutions and procedures for generations. They knew how to operate them; they were comfortable with them. Although economic instability frequently broke down into disorder in wide areas of American society, both rural and urban, the most prevalent instincts of the leading members of political society led them to accommodate these changes with a minimum of structural alteration in the familiar forms of institutions. It is surely relevant that among all the former colonies, as they converted themselves into sovereign states, Pennsylvania and Georgia, the two which had lived with unicameral arrangements—or what amounted to them—were the only two which retained the unicameral form. All the old bicameral colonies retained the bicameral form as states. Habit may not have as much glamour as acquisitiveness or ideology in the pages of historical explanation, but it is not without force in determining the channels in which they will run and the molds in which they will be formed.

In a period of conscious political choices, habits amounted to rather more than the force of inertia; they could be dignified as experience. But it was also true in this turbulent era that institutional habits were reinforced by more positive motives. Pennsylvania had been taken over by ideological radicals, who fastened on the new state the most radically democratic constitution of the age; and the fact that radically democratic versions of republican theory regarded single-chamber legislatures as purer, because more directly under popular control, than bicameral ones had a very strong bearing on what the radical party was trying to achieve. By the same token, or the other side of it, men of even slightly more conservative disposition felt safer with two houses even when they found it difficult to distinguish a separate constituency for the upper house.

Their motives became a little more apparent from the character of the new bodies. Where annual elections prevailed in the lower or popular houses, some states gave their senators longer terms of office. Maryland's distinctively conservative senate had a five-year term; those of New York and Virginia ran to four years, Delaware three, and South Carolina two. All these represented conscientious attempts to create a sense of difference in the character of the upper house. Most states took this effort further by establishing the upper houses on a higher property basis. In some cases, such as New York, property qualifications for voters for the senate were set higher than for the house; Massachusetts and New Hampshire awarded seats in their senates on the basis of taxes paid by the electoral districts. In New Jersey, where each county sent the same number of senators, candidates had to be substantially wealthier than for the house. The county itself formed a different constituency from the town or other electoral division.[14]

While the political conventions of the time offered the bicameral framework as a working model, these devices represented a rather unusual development in eighteenth-century political science. Constitution makers were deliberately striving to use existing institutional forms for the representation of social elements not far removed from class interests, which had never been previously defined as fitting into distinct institutions; and in the process they were contributing to, and strengthening, a sense of class distinction which had in the past only been very indistinctly defined. Much churning was going on in revolutionary America, and in the turbulence of a situation which might at any moment become revolutionary at home, it rapidly appeared that the higher interests of property could find themselves in greater need of protection. It would go rather far to call this an attempt to bring an aristocratic "estate" into existence. But property rendered political power in the colonies, and its owners had to find ways to make that power secure without setting themselves at too great a distance from the common people. The makers of these institutions were very conscious both of their heritage from the classical past and of their responsibilities for transmitting it, purified and strengthened, to their descendants. Their choice of the name "senate" for the upper house was a mark of this sense of responsibility; after all, they could have continued to use the word "council." But the Roman Republic was in their minds, and Americans, in contrast to the Romans, were forging a purified republic out of the ruins of a decadent empire.

If it was not essential to create a political elite, it was because revolutionary leaders were for the most part the men who already formed that elite. To launch a revolution they were supplemented and reinforced by a huge intake of ordinary people who formed the numerous committees which enforced revolutionary decrees in the towns and counties. But these highly populist bodies needed both guidance and restraint from their leaders. Most of the common people had accepted this leadership in the past, and did not resist the idea that men of greater worth and substance, men of learning and superior wisdom, had a rightful place in government. This leadership of "men of wisdom, firmness, learning and the consistency of character exhibited by an aristocracy" was nowhere more clearly joined to a general theory of political obligation than in an important pamphlet which resulted from a convention of the gentry of Essex County, Massachusetts—and so came to be called the Essex Result.[15]

This pamphlet, generally attributed to Theophilus Parsons, a prominent lawyer, accepted all the Whig tenets of republican government and went on without any inconsistency to claim that "equal interests among the people" should have "equal interests in the body of representatives." The distinction to be observed was between persons and property. "If the law affects only the persons of the members, the consent of a majority of any members is sufficient. If a law affects the property only, the consent of those who hold a majority of the property is enough. If it affects (as it will very frequently, if not always), both persons and property, the consent of a majority of the members, and of those members also, who hold a majority of the property is necessary." The answer was to set the representation of property firmly in the senate.

The need for an upper chamber was perceived by another prominent Massachusetts figure, John Adams, in a dual and rather complex light. On the one hand the dangers and imbecilities of a single house were to be avoided, liable as it was "to all the vices, follies and frailties of an individual; subject to fits of humour, starts of passion, flights of enthusiasm, partialities or prejudice, and consequently productive of hasty results and absurd judgments. And all these errors ought to be corrected and defects supplied by some controlling power."[16] But Adams was also impressed by the arrogance of the aristocracy, a class which he regarded as a natural and inevitable element in any society. This led him to observe that it would be safer for legislative purposes to segregate the *aristoi* in a separate chamber. He called it a kind of "ostracism."[17] (He did not notice that this ostracism would have no power to prevent members of that class from getting themselves elected to the lower house, if that was where they could exercise their influence to the greatest effect.)

Another feature of the new forms of state government added a kind of negative reason for not only retaining but giving more strength to the upper houses. This was a result of the position of the newly instituted republican governors. It seems that American experience with royal and proprietary governors—and indeed with the king himself—has led to a revulsion against the executive office; such power was too likely to tempt its holder to aggrandizement and abuse. It did not seem possible to dispense completely with the executive office, but the very general tendency was—as though to punish the royal governors of the past—to reduce the powers of the new, republican governors. This is not to say that they were mere ciphers; but few vestiges remained from the days of royal government, and the new systems left a place of constitutional weakness where there had formerly been exceptional strength.[18] It also meant that nearly all the effective power, especially that of all stages of legislation, was concentrated in the legislature, of which the lower house would inevitably be much the stronger branch. No practice of judicial control over legislation had yet begun to emerge, and even where there were glimmerings of it in the 1780s, it would have been impossible to generalize from these into an effective means of review. A stronger upper chamber was left as the only form of constitutional restraint on the possible excesses of the lower house. It did not prove a very formidable barrier.

Both during the course of the War of Independence and afterward, state politicians had to contend with extremely divisive issues. In several states these concerned monetary policies; the treatment of loyalists, many of whom were deprived of their estates, was also a subject of strong feelings and contentious divisions. In Massachusetts a minor rebellion broke out in 1786 against tax collections and foreclosures on farm property. But it cannot be said that the bicameral arrangement made the kind of difference that its progenitors had hoped and planned for. Very seldom was legislation passed by the lower house rejected by the senate; in only one state did the senate make a determined effort to reject paper money voted by the lower house. Despite the precautions over property qualifications, the men who filled senate seats differed very little from members of the house. Fewer than one in four or five members of senates were genuinely educated men; there were too many seats to be filled and too few men of learning, wisdom, substance. Whether the deficiencies of political representatives were also deficiencies of the vital republican quality of virtue was rapidly becoming a question of party loyalty. Senates did show some tendency to be sensitive to property interests in party struggles; it would be an error to discount them completely. But it was equally likely, where policy issues split along party lines, that the divisions of opinions would be reproduced in both houses rather than that one house would check the other.[19] An important early conclusion from the development of political strife was, however, that bicameralism as an institutional restraint did not prove strong enough to preserve the precious quality of disinterestedness.

But this did not deter the bicameral eagerness of the conservative interests of Pennsylvania, where the most intense party conflicts occurred and where the radical constitution became in itself the object of contention. The radicals called themselves constitutionalists, while their more conservative opponents adopted the name of republicans. When, in 1790, the republicans were able to form a strong enough majority in the assembly, after the adoption of the Constitution of the United States by a convention held, as it happened, in Pennsylvania's capital city, they resolved the political problem by calling a state convention to reform the constitution itself. The dominant feature of the new constitution of Pennsylvania was—effectively for the first time since 1701—a bicameral legislature.

There could have been no way to resolve all of the post-Revolution problems faced by state governments without controversy. But where populist policies prevailed, they often threatened to debase the value of the currency, and gave grave alarm to those for whom the value of money was the most sacred form of security. In other respects, too, even the bicameral legislatures of the first state constitutions showed little regard for the interests of property or the rights of individuals. In Virginia, the legislature ignored the language of the state's bill of rights when it suited it to do so.[20] The movement for a new federal constitution arose from what was conceived of as the weakness of the existing Continental Congress, the unwillingness of the states to give it necessary support, and their own impetuous but uncertain policies.

In these dangerous circumstances, the nationalists who provided the impetus for a new convention were seeking for political forms which would give strength, wisdom, and security to the advancement of the interests they had at heart. When the Virginia delegates arrived in Philadelphia in April 1787 to wait for the arrival of their colleagues from other states, they devised a draft constitution to present as an agenda to the Convention. It comes as no surprise that this draft—known as the Virginia Plan—contained provisions for an upper house or "senate" which would be stronger than those of the existing state constitutions. It was, in fact, evidence of the far-reaching nature of their design that they offered a plan containing a bicameral legislature at all. This point is easy to overlook because we have got used to the existence of the Congress consisting of a House of Representatives and a Senate. But in the historical context of the existing Articles of Confederation, this form represented a subtle but profound transformation in the very character of the Union. The old Congress was in essence a meeting of sovereign states—that in fact was what congresses were in Europe and continued to be with the "Congress System" after the Congress of Vienna in 1815. A constitution incorporating a bicameral legislature would announce the creation of a new type of federal union—a nation rather than a confederation. Nation-states in Europe might be composed of "estates," each sitting in its own chambers, but the states themselves were single sovereignties. Opponents of the new system, dedicated as they were to retaining the sovereignty of the individual states proclaimed in the Articles of Confederation, understood this very well and insistently accused the self-styled "Federalists" of aiming at consolidation.

The Virginia Plan envisaged a fully bicameral state in which both houses were to be based on numerical representation. This would not have abolished states, and would have left the great states in a strong position because they had the greatest numbers. The nationalists, however, had greatly underrated the strength of state feelings, which emerged particularly with the fears of the smaller states that they would be swamped by their large neighbors in the new Union. After some bitter exchanges and a moment when the whole Convention was on the verge of collapse, the prospect of a federal constitution was saved by a compromise over the structure of the Senate. Under the Constitution, the Senate was to represent the states as equal partners in the government, each having two senators regardless of population. The House of Representatives was based on the proportional principle, each state being represented according to its population.

The Senate emerged as a very powerful body, independent of both the executive and the lower house. It retained a faint residue of the character of the British House of Lords. Negatively, this was reflected in the provision that only the House of Representatives could institute money bills—a point based on the fundamental principle which linked taxation with representation, with the reminder that the Senate was not, in that sense, a representative body. Senators were to be elected not by the people at large but by the state legislatures.[21] In another sense, the six-year term of office and the provision of an age qualification beginning at thirty-five, which in a youthful population was intended to make senators "elders" in the original Roman sense of the word, added to the unmistakable dignity of the Senate, creating in this newly devised institution some of the aura of a traditional upper house.[22] The Senate's legislative powers were coequal with those of the House, while it was given the power to ratify treaties and confirm or reject presidential nominations to judicial and ambassadorial offices. These twenty-six men representing the thirteen states would get to know, understand, and connive with each other; a mere fourteen of them would constitute a majority. Was the Republic safe in such hands? It was hardly surprising that opponents of the new Constitution thought they detected signs of oligarchy.

The self-styled Federalists, in defending the Constitution before the electorate, insisted that the Senate would be accountable to the people.[23] But senators were intentionally more remote than the members of the House of Representatives, who were directly elected by the people and could never forget for long to seek reelection. Madison, writing No. 62 of *The Federalist,* urged the case that public councils were dangerously mutable, a condition arising from "the rapid succession of members," to which he tactfully added "however qualified they may be"; all this, which he had had the opportunity of observing in his own state legislature (of which he had been a member) indicated "the necessity of some stable institutions in government."[24] A continual change of opinions, leading to constant change in measures—even good measures—was "inconsistent with every rule of prudence."

The principle historically underlying bicameral institutions was the need to embody different estates or interests in the constitution of a sovereign state; and this typology, whether in Europe or in the various American governments, had nothing in principle to do with the separation of powers. But the American Constitution was also consciously constructed on that principle. The executive, legislative, and judicial branches of government are separately described, their powers indicated in separate clauses of the instrument. The "checks and balances" attributed to the Constitution were meant, in the dialectics of political science, to operate between the branches of government. But the legislature which "checked" the executive was itself a bicameral legislature, in which, as we have seen, some powers are entrusted to one house but denied to the other. The two houses were thus also a sort of "check" on each other. It was a complicated system, whose operations were inevitably time-consuming, and whose institutional character tended to create suspicions and animosities between the two houses.

Madison was forced by the character of the compromise over the basis of the Senate to make the best of a document of which he did not fully approve. He used *The Federalist* to disarm the defenders of state sovereignty with the argument that the equality of states in the Senate safeguarded the "federal" character of the Union.[25] He defended the close character of the Senate by pointing out that larger numbers always diminish individual responsibility. Ancient history, in which Madison had schooled himself for the purpose, was drawn into the argument. "It adds no small weight to all these considerations, to recollect, that history informs us of no long lived republic which had not a senate. Sparta, Rome and Carthage are in fact the only states to whom that character can be applied. In each of the two first there was a senate for life."[26] The enfeeblement of the powers of the senate of Carthage seems to have weakened the state. He also dealt severely, as Hamilton had done in earlier essays,[27] with the consequences of government swayed by popular passion in Athens.

Federalists did not appeal to the idea of virtue as often as one might be led to suppose. Both they and their opponents, however, were familiar with Montesquieu, for whom virtue was the spirit of a republic. It is easy to translate virtue into that highest form of self-interest which identifies the true character of the republic in terms of one's own class. But the idea had a classical lineage; and there is no reason to doubt that they deeply believed in the importance of setting men of substance, learning, and some leisure to reflect on underlying principles. If virtue meant anything superior to private interest, it must mean an ability to speak for the Republic as a whole. The principle that each member of Parliament ought to consider himself a representative for "the whole nation" had already acquired classic status in the language of Edmund Burke.[28] Bicameralism in its American form raised the Senate closer to this ideal; but much of it was lost again in the conscious representation of the states. By 1860 those of the South conceived of their interests as being directly contrary to those of the "whole nation." There was no adequate solution to this problem within the Constitution and it was settled by war. But such dreadful contingencies the men of 1787 hoped to avoid. The Republic would, in their opinion, best be served by men who understood the principles which were intended to survive whatever crisis excited men's immediate passions.

In such a crisis, however, virtue meant nothing at all if it did not mean preferring one policy to another. There has been much emphasis in recent scholarship on the classically derived concept of virtue as though it were somehow detached from policy. A corrective to this approach might be provided by reference to Madison's excoriating attacks on "the pestilent effects of paper money."[29] It was very clear that making paper money into legal tender was not only bad policy but immoral policy. This was a leading case in immediate contemporary history of the disastrous consequences of an absence of virtue in public councils. So was the collapse of public order in Massachusetts in the year preceding the Constitutional Convention. Upper houses in bicameral systems were not intended merely to provide a fund of consultative sagacity: they were intended to be there to check rash or wrong policies of representatives who depended too directly on the people. Since these representatives had consulted the needs of their electors, and in many cases had thought out their policies with great care and prudence, they could hardly be expected to agree that the senates above them were the peculiar repositories of virtue.

The issue of bicameralism found the leading supporters of social order as sustained by these institutions in a dilemma which they never clearly resolved—and which they did not even adequately acknowledge. John Adams declared, for example, that in America the balance was "nine tenths on the side of the people. Indeed, there is but one order; and our senators have influence chiefly by the principles of authority, and very little those of power."[30] Thomas Jefferson and James Madison agreed in finding the two houses in their own state of Virginia too homogeneous with each other; the trouble was that the senate lacked a natural constituency in society; the question could be generalized for America.[31] Yet in *The Federalist* Madison was still trying to convince his readers, and perhaps himself, that the advantages of a bicameral legislature would be found "in proportion to the dissimilarity of the genius of the two bodies."[32] This position implied that they really in some sense represented different constituencies, but Madison himself had difficulty in identifying the character of this genius. The first elections to the first Congress under the Constitution gave Madison grounds for some cruelly ironical reflections on the subject of virtue, to which, whatever its refinements, Federalists attached serious weight. Madison had every reason to expect to be rewarded for his labors with a seat in the Senate. But the arch Anti-Federalist Patrick Henry got the Virginia legislature to deny him that election, and did his best to get the electoral districts drawn to exclude him from the House. (The procedure would later be called a gerrymander.) Madison overcame the latter obstacles. After going to the distasteful lengths of having to campaign for election, he was elected for his own district and duly took his seat in the House of Representatives: he never sat in the United States Senate.

Social and economic fortunes were in a very fluid condition; it was beyond the power of bicameral institutions to summon corresponding estates into existence. There was, however, a general disposition to agree that a upper chamber had its uses. Its revisory powers were seldom exercised without good reason, and second thoughts were not necessarily perverse thoughts. The habits associated with bicameral legislatures were comfortably adapted to the needs of a turbulent political era. In Massachusetts, the elections of 1787 that followed Shays's Rebellion set right much of the damage of the previous year. But if the state senates had not been ultimately accountable, and if they had persistently opposed the representatives and obstructed their policies, the history of bicameralism might have had a shorter life.

Before the federal Constitution had been created, Anne-Robert-Jacques Turgot criticized America's state constitutions for abandoning the true republican unicameral principle.[33] A great opportunity, he felt, had been lost. To this, John Adams replied with his long-winded, repetitive, but indubitably learned and forceful disquisition *A Defence of the Constitutions of the United States*, published in 1786. Adams ransacked ancient history and the Old World to prove that true republican principles had never been safe, and had never lasted long, without the resort of a second chamber.[34] But if Americans emerged from their political turmoil with something of a consensus on this theme, it was a consensus which depended on the underlying principle that senates were expected to exercise the virtues of wisdom and restraint rather than serving as embodiments of different fundamental principles.[35] (It is not irrelevant, as we have noted, that when different fundamental principles were truly at stake, the Senate of the United States was utterly unable to supply a remedy, and the result was four years of civil war.)

Europeans of both the left and the right perceived in the United States an example of democracy. It was a perception which they entertained with divergent feelings. American democracy was liberated both from a European imperial power and from the restraints of hereditary or monarchical power on its own territory. The success or failure of that experiment was of vital importance to the future of Europe. Bicameral government was not America's only or most prominent contribution to Europe's debates, and it was a contribution which had significantly different implications for Americans and America's anxious European observers.

The distinction that needs to be made here was between bicameralism as a solution to the needs of state government and bicameralism in the Constitution of the United States. At the state level, although the existence of two chambers protracted and complicated the legislative process, the behavior of the majorities in both chambers tended to be subject to party interests; the Republican Party of Pennsylvania won their point in 1790, but it is doubtful whether their victory made much difference to the course of the state's political history. But European observers, especially those conservatives who came to admire the stabilizing character of the American system (a system which had proved its powers of endurance in the Civil War) had their eyes on the Senate of the United States.

There would have been a senate under the original Virginia Plan: it was envisaged as a solution to the need for a chamber of revision. But the Senate as it emerged from the Philadelphia Convention and entered into American history had come into existence as a federal solution, rather than as a class solution, to the problems of American government. All the same, it was a federal solution which, with its distant reverberations of aristocracy, so subtly incorporated undertones of class that European conservatives were attracted to the American model when they faced the rise of democracy in the later nineteenth century.

Even at the federal level, party politics dominated all other considerations when major matters of policy were at issue, as was the case throughout the Civil War and most of Reconstruction. But the political configuration of the Congress could be affected by the fact that Senate elections were on a different timescale from those of the House. The two houses were not necessarily dominated by the same party majorities. In the midterm elections of 1874, the Democrats won the House for the first time since the Civil War, while the Senate remained Republican. It was structure as much as party or class interest that tended to produce conservative results in terms of policy. But all this, in 1787, was for distant generations in an unforeseen future. The immediate lesson, which the founding generation did live to see, was that the new Union was strong and supple enough to survive the storms of conflict that swept the American continent during the French revolutionary and Napoleonic wars—storms that would have torn the Confederation apart. When its wider historical implications are under consideration, it is to be remembered that it was this federal aspect rather than the class aspect of America's bicameral system that gave both substance and symbol to the new Union.

8

The Individual, the Region, the Nation

Where Three Roads Meet

An air of Greek tragedy hangs over the origins of the American Civil War—a sort of willed inevitability. Where three roads meet, three roads also diverge: it depends which way you are going. Here in Vienna (at a conference convened by the Austrian Association for American Studies), where the Oedipus complex was discovered, or invented, the invocation seems dramatic but appropriate. The attempted secession of the Southern states, and the formation of the Confederacy, involved all our three terms of reference—the individual, the region, and the nation: it was region against nation; and region or locality seemed for the most part to determine individuals' loyalties, though they were in principle free to decide their own political choices. When one involves oneself in the historical details, there are always choices to be made (for instance, whether or not "to now provision Fort Sumter"). There are always choices to be made; but from a few paces, there is an air of destiny: a tragedy in which people will their own fates. In that sense, I do not think it is overdramatic to hint of the ambience of Greek tragedy.

But American history is rarely presented as tragedy. The Union triumphed and prospered. All the three elements survived, though I shall argue that they survived by changing in their characters and their relationships to each other. The first problem we confront, in relating the three elements before us in this conference, is that none of them can be considered in isolation. Their crosscurrents of mutual influence have been complex, persistent, and powerful. In certain historical situations they have determined one another. To be a citizen of an American state is still a significant political designation: Massachusetts has strict gun control laws; its neighbor, Rhode Island, does not, and as you pass into the Commonwealth of Massachusetts you are confronted by large billboards warning you of the penalties for carrying guns. Some states have abolished the death penalty; most have not. But citizenship of a state means much less, both politically and sentimentally, today than it often did in the past. And even the emotional hold of the states differs from one to another. (Virginia is the one ancient state which seems to have a peculiar retentive power.)

I began by drawing your attention to divergences. But although the divergences between our three entities have often been profound, they have not proved fatal. In the long run—though this was not apparent at the end of the Civil War—the nation has triumphed as a nation with the obligation to respect and the power to protect the individual, while remaining a nation in which a concept of regional diversity has survived and flourished.

The United States, however, has always been and remains a rather peculiar kind of nation. Its federal structure, together with its formalized separation of powers, sets some limits on what the federal government can do, and keeps spaces open for the adaptation of local government to local needs. It would be far from my purpose to argue that the divergences between individual, region, and nation have been overcome by an ultimate fusion into an indissoluble whole.

The United States is not a corporate government or a corporate political body. Lawyers and jurisprudents have experienced extraordinary difficulty in identifying or locating sovereignty in the United States. James Wilson, one of the more philosophical of the early justices of the Supreme Court, went as far as to say that the word "sovereign" was "totally unknown" to the Constitution.[1]

I have always found it difficult to explain the federal character of American government to British students. Accustomed to a unitary system which reposes sovereignty, theoretically at least, in Parliament, they find it hard to believe that the federal government has historically lacked power to enforce its will throughout the states. In the debates over the ratification of the Constitution, the Anti-Federalists hammered incessantly at the threat of "consolidation." This tactic forced their Federalist opponents to deny that the new Constitution had any such tendency. The fundamental question was not so much what the new Union was, but what it would become.

Having acknowledged the limitations expressed in the debates of 1787–88, it should be recognized that the ground that has been covered in the direction of consolidation would have astonished the Founders.

New Deal legislation did much to promote this process. For example: in the case of *Wickard v. Filburn* (1942) the Supreme Court sustained the conviction under the revised Agricultural Adjustment Act of 1938 of a farmer whose family had consumed at their own table bread made wholly from wheat grown on their own farm; none of the products had passed beyond the farmer's own property. This policy was justified under the commerce clause of the Constitution.[2] And once given the premise of federal supremacy over the whole economy, the Supreme Court's reasoning is hard to resist. For if people consume their own produce, they may certainly influence the price of similar produce on the open market. The question essentially is whether the federal government has a constitutional right to prevent people from influencing the price of food on the open market by the otherwise innocent means of eating bread ground from their own grain. (It is worth noting how profoundly this reasoning affects the concept of property, traditionally an inviolable individual right.) European small farmers or English allotment holders who supply their own tables with vegetables would certainly regard this policy as an infringement on their liberties. More recently, in the *Garcia* case (1985),[3] the federal government has been upheld by the Supreme Court in telling the states what wages to pay their own internal employees. I suspect that even Chief Justice John Marshall might have found this extension of the laws of commerce a little on the extreme side—though it is a principle consistent with his style of constitutional reasoning.

The new Republic was thus capable, in theory, of a surprising measure of internal political expansion. It was also capable of indefinite geographical expansion. But I doubt whether it could have survived as a geopolitical entity without the development of steam power and its application to transport. The modernization of communications made the ever-expanding union politically governable, and national ceremonies and symbols contributed to the growth and maintenance of national consciousness. The invention of the telegraph and Morse code created an instantaneous knowledge of events affecting the whole nation—though the national consciousness thereby engendered did not have power to forestall Southern secession. (Abraham Lincoln was the first president to receive the news of his election by telegraph.) Paradoxically, after the end of Reconstruction, a national economy grew rapidly in the hands of private business while the government remained almost inert for two generations. After the significantly brief interlude of the First World War, it was really the New Deal that crucially nationalized the operation of the federal government. The New Deal tackled the national economic emergency on a national scale. Its numerous agencies were federal agencies with nationwide powers. But some credit must also be given to such an agency as the FBI, which was a slightly earlier creation. Since the FBI was called into existence—or at any rate was kept in existence—to fight crime across state boundaries, I suppose we can give organized crime some of the credit for bringing about the nationalization of federal power.

As I have said, it was not like this in the beginning, or for many years after. The United States began its life without even the advantage of a universally agreed national name. The name of the United States was eventually standardized by the adoption of the Constitution. But in the 1770s and 1780s, the designation "United" was generally used as an adjective, and the new country's name was often written as "the united States of America" or even "the u.States." In the mid-1780s men in public life contemplated as a serious possibility that the confederation might break up into separate groups, probably one formed by the New England states, one by the mid-Atlantic states, and another by the southern states; though nothing could be considered certain, and New York, with its great harbor and internal waterway, might have gone it alone. All these dangers were averted by the adoption of the Constitution: for a lifetime.

At intervals in American history, military contingencies had powerful unifying effects, but even these tended to be short-lived. Only with the Second World War did the military aspect of American national life become both pervasive and permanent. (The CIA is actually a postwar creation.) War and preparations for war, together—curiously enough—with the national assumption of responsibility for individual civil rights, have been agents in a nationalization of federal power which would have been impracticable and hardly conceivable in the eighteenth or nineteenth centuries.

My aim is to suggest that continuing—or ever-renewed—tension and interaction among the entities we are examining has actually produced a certain degree of stability. Allowing for failures and lurches in different directions, that stability has made for the survival of a union in which individual equality has been entrenched as a constitutional principle, individual rights have found a modicum of protection, and some regional diversities have flourished. But the price has been a concentration of power in the agencies of central government which many Americans have viewed with apprehension and skepticism.

We must not forget that in all these three instances, we are dealing not with facts but with *concepts*. Concepts may indeed be their own kinds of facts, often very powerful ones, but they are malleable, porous, and subject to historical change, unlike the granite which underlies much of the soil of New England, or a river. (Of course, even a river may be a sort of concept: a boundary and a barrier, or a waterway. It may be a god: when T. S. Eliot described the river as "a strong brown god" he was presumably thinking of the Mississippi.)

In the American case it is particularly significant that the concept of region has been subject to *temporal* perspectives. Region has meant and symbolized many things in the American imagination; region has been future; region has been past.

"The frontier" and "the West," which have played so powerful a part in the American imagination—and survive in the movies—have in fact never been seated in any one place nor fixed in any one character. Frederick Jackson Turner made a general declaration of the transcendent importance of the frontier in American history at the virtual beginning of his career—in 1893.[4] It is significant that this was his only successful attempt to generalize the theme. He spent much of the rest of his life seeking out the differing characteristics of different American frontiers at different times and in different regions. The concept of region had a place of deep historical importance in the Constitution of the United States: but this was a peculiarly American version of history as future. The vast areas lying to the west of the existing states were set aside for future occupation, and provisions were made for their government as territories. The Northwest Ordinance of 1787, which banned slavery from that region, and the subsequent—much less noticed—provisions for the Southwest permitting slavery, predetermined the course of the nation itself. They made regional tension inevitable; perhaps they made attempted separation and civil war inevitable—though if we say that, we fatefully rule out free will.

Region may represent a different past, or a different future, from the perspective of experience and expectation. We are much more conscious now than our predecessors were that the Euro-American future was all too often and all too fatally the Indian's past.

The region has been historically the most conceptually malleable of these three identities. Colonial groupings are largely notional. New England—with Rhode Island standing apart—has probably been the most solid, the most distinctive in holding to a recognized character. But New England impinged on New York, and both New York and Pennsylvania developed as largely autonomous provinces—raising their own produce, importing and exporting through their own ports.

The early Chesapeake, identified as a region, has become a major center for the economic and social historian—a great agricultural and producing area, a great center of overseas trade with the European continent as well as Britain. The more distinctively southern colonies lay below the Chesapeake, which included northern Virginia. Some historians have grouped South Carolina and Georgia with the British West Indies rather than with the Continental colonies, until the American Revolution divided them.

But then stand on the Atlantic shore and contemplate either Europe or the American continent. Hamilton and much of his generation in the mercantile Northeast faced the Atlantic; but if you faced inward, to the continent, Kentucky and Tennessee, then one by one the first northwestern and southwestern states lay on the periphery of the Union. In his early career, Henry Clay of Kentucky was known as "Harry of the West."

Look at Chicago today: from New York or Washington, it is in the Midwest; from California, it is in the East! The individual may be the same, but the change in point of observation alters the concept. Region becomes a construct of the imagination.

In the colonial era there were southern colonies but the standpoint from which they were viewed was British: there was no concept of "the South." But the most historically striking example of the region as a defining concept in American history has in fact proved to be that of the South. Generations of Americans were taught to think of the "Solid South." But this so-called Solid South was a *result* of the Civil War, not a cause. And for generations it exerted considerable influence on the emotions that swayed political allegiances. The *Old South* was by definition a thing of the past, increasingly a subject of legend and myth. It is a paradox, but not I think a historical accident, that the mythology of "the Lost Cause" took root in the

American imagination—and not in the Southern imagination only—when the concept of "the New South" was being forged in the region's political economy.

Region has undoubtedly declined in the face of the nationalization of economic activities, the mobility made possible by railroads, highways, and air travel, by the replication all over the Union of the same media programs, and also, in the last generation, by the enforcement of civil rights by federal agencies operating under the authority of federal courts. This operation is not entirely unlike what happened in medieval history when the king protected the common people from the local power of the barons.

A potent force in diminishing regional attachments has undoubtedly been mass immigration. New states were themselves much more artificial creations than the old ones, and regions came to be more and more loosely defined. The huge masses of immigrants in the post–Civil War world owed their citizenship and their attachments to the United States, and neither state nor region had the same power over the affections. In fact, mere uncertainty as to where one would settle down, coupled with frequent moves, would have dislodged local feelings. Significantly, immigrants not only identified themselves but often came to be perceived socially by their religious or ethnic identification, rather than by their location—with consequences which remain unresolved, and to which I shall return. Often, moreover, the ideas of ethnicity and location are joined: "There are more Swedes in Minnesota than in Stockholm," or again, "more Irish in Boston than in Dublin."

States have legal relationships to their citizens; regions do not. And regions overlap states; yet there are recognizable regional accents, cuisines, customs, attitudes, loyalties. Decisions about these matters devolve upon individuals; mobility and the pursuit of individual advancement have often cut across regional ties. But the nation that emerged from the Civil War was still in constitutional principle a federal union. From a strictly constitutional point of view, what the war had achieved was the *preservation* of the old union. For many years, beginning even before the end of Reconstruction, the Supreme Court interpreted its own role as being to preserve the integrity of states within that structure rather than to preserve the substantive rights of individuals within the state. This helps to account for certain decisions which by modern standards appear perverse, in which the authority of the state appears to transcend the rights of the individual, but in which, from the Supreme Court's position, the state rather than the Constitution had a primary duty of protection.[5]

We are here at the point of intersection between the region—if the state can stand in as representing region—the individual, and the nation. The traffic along these roads frequently collides. And it falls to the Supreme Court to adjudicate. The operative instrument is, of course, the Fourteenth Amendment, and particularly the clause which confers on all persons the equal protection of the laws. For many years, however, the Supreme Court refused to recognize any substantial *content* to the rights protected by the Fourteenth Amendment. The key, I think, to understanding the Court's position is that judges refused to admit that the amendment *conferred* any rights on anyone. And the amendment is silent on the content of rights or where they come from. Do they come from Congress? The Constitution? The states? Or from nature itself?

The Congress certainly thought it knew the answer. In its Civil Rights Acts of 1866 and 1875, it assumed the power to confer and establish civil rights; but the Union remained a union of states, and the Court did not recognize any power to supersede the authority of the states—except where a state or its agents treated citizens unequally in matters pertaining to such crucial issues as legal due process. The Court would thus throw out the conviction of a Negro where the sheriff had picked an all-white jury. But all the Court would essentially say was that whatever rights the state conferred must be equal rights; the Court would not say what these rights should be, and insisted on reserving the power of adjudication to the state authorities.

The resulting settlement was inherently unstable. I am not arguing that the American political system has sustained or been sustained by an equality of force between our three elements; the nation had a reserve of power which it employed with terrific effect to win the Civil War, but which its competent agencies held in restraint after the end of Reconstruction.

The culmination came in the notorious case of *Plessy v. Ferguson* (1896). Confronted with racial discrimination in the assignment of accommodation in railroad trains in Louisiana, the Supreme Court held that the requirements of the Fourteenth Amendment were honored if the conditions were equal, though separate. (The Court did not look into the question of whether the accommodations were in fact equal—which they were not.) As I have argued elsewhere—as others have—this was a contradiction in terms.[6] It was a meretricious affirmation of the equality of blocs of citizens in a manner which cannot be consistent with the equal freedom of *individuals;* the individual is here incorporated into mass group classifications. Neither black individuals nor white individuals are asked whether they have chosen their designation or are satisfied to have their personal choices determined by such group classification. Inequality is also inherent in a situation in which one group imposes its classification on the other.

The loser was the individual. And the Constitution is an instrument which recognizes the rights of individuals, not groups, as I shall have occasion to say later. By the time all this had changed—which we can date with the *Brown* decision of 1954—the nation had changed. It now said, in effect, not only that the laws should be equally applied, but that they must be in substance and content equal laws. And the Supreme Court had by this time found the way to restore the original meaning of the Fourteenth Amendment by making it apply within the jurisdictions of the states.

Is the individual also a concept? I think so. The legal, social, and moral individual has experienced many changes in identity. One may imagine that the inner experience of individuality has also undergone corresponding changes. Under English common law as received in America, the individual was considered to be an infant until the age of twenty-one. Women were different kinds of individuals from men. Married women had no control over their property until the mid- to late nineteenth century. Rights have been conferred by law, enlarging the individual's social and political identity. Here it is either the nation or the state which assumes responsibility. As women have gained political and economic capability, there is a sense in which the concept of womanhood has changed, and it has become controversial to think in terms of "feminine" characteristics. Women in business and the professions have acquired some characteristics of what was previously thought of as male identity.

The concept of the individual has played a particularly important part in American constitutional ideology because at the period of state and nation founding, under the aegis of Lockeian philosophy, the state itself was considered to be a product of compacts among free and independent individuals.

In a deep ideological sense, the United States justified its claim to existence on the basis of the sovereignty of the individual. This rationale appears in early declarations of rights. It underlies the Constitution, which operates without any intermediary on individual citizens. (Leaving to the states such powers as pertain to the local sphere.) That is essentially why I believe the Warren Court was right in its apportionment decisions of the 1960s when it insisted that representation must be based on equal numbers of individuals.

The concept of individualism is not new in Western history. Burckhardt famously located it in Renaissance Florence. Burckhardt's great book was published in 1860, many years after the word *individualisme* had entered the French vocabulary in the 1820s.[7] The name was introduced into English in 1840 by Henry Reeve in the first English translation of Alexis de Tocqueville's *Democracy in America*. The translator apologized to readers for this awkward expression but could find no English equivalent. Clearly we are not dealing with an exclusively American phenomenon. But American usage gives it a new and significant twist. In both France and England, "individualism" was a term of disparagement; it was held to be a divisive force, corroding the bonds of loyalty and obligation. America transformed the concept: in American usage it fairly soon came to be held up as a positive virtue. In America we encounter a form of individualism that has proved peculiarly intense and pervasive.

No doubt every one of us has his or her own America. When I first crossed the Atlantic, in 1949, I knew that I was going to the land, par excellence, of individualism—and the prospect appealed to me. Was I not an individual myself? But after only a few weeks of observation, I admitted that I was puzzled by a paradox that was difficult to explain. It seemed to me that everyone was being individualistic, but in the same way.

From a British viewpoint, the problem can be exemplified by the phenomenon of the standardization of American name styles. There is no law that every American has to have a middle initial. But the social pressure is more intense than most laws. It has forced strong men, such as Harry Truman, into inventing middle initials for nonexistent names. So pervasive is the demand for conformity that on certain documents if you do not have a middle initial you may find that there is a specific designation for you: "N.M.I.," three letters occupying the vacant space of one.

Later I read Tocqueville and found him making a similar observation about the social pressure to conformity—which gave me some comfort, and also assured me that this phenomenon had a peculiarly distinctive American character.[8]

Tocqueville drew an alarming picture of the deracinated individual, having no roots in the past, no collateral obligations, no social bonds other than to the family. And it seemed to be characteristic of this individual that he was masculine, and was driven by a formidable instinct of self-advancement. How much of this was based on American observation, how much was based on fear for the France of his own time (and of Balzac's), is as much a question for the French historian as for the American. Tocqueville's paradox has an enduring quality: the intensely individualistic individual who thinks and acts in crowds.

More than a century later, David Riesman described the "other-directed" American.[9] But he thought—as a sociologist rather than a historian—that this was a degeneration from an earlier "inner-directed" kind. And we are to infer that the inner-directed individual remains closer to an ideal type, the purposeful, thrusting, self-confident individual whose potentialities were set free by the American Revolution.

The persistence of the individualist ethos was illustrated by the investigations of the political scientist Robert Lane, who devised a method of conducting prolonged interviews with skilled workers in late 1950s. The men had had different life experiences, but it was characteristic of them that where things had gone wrong, they blamed themselves—none blamed the firm, still less the system.[10] (The most available popular alternative, of course, is to blame some other ethnic or religious group.) If I may again advert to personal experience, having lived in the United States through several years of the McCarthy era, I found it disturbing that so large a part of the society could surrender its independence of judgment in a way that threatened so many of its own proclaimed values.

"Rugged individualism," on the other hand, often extolled as a kind of primitive American virtue, is a fiction—invented by corporations as a weapon against government regulation. And corporations are not inherently individualistic. The expression, however, deserves to be commemorated as an ingenious rhetorical trick: it imports the values of the wilderness, the ghost of the Turnerian frontier, into the moral justification for the giant bureaucracy of the corporation.

But the isolated individual is also a myth. The individual (with the exception of the occasional hunter, frontier trader, or prospector) has never really been alone. Group affinities and identifications have existed from time immemorial in family; in the church, which in New England was also the meetinghouse; in the village; and in business or trade union, as well as ethnic society. The story of frontier life was a story of community activities and communal survival.

This brings me to a social entity not listed in our title: the ethnic, religious, or racial group. These are as old as America: what concerns me is not their social or religious values or their historical origins, but the recent politicization they have achieved. Minorities of various sorts and designations have emerged in the last twenty-five or thirty years from the politics of civil rights as claimants to special group protections, in which they submerge the identify of the individuals of whom they are all composed. One is identified as a group member before one is identified as an individual—or one takes one's identity from the group. This kind of identity may have much to offer people in their social lives, in their religions, often in their marital decisions. It is in many respects a socially benign phenomenon. But it has gained political force out of proportion to other types of association. This has extended from set-aside provisions in legislation for government contracts to the ingenious drawing of electoral district boundaries.

The merits of the economic policies, at least as interim remedial measures, are arguable. But the political claims are lacking in constitutional legitimacy, since the Constitution acts on persons, not on groups; the *interests* which have at various times claimed operational protection have never been ethnically identified, and are in any case of doubtful validity. Constitutional law cannot sustain claims to political representation on the part of ethnic, religious, or racial groups. It is true, of course, that in one strong typology the principle of group designation was sustained over a long period in the past, in the interests of racial segregation; but to make that the basis of modern plans for ethnic representation is to regress to the bloc-directed reasoning that controlled the Supreme Court in *Plessy v. Ferguson*. It is impossible to reconcile this type of reasoning with the principle of the equal freedom of individuals. The United States does not consist politically of a mosaic of fixed and unalterable ethnic groups, each within its own boundaries, and it is characteristic of a free society that members of such groups, where they exist, are constantly shifting around in every sense—geographically, economically, socially, and even in their basic identities, by intermarrying and crossing or redefining group boundaries. The argument that men and women can be effectively represented only by people who *look like* them is politically divisive and constitutionally unsound.

The Union which has survived the stresses and interactions among our three leading entities has done so by presiding over and adapting to changes in their meanings—in the concepts they have represented. The Union has been able to achieve this by changing its own meaning—from a weakly governed federal republic to a powerful nation-state, making itself responsible for maintaining certain fundamental principles applying to the whole.

The core of all that is that, in the rights they bring into the world as Americans, individuals are held to be equal under the law—and much more than that, equal in each other's esteem.

9

Nation-Making and the American Constitutional Process

The great distinction and historic achievement of the American Constitution was to weld the disparate, shambling cluster of the self-interested original states into a national union. In other words, *to create* a nation of shared principles. The idea that a true political community was to be defined as a community of principle had advocates among the many differing thinkers whose names have been variously linked with the concept or the forerunners of the Enlightenment, notably Machiavelli, Harrington, Locke, Montesquieu, Burlamaqui, Hume, and Rousseau.[1] In the longest of long runs, as Abraham Lincoln was to insist, when he warned Americans that a "house divided against itself cannot stand,"[2] that principle would determine whether the United States could survive as a nation.

American colonists in their defiance of Parliament insistently based their opposition on principles of legal right. Self-interest might be the driving force, but the thrust of self-interest was protected by the glittering armor of law. The Union formed by the Articles of Confederation, however, was a product of political necessity before it was an embodiment of republican principle. The empire from which the Americans had separated themselves did not work to the rules of a written constitution, either domestically or imperially; as colonial dissent turned to opposition and opposition to defiance, any community of principle uniting Britain and its colonies became increasingly difficult to discern. The states for their part had many differences and rivalries among themselves, but they also had the advantages of much common experience. They shared long-established institutional habits of self-government through representative bodies, and they had agreed to the specified intentions embodied in the Articles of Confederation and the principles that were knit into the procedures of the common law. A common legal language had the inestimable advantage of enabling them to agree without internal dissension in characterizing their grievances as violated rights and their expectations as legal entitlements. But permanent unity would require more than a sense of shared indignation; it meant shared principles.

The Articles proclaimed the aim of perpetual union, an aspiration that already carried a strong commitment to the idea of an American nation. But the Articles proved unequal to the needs and responsibilities of an intercolonial government. To mold the confederated states into a permanent union and the union into a nation, a written constitution was indispensable. This made it essential to develop a consensus on the basic principles to which such a union would subscribe. American national sentiments already sprang from shared history as well as the recent experience of war. But so had ominous elements of a centrifugal particularism. If unity was to be achieved it must now grow from acts of will. The formal foundations of national unity were laid when a shared understanding of the common law and a principled recognition of common interests were transmuted into a federal Constitution that declared itself, in words recalling Magna Carta, to be "the supreme Law of the Land." In appearance, however, the written Constitution that emerged from Philadelphia provided first and foremost a structural and procedural plan of government. Apart from a few grand words at the beginning, it still lacked agreement on vital political principles. But such a plan could not achieve operational unity without a certain measure of moral agreement, as was implied by the plan itself—representation, for a leading example, gave government what we may call the machinery of consent; another prevailing principle was to be embodied in the supremacy of federal law. But where differences of principle threatened the prescribed procedures, the best hope that supporters could offer in advocating adoption of the Constitution was that the passage of time would work to unify rather than to divide.[3] Over time, differences of principle have come to be addressed more frequently in the Supreme Court than in legislatures, and in the eyes of many, this has created severe tensions with the constitutional settlement on which national unity originally rested.

Such concerns remain central to American politics because, in a sense that would have been difficult to understand in France or Britain, the very nation incorporated as the United States of America was a *creation* of its own Constitution. When George Washington was about to retire from the presidency, and delivered his Farewell Address to the American people, he emphasized this theme by reminding his fellow citizens that unity of government constituted them "one people."[4] In the same address Washington twice referred to the Constitution as an "experiment," urging Americans to give it a fair trial.[5] No one could be sure that it would work; no one could be sure that republican government over extended territory could protect both individual freedom and territorial integrity. No one could be sure that federal power would preserve the integrity of the states. But Washington was not content to appeal only to a collectivity of self-interests. He extended his appeal to patriotic sentiment. Sympathy was joined to interest. "Citizens by birth, or choice, of a common country, that country has a right to concentrate your affections."[6] And he went on to ascribe to "the name of American" a cluster of common characteristics in descent and religion as well as in political experience that somewhat exceeded the facts of America's less than homogeneous population. There is a thread connecting this appeal of Washington's with Lincoln's repeated claim that the Civil War was a test of whether humankind was capable of self-government. The viability of the written Constitution was crucial to this test.

The intense partisan rivalry that sprang up in the period of Federalist government was in a sense animated by rival claims to genuine patriotism. The politics of what has recently been called "binary polarity" was fed by rapid growth of partisan newspapers, of political rhetoric, activity, and participation in elections.[7] By the time the ferment died down, in the aftermath of the War of 1812, the United States as a nation and a country had become heir to what we may call a more settled constitutional patriotism. After assuming office as chief justice in 1801, no man did more than John Marshall to strengthen federal authority by imposing it on the jurisprudence of the states. In two of the most important cases, Marshall made use of the contract clause of the Constitution to get his result. *Fletcher v. Peck* arose from a corrupt grant by the Georgia legislature of lands by an act that the succeeding legislature repealed. In overriding the repeal, Marshall argued that the abrogation of the legislation making the land grants (by which all the legislators had made personal gains) violated the constitutional ban on impairing the obligation of contract. In defining contract, he cited Blackstone's distinction between contracts executory, which meant those contracts that were remaining to be completed, and contracts executed, those that had been fulfilled.[8] It seems possible that Marshall could have invalidated the repeal of a completed transaction, say through the Fifth Amendment, without evoking the contract clause. (This was long before Marshall was to declare that the Fifth Amendment did not reach into the states.) But from the point of view of Marshall's long-term agenda, the case provided an opportunity for intervening to keep the channels of contract out of the hands of state governments. This was an early and very clear case of imposing the national Constitution against the express will of the local electorate; but the judgment is interesting for Marshall's reliance on the venerable authority of Blackstone, and by the same token his omission to cite J. J. Powell's much more recent tract, which happened to be the first English treatise specifically devoted to the common law of contract.[9] Marshall knew where he wanted to go and he got there by the quickest route; whether he had even read Powell we are in no position to know. In *Dartmouth College v. New Hampshire,* a case in which the state legislature had altered the terms of a state-authorized college charter in order to serve the public interest better, Marshall again ruled that the state's action was a violation of the contract clause.[10] Contract had a long common law history, which Marshall could have searched had he wanted to justify other conclusions; but again he chose the most direct route to the most explicit result. Marshall's strategy was to apply a substantive clause of the Constitution to the situation, at the same time invoking a fundamental common law principle. Many of the Marshall Court's decisions aroused opposition that took the form of demands to restrict federal judicial power over the states; and even of demands for the repeal of the Judiciary Act of 1789 (one clause of which had occasioned the exercise of judicial review in *Marbury v. Madison*). Near the end of Marshall's life, when the nation faced insubordination in South Carolina over the tariff and the power claimed by the state to nullify federal laws, and in Georgia over the rights of the Cherokees, the aging chief justice grew increasingly gloomy about the survival of the Constitution itself. In September 1832 he wrote to Joseph Story, who had similar apprehensions, "I yield slowly and reluctantly to the conviction that our Constitution cannot last."[11] Without a Constitution, there would be no nation. Without a supreme judicial power over the states, he and Story were convinced—rightly, I think—that no centripetal power would exist to hold them together. It was not only the "republic" but the nation that was in danger.

In 1854 a young Georgian student at Harvard, sitting in the Boston court at the trial that would determine the escaped slave Burns's claim to freedom, wrote to his parents that his blood boiled at having to listen to "false Negro testimony." For the claimant, Colonel Suttle, the Georgian professed such an attachment "as only a Southerner can feel for his brother Southerner when he finds himself in a land of abolitionists." He added, "Do not be surprised if, when I return home, you find me a *confirmed disunionist*."[12] For the youthful Charles Jones, who was later elected mayor of Savannah and served in the Confederate army, the Constitution had failed in the task of creating a nation; two separate nations were forming and the Constitution could not hold them together much longer.

Jones had made what proved to be a correct diagnosis of sociological realities rather than constitutional rules. However, the official Southern view both in the slavery expansion crises of the 1850s and in the apologias written by Confederate leaders after the Civil War was that the Constitution did protect Southern property rights and that it was the abuse of these rights by abolitionists, Free-Soilers, and the Independent Democrats that threatened disunion. In this sense, Southern apologists did not admit that their states had willingly rejected their American nationality; they only took that step when popular conventions voted for secession. But there is an important aspect of the question of Southern nationality as expressed in the votes of the secession conventions that historians commonly overlook. The power of the Confederate states to make independent political decisions on a basis of majority votes was exclusively in the hands of a white population whose political order rested on the produce of a black labor force, and that labor force, being enslaved, was completely excluded from political life. If that section of the population, which was everywhere substantial, in some Southern areas nearing or reaching a majority, is given its hypothetical political weight, with the high probability that its votes would have gone to the Republican Party and against secession, the picture of Southern adherence to American nationhood is transformed. This hypothesis is by no means fanciful: once the freedmen had been enfranchised, it was exactly what came about very soon after the Civil War. Where the Constitution failed, however, the armies of Grant and Sherman, backed by the iron will and flexible tactics of Abraham Lincoln, preserved the Union. By a sort of reversal of the earlier process, Northern military supremacy re-created the nation and preserved its Constitution. By the time the Fourteenth and Fifteenth amendments had been enacted, it was as though in this conflict the nation created—or *re*-created—the Constitution.

The Reconstruction amendments were made possible by the Civil War, and there is not the slightest reason to suppose that they could ever have otherwise been adopted (at least in the nineteenth century), but they were not an inevitable outcome; they were products of the fierce and bitter conflicts provoked by Andrew Johnson's highly personal Reconstruction policies. We cannot be sure that the Fourteenth Amendment would have been engrafted into the Constitution if Lincoln had lived. If this conclusion has paradoxical implications it is because the Fourteenth Amendment's clauses protecting human rights actually elaborate fundamental principles implicit in the original language of the Constitution, transforming them from implied principles into concrete law. Such implied principles were already present in Article IV, Section 2, known as the comity clause—itself a simpler and better drafted version of a similar principle in the Articles of Confederation—which lays down that citizens of each state are entitled to the same privileges and protections in the other states as those states afford to their own citizens. The clause assures American citizens of equality in the rights afforded by the states, without conferring on interstate travelers benefits that they would not enjoy at home. But South Carolina objected to the presence of free black mariners who were citizens of New England states and who, when their ships docked in Charleston, enjoyed liberties not available to the state's own black population. The result was a law passed in 1819 confining black sailors from other states to their ships while in harbor. The failure of federal authorities to enforce the Constitution against this violation was a small (and distant) but ominous sign, that of the dangers to the unity of the constitutional fabric from the growth in different sections of social mores embodying fundamentally divergent principles.

Equality of civic and political rights and privileges under federal authority among all American citizens regardless of the laws of individual states was implicit in the language of the Constitution. The power to define federal citizenship was expressly conferred on the Congress; although the matter was subjected to certain qualifications by state governments, it is hard to discern any constitutional authority by which a state could lawfully curtail the rights of citizenship.[13] Although the language of the first eight amendments was more susceptible to variable interpretation than that of the formal Constitution, the general character of the Bill of Rights reinforced the principle of equality in those rights that pertained to citizenship; and through the comity clause, to state as well as federal citizenship. In these respects, the Fourteenth Amendment may be said to have completed business left unfinished when the Constitution was ratified and the Bill of Rights adopted. If the United States was to be a nation of equals, then the Constitution was again proving itself to be the central instrument in the cause of making the nation. The Fourteenth Amendment implemented one of the doctrines of Enlightenment constitutionalism derived from Machiavelli: that a republic must restore its purity by periodically returning to first principles.[14]

Even first principles, however, could be open to disagreement. The Constitution was not chiseled in marble, and its most eloquent defenders knew that its language would be subject to changing interpretations in the light of changing needs, conditions, and demands. James Madison warned American electors in *Federalist* 37 that language, even when used by the Deity, was a cloudy and imprecise means of conveying meaning.[15]

Marshall himself ultimately failed to maintain a consistent focus on the centrality of federal jurisprudence. Late in his life, the opportunity to redress some of his encroachments into state autonomy arose in *Barron v. Baltimore.* The case, which involved conflict between the rights of private property and the supremacy of public interest, turned on the "takings" clause of the Fifth Amendment forbidding government to take private property for public purposes without just compensation. Barron, who operated a Baltimore wharf, alleged that civic improvements undertaken by the city of Baltimore had adversely affected the water supply on which his business depended.

It seems, for want of controversy on the subject, to have been assumed before Barron's challenge raised the issue that "the supreme Law of the Land" carried the "takings" clause into the states, and that a conflict of jurisdictions would resolve in the federal government's favor. But two styles of prohibition are employed in these amendments: general and specific. The Fifth Amendment belongs to the group in which the prohibition is stated in the most general terms: "No warrant shall issue"; "No person shall be held to answer." By contrast, where the restriction is specific to the Congress, the words are specific: "Congress shall make no law." The literal inference appears to be that in the first instance, in which the terms are open, no authority, federal, state, or municipal, shall encroach on the rights so protected, from which it would follow that the prohibition restrained state as well as federal governments. Marshall did not think so, and, making short work of the carefully prepared arguments of Barron's distinguished counsel, declined to enter into the merits of the case on the ground that the Fifth Amendment could not have been intended to apply to the states.[16] The history of the amendment up to that date was inconclusive, having yielded differing inferences, but it hardly warranted such peremptory dismissal. Marshall himself, in earlier cases, had pressed the contract clause to its limits in order to reverse state actions;[17] William Rawle, whose textbook on the Constitution was widely used and regularly assigned by Joseph Story to his students at Harvard, was clear that the open-worded amendments *did* apply to the states; moreover, before 1833, at least six state appellate courts had regarded it as self-evident that "the supreme Law of the Land" was superior to state laws.[18] It might have been argued that in case of conflicting opinions, this self-assertion of federal supremacy would settle the question. Marshall, however, was clear, confident, and positive in his own opinion, was strikingly lacking in respect for alternative views, and carried a unanimous Court. This, however, did not conclude the matter, for state supreme courts—notably Georgia's—frankly disagreed with and ignored the *Barron* judgment on several occasions before the Civil War.

Other interpretations were available, plausible, and in fact widely held. Marshall had a powerful argument but it was an argument, not a rule of law; had he chosen to find otherwise, he could have found other reasons. It is not unreasonable to ask whether Marshall might have had motives in the era of the Nullification Crisis that had not influenced him in the past. A plausible alternative view would attribute his decision to political expediency.[19] Times were changing in threatening ways, as Marshall and Story were painfully aware. Expediency might have suggested that it would be timely to avoid provocation by leaving to the individual states more latitude in providing for their internal affairs in a period, for other reasons than Barron's, of increasing tension in federal relations. If so, this was policy rather than jurisprudence, and policy of dubious long-term wisdom. The exclusion of the Fifth Amendment from the states had no inherent tendency to encourage the growth of an organic national unity.

The generation of state judges who differed from Marshall on the issue was equally close in time to the actual creation of the Bill of Rights. Marshall's confident language seems a shade opportunistic. If a poll could have been taken among contemporary state and federal judges, it would be difficult to be as sure of the outcome as Marshall made it appear. Whichever the intention, the states' rights standpoint could take more comfort from the decision than from many of its predecessors as handed down by Marshall's Court.

The *Barron* case did not involve judicial review of congressional legislation, which had been exercised only once, in 1803, was not anticipated as a normal event, and did not at that period involve the Court in controversy. Chief Justice Taney's attempt to lay the slavery issue to rest in the notorious *Dred Scott* case in 1857, in which the Supreme Court declared that the act of Congress constituting the Missouri Compromise of 1820 had been unconstitutional throughout the thirty-four years of its existence (it had been superseded in 1854) not only failed in its objective but involved the Court in charges of illegitimate exercise of judicial power. The fallacies in Taney's reasoning were devastatingly exposed in the dissenting opinion of Justice Curtis and need not detain us now; but from the point of view of the Constitution's contribution to the making of the nation, Taney's logic has a certain anthropological interest. Taney tried to construct a picture of American citizenship as the formal embodiment of a homogeneous, organic relationship among Americans, based as much on descent as on values; this association he designated a "political family." This postulate enabled him to argue that the African population had never been members of "the political family" to which the Constitution applied, and therefore had no rights that a white man need respect. This reasoning was specious. It failed to acknowledge that its premise of the family was merely an unexamined metaphor. It failed to explain why immigrants whose ancestors had not even been present at the formation of the Constitution had any better claim to "family" membership, especially since black Americans were among the earliest of immigrants, and they exercised the right to vote and enjoyed the protections of citizenship in several states.[20]

Citizenship was the issue in the first major case to arise under the Fourteenth Amendment. The Louisiana legislature had granted a monopoly over the butchering business in New Orleans. Rival firms complained that this deprived them of the equal protection promised by the amendment. In *The Slaughter-House Cases*[21] the Supreme Court ruled, first, that the Fourteenth Amendment was designed exclusively for the protection of the Negro race and therefore had no general application; and second, that its application was restricted to the rights appertaining to federal citizenship. This was never likely to be more than a small class of complaints. By this decision, the vast majority of civil rights cases—the real substance of the complaints, and the reason for the Fourteenth Amendment—were remitted to the care of the state and thus excluded from the Fourteenth Amendment's protection. Justice Stephen Field, in dissent, caustically observed that if this were the case, the Fourteenth Amendment was "a vain and idle enactment, which achieved nothing, and most unnecessarily excited Congress and the people on its passage." The Court by a five-to-four majority had indulged in a conscious act of judicial lawmaking.[22]

This decision began a process by which the federal judiciary steadily undermined the Fourteenth Amendment and, by separating American citizens into discrete, racially defined blocs, corroded the fundamental principle that the Constitution bore equally on Americans as individuals. *The Slaughter-House Cases* involved state legislation, not an act of Congress. But in 1875 Congress enacted a comprehensive Civil Rights Act. Showing no reticence about moving from jurisdiction over state to federal legislation, the Supreme Court collected a series of challenges to that act, which it invalidated in *The Civil Rights Cases* in 1883.[23] The process culminated in the Louisiana railroad accommodation case of *Plessy v. Ferguson*,[24] which authorized the spurious doctrine of "separate but equal."

By these and many other rulings, which have taken their place in the mainstream of American constitutional history, and without encountering significant contemporary protest, the Supreme Court entered into the process of declaring, which has effectively meant making, substantive law, frequently in matters that were regarded as subject to normal and historic process of political policy. The Court has come to be commonly if informally referred to as "the unelected branch of the legislature." This adoption of a quasi-legislative role probably represents the greatest of all deviations from the Founders' intentions in the history of the Constitution.

The practice has rested on two foundations: first, that since legislation can be challenged only after it has been passed by the Congress and signed by the president, the judiciary necessarily has the last word. But this is merely a result of procedure, not of constitutional reasoning. The order of events does not determine the merits of the argument. The last word is not by definition the best policy; nor does it follow that the Supreme Court is the only judge of what is and what is not constitutional. Both the legislative and executive arms operate under the Constitution and are equally entitled to their own interpretations. A second and more persuasive argument begins with the Constitution's self-description as "the supreme Law of the Land"; and since judges determine questions of law, it would appear to follow that judges must uphold the supreme law against any inferior law. While it may be true that judges are trained to interpret law, nominations to the bench are seldom made exclusively for reasons of legal preeminence, and the frequency with which Supreme Court justices disagree among themselves would alone be ground on which to raise doubts as to the finality of their judgment. The supreme law doctrine, however, is the essence of Hamilton's argument in *Federalist* 78, which is generally recognized as the principle contemporary statement of the case.

That case, however, can be correctly understood only in its historical context. Madison had observed in *Federalist* 51 that "[i]n republican government, the legislative authority, necessarily, predominates." For defense against legislative excesses, of which Madison in particular had seen all too much in Virginia, a judicial arm was essential. But on the other hand, Hamilton's tactical purpose in essay No. 78 was to give a convincing reassurance against the forceful arguments advanced by the Anti-Federalist pamphleteer "Brutus," who had warned of an excess of quasi-legislative power by the federal courts. The balance was delicate. Might not a judiciary strong enough to check the legislative power subvert the basis of representation? Hamilton's answer sought to convey reassurance by explaining that, having no executive arm of its own, the judiciary would be "the least dangerous branch" of the tripartite constitutional system. The issues had been somewhat cursorily debated in the Constitutional Convention, probably because the case was already broadly understood and occasions for judicial review of legislation seemed likely to be very rare.

Yet Madison was not so sure. In *Federalist* 39 he anticipated the argument that Hamilton was late to elaborate; but he also recognized the danger of permitting the judiciary to become predominant, and a few months later he cautioned against making the judiciary department paramount, "which was never intended and can never be proper."[25] In June 1789 with the Bill of Rights in place, he again changed emphasis, anticipating that the courts would become its guardians.[26] Although Madison had much more than Hamilton to do with the drafting of the Constitution, he could find no stable solution for the problem of conflict between the legislature and the judiciary, and his comments can hardly be regarded as a definitive guide to whatever intentions may be attributed to the Founders. Hamilton, meanwhile, had reinforced his case in *Federalist* 78 by exalting the Constitution as the will of the people. This thesis, when viewed from the twenty-first century, assumes that the people have remained an unchanging entity with an unchanging will over more than two centuries. In its own time it failed to explain why the will of the people expressed once, at the founding, should be considered superior to the will of the people as expressed through their elected legislators two centuries later.

Nothing in the language of the Constitution mandates the power of judicial review of congressional legislation. If a congressional majority, resolved to place public policy in the hands of the people's elected representatives, were to seek a means, they would find a remedy not only available but also with the force of historical precedent. It can be stated simply: in the event—by no means infrequent—of a judicial veto, both houses could repass the same bill, which on being re-signed by the president, would become law. It is reasonable to presume that members of Congress are capable of reading and understanding the Constitution, but presumably a judicial decision of unconstitutionality would not be lightly overridden. If this procedure were adopted, it would be desirable that it should enter into the conventions of unwritten law; but if the Supreme Court persisted in its veto, the Congress could exercise its authority under Article III, Section 3, which gives it power to make "exception and regulations" to the appellate jurisdiction of the Supreme Court.[27]

The principle that Supreme Court judgments should be definitive was not clear at the time of the *Dred Scott* decision. Lincoln confronted the problem in his debates with Douglas in 1858 by declaring that although he would accept the Court's decisions in the specific cases to which they applied, he would not feel obliged to accept them as a general rule of policy. Although he held the Supreme Court in high respect, if he were a member of Congress he would vote to reverse the *Dred Scott* decision.[28] At that time, Lincoln evidently believed that Congress could override the Court. When he returned to the issue in his First Inaugural Address, he seemed to modify his position somewhat, explaining that he would accept the decision as it stood but would work to get it judicially reversed in a future case involving the same issue. Precedents were not conclusive; an obnoxious particular decision instead of becoming fixed precedent might be overruled by a subsequent decision. He was aware of the dilemma, which remained unresolved, since the principle at stake was self-government. "At the same time, the candid citizen must confess that if the policy of the Government upon vital questions affecting the whole people is to be irrevocably fixed by the Supreme Court . . . the people will have ceased to be their own rules, having to that extent practically resigned their Government into the hands of that eminent tribunal."[29]

Thirty years as chief justice did not chasten Taney's conviction of judicial prerogative. His last act was to write a memorandum declaring that the Supreme Court's decisions on constitutional questions were to be considered as definitive. But Taney died before he could pronounce it from the bench.[30] This gesture may well have been provoked by the action of Congress in an act of 1862 banning slavery from the territories, which clearly contradicted the *Dred Scott* decision.[31] In 1866, hardly a year from the Civil War, Congress enacted the first federal Civil Rights Act.[32] This historic measure, which in part anticipated the Fourteenth Amendment, was the first federal law to enact that all persons born or naturalized in the United States were to be citizens of the United States. In both these acts the Congress *reversed* an existing Supreme Court decision.

Congress could now return to these precedents if it wished to establish itself as the embodiment of the full legislative power with which it began its existence. In doing so it could recall that the abolition of slavery and the elevation of all Americans to equal citizenship in principle completed the work of creating a nation.

Barely twenty years had elapsed since the adoption of the Fourteenth Amendment when James Bryce famously distinguished for purposes of comparison between "rigid" and "flexible" constitutions, meaning the written American and the unwritten British constitutions.[33] The constitution of England, he observed, was constantly changing; that was its character and the key to its survival. But he promptly proceeded to undermine this distinction by noting the numerous ways in which the American Constitution had itself been adapted to changing circumstances. It had stood the test of time, he observed, "because it has submitted to a process of constant, though scarcely perceptible, change which has adapted it to conditions of a new age." The word "process," which appears in the title of this chapter, therefore claims some historical authority. "Habit," Bryce also remarked "fixes some things, time remoulds them."[34]

This at last brings me to the Argonauts, a bunch of rough seafaring men not much given to philosophical speculation. But one speculative problem did engage their attention and that was whether their ship, which had been repaired and its fabric restored every time they put into port, was the same ship in which they had first embarked. They concluded that it was indeed the same ship. The same question and the analogy of a much repaired ship occurred to John Selden, from whom it was picked up in the 1660s by Sir Matthew Hale, chief justice of the Common Pleas, both of them referring to the common law of England.[35] And both reached the same conclusion. The author reckoned himself in good company when the analogy occurred to him with reference to the Constitution of the United States.

Is it the same Constitution? I think it is. But whether the Founders would have agreed is another question, which, perhaps happily, must remain unresolved.

10

The Performance of Representative Institutions, 1776–1876

Ideology, Estates, and Interests

The great revolutions of the later eighteenth century set in motion a vast transformation of government which it is impossible to think of as ever in any one period having become formally complete. After the passage of a century or so, however, its outlines and character were clear enough for some sort of summary; and an informal, temporary completeness might be discerned in certain very distinct events. It was symbolized, and in part effected, by the passage of the British Reform Act of 1867; by the establishment of the Third French Republic; by the American Civil War and preservation of the Union and the passage of the Reconstruction Amendments to the Constitution; and in Germany by the creation of national unity under Prussian hegemony. Italy had regained national identity under a constitutional monarchy. The perspective is Western. It is arguable that the process of consolidation advanced the cause of European imperialism.

The American Revolution, which split the British Empire along the seam joining sovereignty with legitimacy, gave an original impulse to these events. Although the rending noise was heard around the world, the principle of representation remained comparatively unscathed. Parliament remained notoriously unreformed until 1832; and many of the institutions of representation not only in Britain but in effect throughout most of the early American states retained the "virtual" character which had been ascribed to them, and to the British people themselves, before the Revolution.

But notwithstanding these and similar evidences of institutional continuity, an earthquake of such proportions was bound to have seismographic consequences. Before 1776 the popular principle in government, despite occasional rumbles, was confined principally to the realm of theory. But during the next half century many states, including Britain, France, and the United States, found themselves in their different ways struggling with the problem of redefining political legitimacy in language and institutions which in some way, however obscurely, recognized the claims of the mass of the population—at least the male population. Some of the most important reforms of the period, however, could be achieved, not from expansive claims to democracy, but largely for the opposite reason, because they claimed to set restraints on those claims; any claim for "completeness" is paradoxical, at the best unresolved. In the United States formal democracy, though institutionally hedged and qualified, became fact as well as creed; but in Europe, regimes reflecting a wide assortment of estates gradually broke down into political systems representing much more multifarious and less clearly defined or historically derived clusters of interests. Yet government by representatives not only survived these changes but in some ways proved instrumental to them. While legislative chambers retained their historic style, they were effectively transformed from representatives of estates to representatives of interests. And during a further half-century they functioned in this character.

The century under review acquires more coherence when we see it as encompassing certain definitive phases of movements toward national unification. These involved both the constitutional structure and the economic character of the modern state. In the United States, the Union created in 1787–88 was challenged four score and seven years later by the attempted secession of the Southern states, and saved by the Grand Army of the Republic; to which it is important to add, not only the Union's superiority in resources, but its superior ability to apply and deploy those resources. The industrial character of the modern American state made an indispensable contribution to its survival against the South's largely agrarian challenge and looked for its inspiration in another historic direction. Abraham Lincoln received the news of his election in the telegraph office in Springfield, Illinois; it is doubtful whether the South possessed a telegraphic system of communications. Even in its preserved condition, however, the powers ascribed to the Union in civil government were subject to restraint by rulings of the Supreme Court. However, the United States had undoubtedly emerged as a nation capable of doing things that other nations expected to be able to do. The unification of Germany was achieved on the other hand by unsteady steps. If the Zollverein was a successful indication of the possibilities of unity, the Frankfurt Parliament of 1848 was a striking example of the practical limitations of the role of representative institutions in that process. And even while it sat, other assemblies continued to exercise their functions in some of the German states. Eventually German unification was brought about not by the kind of voluntary adherence of which representative institutions were the instruments—as had occurred in the formation of the American Union—but by war. It was perhaps a coincidence of chronology but one of symbolic significance that the need for force to preserve the American Union occurred within a few years of Bismarck's use of force to create that of Germany.

In countries not earlier unified by monarchical power, the corresponding change in the economic character of the state was often brought about because an increasing proportion of national wealth was being generated by merchants and industrialists, serviced by banks, insurance companies, mechanized transport, the electric telegraph, and the many other agencies of the impersonal capitalist economy. All these required larger markets, unobstructed by internal divisions and local customs barriers; they required freer movement of the labor force and rapid communication of information. The transforming effect of capitalism in this period arose from its insistent drive toward national unities—and, of course, in many respects, international unities. The Standard Oil Company and United States Steel were in certain respects more unified elements in the American nation than was the American nation itself.

These economic forces took political forms. They brought into existence the elements which demanded effective representation in public policy and thus constituted new sets of political interests. They could not be contained in the older forms of estates, and they had no desire to merge themselves with the people at large: in fact they formed some of the most determined resistance to universal suffrage. But it was only through the reform and enlargement of eligibility for and membership in representative institutions that they could take an effective part in the work of lawmaking that was required for their own development. These were not merely matters of self-esteem.

Parliamentary institutions experienced an interrupted existence in Britain, a much more checkered life in France. But neither of these countries had to confront the basic structural problem of national unity. Certain internal restrictions and remnants of provincial autonomy that had survived in France were swept away by the Revolution. In each country parliamentary institutions became the agencies of the economic processes of capitalist advance, although the strong parliamentary representation of the landed interest created such effective resistances in Britain that the repeal of the Corn Laws was delayed until 1846. In the United States these restraints were weaker. Where the landed interests were not actually on the same side as the advance of capitalist enterprise, they were in no position to resist—except in the South, which fought its own battles through its representatives in Congress. Apart from the protective tariff, it was in the individual states rather than in the federal Congress that most of this enabling legislation was passed. Charters incorporating new companies, limited liability laws—all these measures were pressed through the existing agencies of legislation. State legislatures incorporated new companies and in the 1830s began to pass laws laying down general and uniform provisions for incorporation; it was the states, especially after the expiration of the federal charter of the Bank of the United States in 1836, which authorized and standardized the laws governing banking.

When concentrating on one form of institution it is sometimes desirable to draw attention to the obvious. Representation always operated within complex frameworks of government and was subject to the power of other institutions: the monarchy, the judiciary, the bureaucracy, and, particularly in Prussia, the army. The very great differences among the nations make comparisons hazardous; and though there is no point in pursing comparisons merely for the sake of ending up with something, however tenuous, to compare, the process of comparison will sometimes illuminate more striking contrasts; and the historian should not look solely for the outcome of the larger processes but should direct his or her thoughts to the situation at discrete periods. No Frenchman in 1860 would have been likely to say that France was moving ineluctably toward parliamentary democracy, and a great many Frenchmen lived and died between 1789 and 1871. But the sharpest contrast was nevertheless that between the Western nations and Germany. Representative government had no place in French life under the empire until after the crisis of 1862, and then only within limits; in the German states, assemblies and diets convened, listened, debated, sometimes remonstrated with the ministries, but with some exceptions they made little difference to the way the state was run. Bismarck conducted the wars against Denmark and Austria without parliamentary approval or taxation.[1] But representation was restored as the means of government in France, by which time it had been virtually eclipsed in Germany. The parliament of the Second Reich never rejected a ministerial budget.

It would be a somewhat artificial exercise to assign theoretical principles to the element of representation that existed in the various governments of the eighteenth century. Great Britain's was much the most celebrated—but under analysis it seems to have been extolled by the best political minds of the Enlightenment not so much because of its representativeness as because it managed to give a certain amount of play to the liberties which Englishmen prized and which enlightened thinkers on the Continent so badly missed in their own governments. The British system of representation was notoriously unrepresentative. It did, however, have the virtue of a certain pragmatic adaptability, which (as apologists pointed out) allowed many able men to get into the House of Commons, and helped to make that chamber a sounding board for opinion about public affairs. Ministers who failed to tune themselves according to that sounding board would not last very long. At the theoretical level, however, its defense had to rely on the specious theory of "virtual representation"—a doctrine significantly spun from the constitutional fabric to counter the outraged cry of the American colonies that they were being taxed without representation.[2]

The inhabitants of the British Isles were even less well represented in practice than in theory. The effective forms were the haphazard deposits of centuries of botches and adjustments in which it was impossible to discover any consistent principle. True, the county forty-shilling freehold had survived since 1430; but the counties themselves had experienced enormous drifts of population, and differed greatly from one another in their social and economic characters. Yorkshire and Middlesex with their large number of freeholders were thus politically robust to an extent that could not be characteristic of most other counties.[3] Their vitality (together with certain other aspects of the Wilkes affair) deceived the Americans into overestimating the strength of radical sentiment in England in the late 1760s down to the general election of 1774. The counties, each with two knights of the shire in Parliament, gave the landed interest a very substantial political solidity. Perhaps the system exaggerated the consistency of that interest. It was in the variety of borough constituencies that room had to be found for the emergence of those other interests that were beginning to gain a political character; this new development was recognized in 1770 by Edmund Burke: "A great official, a great professional, a great military and naval interest, all necessarily comprehending many people of the first weight, ability, wealth and spirit, has been gradually formed in the kingdom. These new interests must be let into the share of representation, else possibly they may be inclined to destroy those institutions of which they are not permitted to partake."[4] The basic idea of interest representation had earlier been expounded by David Hume, but Burke was the first practicing politician to urge its adoption into the vocabulary and practice of British politics.[5]

The parliamentary reform movement that gathered strength largely as a result of the failure of the war in America may be called radical in its desire to rationalize representation in the boroughs; but it was also inspired by a radicalism of a deeply conservative character, which aimed to restore the purity of a supposedly corrupted system by increasing the representation of the shires.[6] The fundamental purpose was to strengthen the independence of the legislature on which the crown had so dangerously encroached. Independence lay, more than anywhere else, in the land. The movement is frequently treated as a step in the direction of reform. But if it had succeeded it might well have barred the advance of the urban-centered reform movement which came to a head half a century later.

The provincial *parlements* of France were law courts and made no claim to form part of a national representative government. To the extent that royal *intendants* consulted them and made use of their local administration it might be said that a form of consultative representation existed; the estates of Burgundy, Languedoc, Provence, Artois, Béarn, and Brittany came closer to performing a representative function, in each case on a basis restricted to the province. The best they could be expected to do was to become more efficient and vigorous spokesmen of the causes of the nobilities scattered throughout the provinces. To that extent they were perhaps local embodiments of forms of interest representation. They were not actuated by any inherent tendency to develop into the components of a national system. But the Parlement of Paris, with its jurisdiction over half of France, did claim increasingly to have a representative character after about 1770. The First Estate, of course, was clerical.

A nation made of so many provinces, each capable of sophisticated methods of obstructing the operations of a self-styled absolute monarchy, might be expected to have many difficulties in the way of seeing itself, or acting, as a whole. But there was, of course, another point of view. Louis XV expressed it in 1766:

> It is in my person that sovereign power resides, without dependence and without sharing, it is by my authority alone that the officers of my courts proceed not to the formation but to the registering and publication of my law. . . . The public order in its entirety emanates from me, I am its supreme guardian; my people is at one with me, and all the rights and interests of the nation . . . are necessarily united with mine and repose only in my hands.[7]

The assertion of personal authority is sustained by an equally sweeping and theoretically more significant assertion of the unity of the state. Notions of this sort were not in any sense exclusive to the theory of absolute monarchy. Rousseau's concept of the general will requires us to believe in and subscribe to a unity which would have been far more overpowering than the absolute but irregular government of the ancien régime; it would have left no room at all for social orders such as the clergy or the nobilities, or for the groupings of economic interests, or for individuals finding themselves in a minority.

It was not therefore a wholly new concept that Sieyès articulated when he declared, "The nation exists above all, it is the origin of all, its will is always legal and is the law itself. Before it and above it there is nothing but *natural* law." In conformity with this spirit he could then declare: "The assembly of representatives of the people should take no notice of the division into orders, vestige of feudalism: voting should be by head count."[8]

On October 5, 1789, Sieyès's theory passed into fact; the Constituent Assembly declared itself to be the representative of the supremacy of the nation and empowered to exercise a legal dictatorship. For practical purposes, Sieyès himself decided that representation was safer than democracy; the great majority of Frenchmen, he held, did not have enough leisure to wish to concern themselves with the laws governing France.

Three distinct ideas of the state can be discerned in the turmoil. The first is that of the nation as a whole, knowing nothing of internal divisions or orders requiring separate representation. The second is of the state or realm as an emanation of orders. In this view the church is the first order—as it was in Britain—and the nobility have a legitimate claim to representation by virtue of birth, though this had been watered down by the policy of creating highly dependent forms of nobility subordinated to the administrative system. Where they (literally) grounded their claims in the land, those claims were correspondingly stronger. This view of the structure of the state survived in Britain through the agency of the House of Lords. A third view regarded the state as containing, but not as emanating from, various interests, these interests resulting and deriving their legitimacy from certain essentially useful functions.

The long-term consequence in France, and in a more modified way in Britain, was a continuing, intermittent, but occasionally intense struggle between the claims of landed aristocracy for representation in its own upper house, and the claims of newly significant, mainly bourgeois, interest groups which proved themselves generally competent to rule through alliances and mergings rather than through conflict. Nor could the division between the houses ever be distinct. In Britain, landed interests had the advantage of effective representation in the House of Commons throughout the nineteenth century. But both the landed and the middle-class interests had to keep an eye on the lower orders, who had a strong tendency to appear not only below but on the left. Both the occupants of the lower houses and those who sought more representation there had to find grounds that would satisfy their own interests without being drowned by the voice of the industrial masses. This problem gave concern to genuine liberals of the new order in both Britain and France. But the revolutionary tradition and the immense claims that had been made, even temporarily enforced, during the Revolution made the matter more urgent in France.[9] The French left could manage a theoretical marriage of the unified nation with the liberated individual; it could even manage some gestures toward the equality of individuals. It had a power base in politics and a foothold in history. But the Constituent Assembly was very quick to introduce distinctions between "active" and "passive" citizens. Napoleon was the first to make use of the plebiscite; but at no period were the masses invited to feel the muscle of their citizenship until the introduction of the plebiscite by Louis Napoleon; and then—as under the first Napoleon—it was to validate a new form of dictatorship. Throughout this period, however, earlier expressions of unity left a legacy not merely of rhetoric but of principle to later democratic reformers, not to say revolutionaries.[10]

The struggle between the aristocracy and the bourgeoisie of commerce and manufacturers in France was most acute under the restored Bourbon monarchy. Representative institutions between 1815 and 1830 had an ambiguous status and an uneasy history; but they were sufficiently effective to be the agency of the fall of Charles X's ministry after liberal successes had marked the elections of 1827.

The restoration of the Bourbons did not restore the feudal attributes of the old order. There were no doubt many reasons why it could no longer have been possible to impose an ancien régime monarchy supported by an ancien régime aristocracy on the French people in 1815. But one reason was certainly the altered distribution of economic power; the nobility were surrounded by capitalists, from whom they could sometimes not be distinguished; in the Northeast, some 50 percent of the notables themselves were manufacturers. In these circumstances it was the representative institutions which carried most of the hope for a form of government that would respond to the dynamics of the economy. The mistake—a mistake characteristic of a certain kind of Whig historiography—would be to conclude that the same elements necessarily carried in their political baggage the dynamics of advancing democracy. The rival mistake is to conclude that there could have been any better prospects for democracy without a liberal-bourgeois system of representation. The historical alternative to that was the revival of Caesarism by Louis Napoleon.

The principles of representation gained their most triumphant vindication in the creation of the July Monarchy. The charter as revised in 1830 was not granted to the nation: it was amended by the two chambers and accepted by the duc d'Orléans. An Orléanist monarchy was not a new idea; but from the ranks of possible contenders for the succession Louis Philippe was chosen not by exclusive hereditary right but by the decision of the two chambers; it was they who, like the Convention Parliament of England in 1689, declared the throne vacant by virtue of the king's having broken the charter and left the realm. Institutions of representation could not have made a more fundamental assertion of their power to determine the legal character of the state.

The revised charter declared that the power of proposing laws belonged to the king, the Chamber of Peers, and the Chamber of Deputies, whereas the charter of 1814 had reposed it in the king. In many respects the new régime opened itself to those liberal principles which in turn stimulated the representativeness of the system of government. The age of eligibility for deputies was reduced from forty to thirty; for voters from thirty to twenty-five. The Chamber of Deputies was to elect its own president. Sittings were to be public; peers, to be nominated by the king, were to sit for life. Liberty of the press was restored. It cannot be said, however, that the suffrage basis on which all this rested was very generous; the 168,000 electors would in fact amount to only one-sixth of the proportional suffrage in Great Britain (excluding Ireland) after 1832. It is also noteworthy that the powers of the upper chamber were slightly increased.

Under the July Monarchy the Chamber of Deputies took the initiative and effectively made itself—or rather, was made—into the agency of those ambitious business interests which had been seeking so long for positive representation in government. It was a long time since the phrase "laissez-faire" had been invented, but never before Guizot had it been so effectively manifested in the person and government of France.

It is interesting to compare the different phases of the French trinity. The era of Louis Philippe was the era of Equality. And the king himself, a man of great intelligence and remarkable memory for significant detail, could easily have been mistaken for one of the more successful businessmen of his own reign. But equality for whom? There never was a clearer case of some being more equal than others. For in addition to their struggle with the aristocracy, in which Tocqueville so clearly saw his own class as doomed, the business classes had to keep up a perpetual watch on the political consciousness of the workers. This threat at least sufficed to bring about some reciprocal appreciation between the aristocracy and the bourgeoisie. In the 1840s the régime came increasingly to serve the business interests of the latter, while the Chamber of Deputies itself was a forum for eloquent and irrelevant debate. Two observations of Tocqueville's penetrate the disease with fearful diagnostic intelligence. After observing that the spirit of the middle classes became the general spirit of the government, he adds:

> Posterity, which sees only striking crimes and generally fails to notice smaller vices, will perhaps never know how far the government of that time took on the features of a trading company whose every operation is directed to the benefit that its members may derive therefrom. These vices were linked to the natural instincts of the dominant class, to its

> absolute power, and to the enervation and corruption of the age. King Louis-Philippe did much to make them grow. He was the accident that made the illness fatal.[11]

Yet the chamber itself was in no sense made up of banal or trivial minds. Tocqueville says a little later:

> I doubt if a parliament (and I do not except the Constituent Assembly of 1789) has ever contained more varied and brilliant talents than ours in the closing years of the July Monarchy. But I can assert that these great orators were very bored with listening to each other, and, what is worse, the whole nation was bored with hearing them. Gradually the nation came to regard the debates in Parliament as exercises of wit rather than serious discussions, and to thinking of the parliamentary parties—majority, left-centre, and dynastic opposition—as quarrels between children of one family over the distribution of their inheritance. Some glaring instances of corruption, accidentally discovered, suggested that other scandals lay hidden everywhere and convinced the nation that the entire governing class was corrupt. So the nation conceived a quiet contempt for that class, which was generally interpreted as a trusting and satisfied submission.[12]

It is hardly surprising that the socialists and their allies constituted themselves the heirs to the one-nation tradition in French thought, and that they insisted on expressing the will of the nation through the institutional form of a single chamber. If the will of the people was a unified will, so should it be expressed in a single delegation. And it was, as the demand for the single chamber prevailed. It prevailed over the resistance of a small group of parliamentarians—Barrot, Thiers, Tocqueville, Duvergier de Hauranne—who regarded the separation of powers as the first principle of free government. For them bicameralism was a compromise between aristocracy and democracy which could check the onslaught of unitary democracy.

Instead of being checked, that impulse was tamed and harnessed by Louis Napoleon, who crushed whatever democratic aspirations might have been at large among the masses and transmuted them into a mere device which, by means of universal suffrage, legitimized a new form of dictatorship. For about ten years the régime survived the extinction of parliamentary government; the *corps législatif* merely received and approved the proposals of the emperor and his cabinet. But a crisis sprang up in 1862 when the small opposition group renewed the defense of parliamentary fundamentals, including the principle that the elected chamber was to control public expenditure and that ministers were to be collectively responsible to the chamber.[13] These were straws in a rising wind. The elections of 1863 multiplied by six the number of opposition deputies and gave the Democrats a majority in Paris. The empire was passing not smoothly but by a series of hesitant jumps toward a legitimate parliamentary form of government at the time it fell. Tocqueville, who did not live to see these events, had always believed in the historical continuity of the revolutionary process in France, and would not have been surprised by the emergence of the Third Republic.

Everywhere in Germany, even in Baden with its comparatively liberal representation and in Bavaria, already extolled by some as a liberal state in the *Vormärz* period, the possibilities of representative institutions were subject to limitations resulting from the multiplicity of states. Germans owed the idea of national unity, and indeed of the status of the liberated individual under its aegis, to the French; and certain representative forms—notably, however, in the cities—were established by Stein under French hegemony. This new concept of national unity is to be distinguished from the venerable unity-in-diversity by which many small states had flourished under the Holy Roman Empire. But the promoters of German nationality were victims of a historical irony. They were the strongest supporters of representative government, and as liberals they believed through at least the first seventy years of the nineteenth century that they spoke for the true voice and understood the soul of the German *Volk*, the soul being truly a liberal soul. But in the historical nature of the case these representative institutions were seated in the several states. Instead of becoming beacons of nationalism they tended instead to become bastions of particularism.

The overrepresentation of the aristocracy further restricted the effectiveness of these notional legislatures as vehicles for national expression. Aristocracies were after all very deeply rooted in their own territories; even as late as 1870, a substantial proportion of the German nobles would have been more content with a reformed version of the German Confederation than with the new, Prussian-dominated empire. The elective chambers always contained a high proportion of civil servants, who in most states enjoyed the benefits of a system of tenure which gave them freedom to pursue political roles. They were overwhelmingly liberal in their commitment to such causes as press freedom, personal liberty, and equality of rights. But civil servants tend nevertheless to be attached to the governments that employ them, and it would be surprising if this quite influential class of parliamentarians really added their weight to the nascent national cause. The political effectiveness of these little parliaments was in any case very restricted by a princely or monarchical power after 1815. Of the various types of framework which everywhere affected the power of representative institutions, those of the German states seem to have been the most discouraging. Prussia, indeed, got its first real parliament only as late as 1847; and elaborate electoral arrangements kept the political effectiveness of the masses at a controlled minimum. At the meeting of the United Provincial *Landtag* in 1847 King Frederick William IV told the assembled representatives, "[Y]ou have been called together to represent rights—the rights of estates and those of the throne. It is not your task to represent opinions."[14]

It would be a mistake to regard the advocates of parliamentary government as identical with the representatives of the industrial, commercial, and business interests whose demand on representative institutions was to promote their activities. In the first place, the large numbers of civil servants, lawyers, and teachers, as well as middle-class farmers, who got into the parliaments did not necessarily share these interests or opinions; and in the second place, many German liberals tended to be fascinated by the power and symbolism of the state. Yet the state was always for the representative organs a rival in aspirations to legislative power—as Frederick William's injunction makes clear.

German liberals were very slow and reluctant to think through the constitutional implications of their own beliefs. Few of them really wanted the legislature to take power away from the bureaucracy; and they talked about "responsibility" without knowing what its English usage meant and without understanding the role of Parliament in Britain. What most of them meant was responsibility to the law rather than to a parliamentary majority.

The Frankfurt Parliament reflected with great fidelity these difficulties, which were partly intellectual and partly rooted in the very varied constituencies to be found among the German peoples. The constitution finally produced by the Parliament failed to make the government responsible to a majority in Parliament. The long debates on the difficult theme of common citizenship exposed the very real problems involved in trying to create some form of unity while retaining the independence of the states. One consequence of the Parliament's deliberations was a certain disenchantment with the liberal hope of unity through legislative action. The object was in fact never to be achieved.

By this time, however, the more aggressive economic forces, which wanted to open up the country and which needed much more freedom of movement for labor, goods, and communications, as well as the other protections required by investment capital, were pushing their way into the legislative system. But German liberals now faced a formidable dilemma. The plebiscitarian dictatorship of Louis Napoleon had arisen across the Rhine to reinforce all their natural fears of universal suffrage. Whether the masses seized power in a red revolution or whether they were manipulated by a skillful dictator, the dangers were frightful on either side. Johann Gustav Droysen described the absolutism of democracy as "just as unbearable as that of the court party. . . . In our days flattery of the people is about as dangerous as flattery of the princes." Julius Fröbel denounced "democratic absolutism with its universal suffrage"; and Heinrich von Sybel observed that the introduction of general, direct, and equal suffrage was always the beginning of the end for "any form of parliamentarianism."[15] The liberal hostility to any form of government that would lead to the disintegration of either the organic or the functional groups forming the older society was expressed by Friedrich Julius Stahl as a spokesman for what he called "the party of legitimacy," which, he explained,

> wants the natural organization of the people. It wants an organization in keeping with the natural foundations, needs, and purposes of society . . . in other words, in keeping with property, occupation, and walk of life. This is in opposition to the aggregativeness of revolution. It wants estates of the realm. . . . It wants corporative bodies, unifying associations of the estates of the realm, and the communities, counties, provinces. And it wants the autonomy of these corporative bodies. . . . That is organization of society, while the reverse is leveling.[16]

From this point of view Lassalle and Bismarck were about equally to be feared. Marx, in London, failed to understand the danger because he failed to appreciate the innate conservatism of the masses; in the Franco-Prussian

War he hoped for a Prussian victory on the ground that Prussian hegemony would nationalize the German working class. But Lassalle had warned him some years earlier: "You seem over there, ten years removed from here, to have as yet really no idea at all how little our people are alienated from the monarchy."[17] It was a view that Bismarck was able to confirm. Opposing an electoral system based on class lines translated into collegiate forms, he declared,

> At the moment of decision the masses will stand on the side of kingship regardless of whether the latter happens to follow a liberal or a conservative tendency. . . . May I indeed express the conviction based on long experience that the artificial system of indirect and class elections is much more dangerous [than direct and general suffrage] because it prevents contact between the highest authority and the healthy elements which constitute the core and mass of the people. In a country with monarchical traditions and loyal sentiments the general suffrage, by eliminating the influences of the liberal and bourgeois classes, will also lead to monarchical elections.[18]

The distinctively class-bound orientation of liberal policy could hardly have been more realistically stated than by Julius Fröbel in his *Theorie der Politik*, published in Vienna in 1861 and 1864:

> Liberalism, moreover, which currently plays a dominant role in the life of European peoples and states, is by no means to be understood as the system of popular freedom in general, but as a system in the special interest of quite specific elements of society which are assembled in the commercial and industrial middle class. The liberal state in this conventional sense is the state which represents the interest of this social group. But that does not in any sense mean that it must represent the interest of . . . the true majority of the people.[19]

Fröbel was a firebrand of 1848 turned, not so much into a moderate, as into a strong spokesman of a special interest.

It was after the fundamental matters of the unity of the German state had been settled by force of arms under Prussian hegemony that the Reichstag could become an instrument of these interests. But liberals by this time were both divided and confused. Some of them were magnetized by the power of the monarchy; many others were trapped in Bismarck's *Kulturkampf* because they believed that the Roman Catholic Church was the greater enemy; nearly all of them feared the masses; none could cope politically with Bismarck. It might be said that he had taken over where Napoleon III had failed. In 1876—which ends our period—Felix Freiherr von Stein made a remark which established a close parallel with comparable events, at different periods, in Britain and France, and in a sense with the United States:

> Some of the purely political questions which were paramount in 1866 have been solved since 1871, and some will solve themselves as time goes on. Economic questions have now taken their place and have pushed into the foreground with increasing insistence. It is very probable—because of an intrinsic necessity—that these questions will lead to a fragmentation of the existing parties; indeed this has already begun to take place.[20]

Bismarck, who hated parliaments and had conducted his wars without their assistance, established a regime which had no tendency to lean in the direction of a more parliamentary government as time went on. As Fritz Stern remarks: "The Prussian Diet quickly capitulated in face of Bismarck's triumph. The unpolitical German had begun to play his fatal role."[21] Germany issued to Europe a formidable warning that great power backed by massive and technically advanced industry, generating prosperity and popular satisfaction, might function through the agency of representative institutions, but had absolutely no necessary or historical connection with representative government.

Great Britain did not confront the great issue of national unity, which the Americans solved before the end of the eighteenth century by voluntary association and reinforced between 1861 and 1865 by force; and which the Germans solved by a series of wars culminating in 1871. Nor was Britain convulsed by a revolution in serial form as was France. But there remain certain similarities, concealed beneath the forms of parliamentary government but highly significant. Britain had to confront and resolve the major question of Catholic emancipation, settled in 1829; the great crisis of Parliamentary Reform, settled between 1830 and 1832; the related question of the constitutional standing of the House of Lords, raised to serious proportions by the possible need to create enough peers to pass the Reform Bill; and the standing both of the Church of England and of the Dissenters within the constitution. When these great constitutional questions had been resolved, or seemed to have settled down, the House of Commons was freer than before to take up—in some sense to resume—its role as the agency of those increasingly pressing economic interests which made their weight felt everywhere, and as a forum where the problems of economic and political policy were debated and sometimes resolved.

It is a mistake to regard these reforms as links in an advancing chain of enlightened public opinion. On the contrary: the reformed House of Commons would probably have passed Catholic Emancipation with greater difficulty than the old one, and a fully representative House not at all. The very fact that the House of Commons passed the Emancipation Bill was used as evidence of its unrepresentative character! It is another and connected mistake to treat the history of Parliament as though Parliament was always on the point of being reformed—each reform simply preparing the ground for the next. Parliamentary history should be considered primarily as the history of the function of Parliament. But contemporaries had reason to believe that the reformed Parliament functioned very differently. So it is necessary to ask what was at stake in the great debate on reform both in the eyes of the contending parties and in actual consequences. It is not my intention to dismiss reform from the legitimate history of Parliament. The nature of Reform itself throws light on the question of function.

Earl Grey believed himself to be proposing an aristocratic measure, and was able to carry it through its long travail, because he was able to convince a substantial number of his party in both houses that it would protect the constitution against the dangers of democracy. Lord John Russell himself believed so firmly in the finality of this as the only reform that would ever be needed as to earn the soubriquet of "Finality Jack." Ironically—for we can hardly attribute this aspect to tactical shrewdness—the Reform Bill had a democratic appearance and was in fact so much more democratic than any that had yet been brought forward that it captured the imagination of the left wing of the Whigs and the vast majority of radicals.[22] Still more important in the process of identifying the bill's political character was the experience of fighting for its passage through two general elections and a threat to swamp the House of Lords. If Grey had known what the struggle would entail he would probably never have embarked on it.

There is no single key to open the historical meaning of the Great Reform Act, but a double key will explain its essentials. (Its details are immensely complex.) The first is formed by the new political leverage exerted by the combination of property and population. "To property and good order, we attach numbers," the Earl of Durham explained.[23] The numbers were not large; reapportionment was a much more significant aspect of the practical effects of the act than the increase in the suffrage. But the enfranchisement of the ten-pound householders in urban constituencies and ten-pound copyholders in the counties was the first general increase in voting numbers brought about by legislation since Cromwell, and the first under royal government since 1430. Radicals understandably looked on it as a fundamental gain in principle. The combination of population and concentrated industrial property had been crucial to this process. It was carefully balanced by sixty new county seats; Althorp thought too many concessions had been made to the landed interest. But the principle of the reform was new, and was propelled by a new force. And it may be worth repeating that although its effects were much more muted in Britain, this combination, which brought the numerical element into the accounting principles of modern democracy, was also instrumental in bringing about a similar result in the United States.[24] There the period already lay half a century in the past, for these crucial changes took place in the political reconstruction that accompanied the American Revolution and the making of the Constitution. And similarity of principle was modified in effect by the great differences between the American and British social orders. But similarity of principle can be discerned.

The second key is provided by the concept of interest representation. As we have seen, it had been proposed by Hume and Burke in the eighteenth century; but it acquired its parliamentary sanction gradually and was acknowledged with reluctance. Interest representation did not seem to have the constitutional dignity of the concept and frame which it was in time to displace; men preferred to think of their great institutions as reflecting the estates of the realm. But after the turmoil and debate and the underlying threat of civic disorder, what emerged from the Reform Act was an extended and reshuffled representation of interests.

I have suggested that the politics pursued in the reformed Parliament flowed directly from its reformed character. This, ironically, was no less true of the prolonged life of the Corn Laws than of their ultimate repeal. But the

House of Commons moved closer into line with the cautious liberalism of much well-informed opinion of reflective men in the country. Subtly but perceptibly a change of emphasis came to pass. A House of Commons which had once stood apart, thinking of itself as giving laws and opinion to the nation, came by its very nature to justify itself as giving laws which reflected opinion. Walter Bagehot observed that it had been said of Peel that he was converted at the conversion of the average man, and added that the same could not be said of the present Parliament—that of the mid-1850s.[25]

Radicals regarded the Reform Act as the first step in an incomplete process. Once this step had been taken, they had on their side the logic of the argument that further reform was necessary in order to keep pace with further changes in the distribution of population and wealth. Between 1837 and 1857, the population of the county seats increased by 6 percent, that of borough seats by 17 percent. Reform of some sort became a sheer necessity; reform of what sort would depend, as Cowling has cogently argued, on parliamentary politics.[26]

Yet once again, reform was carried, in 1867, in the name of conservatism and the protection of the main fabric against the advance of democracy. And to take the other key point, Cowling has argued: "Throughout these years Disraeli was addressing himself, not to the *Edinburgh Review* [which might be expected to voice liberal-radical opinions] but to a House of Commons over half of whose members were unalienated aristocrats, gentry or adventurers who had adopted aristocratic ways of thinking, and most of whom thought, not in terms of equality or the rights of man, but in the language of the representation of interests."[27] Bagehot had argued for parliamentary reform to preserve the "character" of constituencies—which would be threatened by numerical reform. He was not specifically urging interest representation, but the central themes are consistent. And there can be no doubt that the passage of the act of 1867 was made possible only by the votes of members whose interest in it was profoundly conservative.

Throughout these debates, the great enemy was Democracy, and its great exemplar was the United States. Time and again, speakers and writers pointed to the American example as being the definitive proof of the dangers inherent in giving way to the doctrine of numbers; and these fears were often reflected in German debates as well. That the better classes had dropped away from politics in America was an indication of all that the enlightened reformers had to fear.

Europeans were essentially correct when they held the United States up as the supreme example of democracy, not only because of its open society, but because the constitutional logic of American institutions did press toward the principle of one man, one vote in equal constituencies. And it is probable that in this respect American constitutions were more democratic in the 1860s than a century later, when population drift had rendered the uncorrected distribution of representatives archaic. It was only then that the Supreme Court intervened to establish the whole system on a basis protected by the Constitution.

European reformers wanted in general to preserve inequality among persons, but to redistribute the franchise so as to increase the actual number of represented interests—by representing the individuals identified with those interests. It was far more important that a significant interest should be represented than that any egalitarian aim were fulfilled. Bagehot expressed the central aim, some ten years before Reform was carried, by explaining the importance of organizing a means of expression for the lower orders but at the same time forestalling any tendency to democracy.

In the United States, representative institutions had failed to preserve the Union; they had, on the contrary, been instrumental to its dissolution. But the North which won the Civil War was governed by the most democratic of all existing forms of representative government. That, too, was an achievement for Europeans to reflect on, for it proved that even Democracy could organize power. And to what ends?

Notes

Preface

1. Sir Henry Maine, *Dissertations on Early Law and Custom* (London: John Murray, 1883), 389.

Introduction

1. *Baker v. Carr* 369 U.S. 186 (1962).

2. *Reynolds v. Sims* 377 U.S. 533 (1964).

3. Oscar and Mary Handlin, eds., *The Popular Sources of Political Authority: Documents on the Massachusetts Constitution of 1780* (Cambridge, Mass.: Harvard University Press, 1966), 152–53.

4. *The Works of John Adams*, ed. Charles Francis Adams, 10 vols. (Boston, 1850–56), 4:193–209.

5. William Livingston, *Observations on Government* (New York, 1787), 53.

6. Samuel Eliot Morison, ed., *Sources and Documents Illustrating the American Revolution, 1764–1788, and the Formation of the Federal Constitution*, 2nd ed. (Oxford: Oxford University Press, 1962), 149.

7. J. R. Pole, ed., *The Revolution in America, 1754–1788: Documents and Commentaries* (London: Macmillan; Stanford: Stanford University Press, 1970), 479.

8. Winton U. Solberg, ed., *The Federal Convention and the Formation of the Union* (Indianapolis: Bobbs Merrill, 1958), 363–64.

9. In arguing this thesis I am in agreement with Adam Tomkins, whose recently published, persuasive book on the republican element of the British constitution came to hand too late for adequate engagement in this chapter. There may seem to be some inconsistency between Tomkins and myself in our approach to the common law as a sustaining element in the constitution. Tomkins argues that the English constitution has not been historically upheld by the common law and that it cannot be called a common law constitution, whereas much of my emphasis is placed on the operation of the common law. The difference can be reconciled, I think, by observing that we both regard representation and its sustaining institutions as essential to republican government, no less in the American Constitution than in the British, a position which loses none of its force from my central argument about contract. The word "contract," inci-

dentally, does not appear in Tomkins's index. Adam Tomkins, *Our Republican Constitution* (Oxford: Hart Publishing, 2005), chap. 3, 108–9, 123–24.

1. Where the Law Comes From

1. J. H. Baker, *An Introduction to English Legal History*, 3rd ed. (London: Butterworths, 1990), 232.

2. Hans S. Pawlisch, *Sir John Davies and the Conquest of Ireland: A Study in Legal Imperialism* (Cambridge: Cambridge University Press, 1985), 165.

3. Shakespeare, *The Tempest*, 5.1.25–58:

> Though with their high wrongs I am strook to th' quick,
> Yet, with my nobler reason 'gainst my fury
> do I take part.

4. *Coke's Reports*, 91a; A. W. B. Simpson, *A History of the Common Law of Contract: The Rise of the Action of Assumpsit* (Oxford: Clarendon Press, 1975), 292–302; Kevin M. Teeven, *A History of the Anglo-American Law of Contract* (Westport, Conn.: Greenwood Press, 1980), 48; J. H. Baker, *Introduction*, 392–98; Baker, *The Common Law Tradition: Lawyers, Books and the Law* (London: Hambledon Press, 2000), 289–92; D. J. Ibbetson, *A Historical Introduction to the Law of Obligations* (Oxford: Oxford University Press, 1999).

5. *The English Works of Thomas Hobbes*, ed. Sir William Molesworth (repr., Aalen: Scientia Verlag, 1966), 6:1–160.

6. Norma Landau, ed., *Law, Crime and English Society, 1660–1830* (Cambridge: Cambridge University Press, 2002), 10.

7. Cynthia Herrup, *The Common Peace: Participation and the Criminal Law in Seventeenth-Century England* (Cambridge: Cambridge University Press, 1987), 7; Arthur R. Hogue, *Origins of the Common Law* (Bloomington: Indiana University Press, 1966), 154–58; Sir Frederick Pollock and F. W. Maitland, *The History of English Law before the Time of Edward I*, 2nd ed. (Cambridge: Cambridge University Press, 1952), 1:200–203. The argument will be developed in chapter 2.

8. A. W. B. Simpson, *Legal Theory and Legal History: Essays on the Common Law* (London: Hambledon Press, 1987), 146–67; Baker, *Introduction*, 319–20.

9. David Thomas Konig, "Legal Fictions and the Rule(s) of Law: The Jeffersonian Critique of Common-Law Adjudication," in *The Many Legalities of Early America*, ed. Christopher L. Tomlins and Bruce H. Mann (Chapel Hill: University of North Carolina Press, 2001), 102.

10. Another example is the invention of trover and conversion as a means of reclaiming property which had passed into hands other than those of its original owner. Konig, "Legal Fictions," 100; Baker, *Introduction*, 237, 292–93, 323–30.

11. Pawlisch, *Sir John Davies*.

12. Carl Bridenbaugh, "The New England Town: A Way of Life," in *Proceedings of the American Antiquarian Society*, vol. 56 (Worcester, Mass.: The Society, 1947), 19–48; J. R. Pole, *Political Representation in England and the Origins of the American Republic* (1966;

Berkeley: University of California Press, 1971), 38–54; Stephen Innes, *Creating the Commonwealth: The Economic Culture of Puritan New England* (New York: W. W. Norton, 1995), 306.

13. Innes, *Creating the Commonwealth*, 198–99, 218–19, 248–50, 215.

14. W. W. Hening, ed., *The Statutes at Large, being a collection of all the Laws of Virginia, 1619–1772*, 13 vols. (Richmond, 1809–23), 3:333–35; on law, patriarchy, and the distribution of power in society, see Rhys Isaac, *The Transformation of Virginia, 1740–1790* (Chapel Hill: University of North Carolina Press, 1982), 132–34.

15. J. H. Baker, "Personal Liberty under the Common Law of England," in *The Origins of Modern Freedom in the West*, ed. R. W. Davis (Stanford: Stanford University Press, 1995), 178–202, 185. Bracton asserted that a villein was unfree only against his lord, and free against the rest of the world.

16. A. Leon Higginbotham Jr., *In the Matter of Color: Race and the American Legal Process: The Colonial Period* (New York: Oxford University Press, 1978), 320–24.

17. George Lee Haskins, *Law and Authority in Early Massachusetts: A Study in Tradition and Design* (New York: Macmillan, 1960), 129.

18. Elizabeth Gaspar Brown, *British Statutes in American Law: 1776–1836* (Ann Arbor: University of Michigan Law School, 1964), 11.

19. The same point might be made in connection with the notorious American case of *Dred Scott v. Sandford* (1857).

20. George Van Cleve, "Somerset's Case and Its Antecedents in Imperial Perspective," *Law and History Review* 24 (Fall 2006): 641–46.

21. William Blackstone, *Commentaries on the Laws of England* (London, 1765–69), 1:123; 3rd ed. (Dublin, 1769), 1:127.

22. Thomas Bayly Howell, ed., *Cobbett's Complete Collection of State Trials* (London, 1809–26) (hereafter cited as Howell, *State Trials*), vol. 20 (1815). David Brion Davies, *The Problem of Slavery in the Age of Revolution, 1770–1823* (Ithaca: Cornell University Press, 1974), 469–89; James Oldham, "New Light on Mansfield and Slavery," *Journal of British Studies* 27, no. 1 (1988); Oldham, *The Mansfield Manuscripts: The Growth of English Law in the Eighteenth Century*, 2 vols. (Chapel Hill: University of North Carolina Press, 1992), 2:1221–40. Higginbotham, *In the Matter of Color*, 320–55; and Van Cleve, "Somerset's Case," 623, 638, with comments by Daniel J. Hulsebosch and Ruth Paley, *Law and History Review* 24 (Fall 2006): 647–58 and 659–64. Simon Schama, *Rough Crossings: Britain, the Slaves, and the American Revolution* (London: BBC Books, 2005), 35–74, gives the most comprehensive and satisfying account. What Mansfield actually said has been much disputed; Capel Lofft's report had Mansfield concluding "the Black must be discharged," but according to Schama, the above version, which was published in the *Gentleman's Magazine*, was approved by Mansfield (72).

23. Van Cleve, "Somerset's Case," 638.

24. I owe my original information on the limitations of Mansfield's judgment to a conversation with the late Professor Jacob Viner in Princeton in 1957.

25. Worcester County Court, April 1783, Cushing Papers, Massachusetts Historical Society.

26. The colonial newspapers carrying these reports were, among others, the *Connecticut Courant*, the *New-York Gazette*, the *New-York Mercury*, the *Boston Gazette*, the *Virginia Gazette* (several versions), and the *South Carolina Gazette*.

27. Sir Charles Grant Robertson, ed., *Select Statutes, Cases and Documents* (London: Methuen, 1947), 440–58, at 453–54; Howell, *State Trials*, 20:1167.

28. The Writs of Assistance case in 1761 has also been claimed as the origin of the Fourth Amendment; see Bruce H. Mann in *Law in the American Revolution and the Revolution in the Law: A Collection of Review Essays on American Legal History*, ed. Hendrik Hartog (New York: New York University Press, 1981), 5. The case made a great stir in Massachusetts and famously impressed John Adams, but may not have been as widely reported elsewhere.

29. Howell, *State Trials*, 20:473.

30. Baker, *Introduction*, 239–40.

31. As late as 1670, Chief Justice Vaughan denied the authority of Slade. Ibid., 394 n. 88.

32. *Omichund* [or *Omichand*] *v. Baker* (1744–45), *English Reports*, 26:13–34.

33. Ibid., 21.

34. *Smith v. Gould*, 1705–7, 2 Salk. 666; Baker, *Introduction*, 541 n. 45.

35. 381 U.S. 479 (1965); Kermit L. Hall et al., eds., *The Oxford Companion to the Supreme Court of the United States* (New York: Oxford University Press, 1992), 351–53; Robin West, review of *Liberty and Sexuality*, by David Gonoy, *Law and History Review* 13, no. 2 (Fall 1995): 433–37.

36. 410 U.S. 113 (1973); Anita L. Allen, "Constitutional Law and Privacy," in *The Oxford Companion to the Philosophy of Law and Legal Theory*, ed. Dennis Patterson (Oxford: Oxford University Press, 1999), 146–50.

37. 19 Howard (60 U.S.) 393 (1857); Don E. Fehrenbacher, *The Dred Scott Case: Its Significance in American Law and Politics* (New York: Oxford University Press, 1978); J. R. Pole, *The Pursuit of Equality in American History*, rev. ed. (Berkeley: University of California Press, 1993), 180–85.

38. 163 U.S. 537 (1896); *Oxford Companion to the Philosophy of Law*, 637–38; and for an analysis (one among many), see Pole, *The Pursuit of Equality*, 24–29.

39. 347 U.S. 483 (1954).

40. David Ibbetson has called this "a mature theory of contract," in *Historical Introduction*, 264–93.

41. Coke, who kidnapped his own daughter to force her into a marriage advantageous to his career, should have been a witness to this!

42. *Bennett v. Bennett* (1876). Both cited by Patrick Atiyah, *The Rise and Fall of Freedom of Contract* (Oxford: Clarendon Press, 1979), 213, 388.

43. James Kent, *Commentaries on American Law*, 4 vols. (New York, 1826–29), 2:3801. This is an example of the senior American judiciary's staunch adherence to the common law at a time when it was a politically divisive issue, under attack from proto-Jacksonian forces which were gaining support in many states for a general legal codification.

2. John Slade's Other Harvest

1. Charles Fried, *Contract as Promise: A Theory of Contractual Obligation* (Cambridge, Mass.: Harvard University Press, 1981).

2. John Wise, *A Vindication of the Government of New England Churches* (Boston, 1717), in *Puritan Political Ideas*, ed. Edmund S. Morgan (Cambridge, Mass.: Hackett, 1951), 16.

3. Christopher Grasso, *A Speaking Aristocracy: Transforming Public Discourse in Eighteenth-Century Connecticut* (Chapel Hill: University of North Carolina Press, 1999), 66–67.

4. Howell, *State Trials*, 4:1016.

5. Hooker's statue sits before Exeter Cathedral.

6. But for that matter, the legal profession did not bestow an unrestrained blessing on Slade's case; two great seventeenth-century justices, Sir Matthew Hale and Sir John Vaughan, disapproved of its consequences, in particular its ratification of "informal" contracts, and some clauses of the Statute of Frauds in 1677 reflected this disapproval. J. H. Baker, *An Introduction to English Legal History* (London: Butterworths, 1980), 394; A. W. B. Simpson, *A History of the Common Law of Contract: The Rise of the Action of Assumpsit* (Oxford: Clarendon Press, 1975), 295–97. There may subsist, however, a difference between criticism of the reasoning which determined the outcome of a particular case, and criticism of the importance attributed to the outcome by legal historians. (I say "legal historians" because Slade is hardly ever mentioned by political or social historians.) I myself am content with Professor J. H. Baker's summary: "Slade's Case marked the final stage in the unification of the law of parol contracts through the action of assumpsit. [There were objections:] Nevertheless, 1602 may be regarded as the date whence the modern law of contract traces its life as a single entity" (*Introduction*, 394). Legal scholars continue to differ on these questions, as I have found in presenting my own (pro-Slade) views.

7. Coke, *On Littleton*, 91a.

8. The writ system survived into the nineteenth century, when it was simplified, and then gradually dismantled by a series of acts of Parliament, beginning in 1832–33 and 1833. J. H. Baker, *Introduction*, 80–81.

9. Alexander Hamilton, James Madison, and John Jay, *The Federalist*, ed. J. R. Pole (Indianapolis: Hackett, 2005).

10. Francis Wharton, ed., *State Trials of the United States during the Administration of Washington and Adams* (Philadelphia: Carey and Hart, 1849), cited in Holly Brewer, *By Birth or Consent: Children, Law, and the Anglo-American Revolution in Authority* (Chapel Hill: University of North Carolina Press, 2005), 135.

11. D. J. Ibbetson, *A Historical Introduction to the Law of Obligations* (Oxford: Oxford University Press, 1999), 264–93.

12. A point I owe, with much else, to Joshua Getzler.

13. *Hamlet*, 5.1.

14. J. Davies, *Le Primer Report des Cases et Matters en Ley Resolues et Adiudges en les Courts del Roy en Ireland* (1615), preface.

15. Coke, *On Littleton*, 91a.

16. Ibid.

17. Patrick Atiyah, *The Rise and Fall of Freedom of Contract* (Oxford: Clarendon Press, 1979), 405–8; but for early formalization, see J. J. Powell, *Essay upon the Law of Contracts and Agreements*, 2 vols. (London, 1790); and for an excellent recent statement, Ibbetson, *Historical Introduction*.

18. *Elias Bland, Ex. of Jas. Yeomans (dcd) v. John Bailey, defendant* (1772), Lawsuits A–B, 1772, John Tabor Kempe Papers, New-York Historical Society.

19. Alan Macfarlane, *The Origins of English Individualism* (Oxford: Blackwell, 1978), 104, 121.

20. Hugo Grotius, *De Jure Belli ac Pacis* (1625), trans. Francis W. Kelsey (New York: Oceana, 1964), x, 348.

21. "The story of seventeenth century Whig thought is the story of the rise to dominance of Grotius." Michael Zuckert, *Natural Rights and the New Republicanism* (Princeton: Princeton University Press, 1994), 16. An exaggeration, perhaps, but a useful direction finder.

22. *Hamlet*, 3.1.71.

23. Ibid., 5.1.

24. For one example: "Farewell, thou art too dear for my possessing / And like enough thou knowst thine estimate . . ."; for another: ". . . And summer's lease hath all too short a date."

25. Ben Jonson, *The Alchemist*, 1.1.

26. Keith Thomas, *Religion and the Decline of Magic* (London: Weidenfeld and Nicholson, 1971), 442–43.

27. *Macbeth*, 4.1.117.

28. The Riverside Shakespeare (Boston, 1974), 1309.

29. Luke Wilson, *Theaters of Intention: Drama and the Law in Early Modern England* (Stanford: Stanford University Press, 2000), 23, 201–8.

30. Ibid., 82.

31. *The Tempest*, 5.1.24–28.

32. Elizabeth Read Foster, ed., *Proceedings in Parliament, 1610*, 2 vols. (New Haven: Yale University Press, 1966), 1:xviii–xx, 154–56, 2:316–19; Conrad Russell, *The Crisis of Parliaments: English History, 1509–1660* (1971; Oxford: Oxford University Press, 1990), 277–80.

33. Margaret Atwood Judson, "Henry Parker and the Theory of Parliamentary Sovereignty," in *Essays in History and Political Theory in Honor of Charles Howard McIlwain*, ed. C. F. Wittke (Cambridge, Mass.: Harvard University Press, 1936); J. R. Pole, *The Seventeenth Century: The Origins of Legislative Power* (Charlottesville: University Press of Virginia, 1969), 9–11.

34. Foster, *Proceedings in Parliament*, 2:331–32. I am much indebted to Maija Janssen at this point.

35. Thomas Hobbes, *Leviathan*, part 2, chap. 17; Sir Thomas Smith, *De Republica Anglorum* (1583), ed. Mary Dewar (Cambridge: Cambridge University Press, 1982), 78–79.

36. *Leviathan,* part 1, chap. 14. Hobbes's language on "signs" of contract suggests that he may have looked up Coke on Slade, but this is speculation.

37. *St. German's Doctor and Student,* ed. T. F. T. Plucknett and J. L. Barton (London: Selden Society, 1974).

38. *Leviathan,* part 1, chap. 14. Ibbetson, *Historical Introduction,* 215–17; Robinson A. Grover, "The Legal Origins of Thomas Hobbes's Doctrine of Contract," *Journal of the History of Philosophy* 18 (1980): 177.

39. Smith, *De Republica Anglorum,* 79.

40. Genesis 17:1–7.

41. Sydney E. Ahlstrom, *A Religious History of the American People* (New Haven: Yale University Press, 1972), 390.

42. Quentin Skinner, *The Foundations of Modern Political Thought,* 2 vols. (Cambridge: Cambridge University Press, 1978), 1:4–7. Professor Skinner confirms the argument here presented that Hobbes subscribed to a will theory: "As this account reveals, Hobbes has no objection to speaking in traditional terms about the faculty of the will in relation to human actions" (7). The human action under consideration is that of entering into the contract of government.

43. See Peter Laslett's edition of John Locke, *Two Treatises of Government* (Cambridge: Cambridge University Press, 1964), 112–13. Laslett, who does not seem to have consulted Cowell, dwells on the more general meaning of compact and argues that Locke is deliberately avoiding a legalistically contractual political commitment. From a commonsense point of view, it is easy to agree; after all, men at large in a state of nature could have had no opportunity of learning about the law of contract; if the words had different values, a compact—no less binding, but not necessarily recognized as a legal document—would have been the nearest they could have come to it. Laslett does not consider this point—and Locke himself does not mention it. Laslett points out that Locke uses compact far more frequently than contract. However, the next step in the argument would logically be to show that he uses them in different senses, which Laslett does not do. My argument prefers to suppose that the distinction between "contract" and "compact," at least in legal terminology, is relatively modern. Even as late as the mid-eighteenth century, Johnson defined the noun "contract" by reference to "compact": "1. A bargain; a compact. Temple, 2. An act whereby a man and a woman are betrothed to one another. Shakespeare. 3. A writing in which the terms of a bargain are included." Samuel Johnson, A.M., *A Dictionary of the English Language in two volumes,* 5th ed. (London, 1773). If there was a difference it may have been in nuance rather than lexicography. Laslett also observes that Locke's frequent use of the concept of "trust" is probably only loosely related to the type of property trust with which his landed friends were familiar. Laslett considers that Locke holds all official responsibilities to be of a fiduciary nature. However, some significance surely attaches to his frequent use of this common law terminology.

44. Hobbes, *De Cive* (1642), chap. 5, quoted by Skinner, *Foundations,* 1:12.

45. Locke, *Second Treatise,* chap. 2, secs. 14–15, 23–24.

46. Smith, *De Republica Anglorum,* book 2, chap. 1.

47. Jerome Huyler, *Locke in America: The Moral Philosophy of the Founding Era* (Lawrence: University Press of Kansas, 1995), 44–45, 147.

48. Foster, *Proceedings in Parliament.*

49. Sir Jeffrey Gilbert, LCB, *The Law of Evidence,* enlarged by Capel Lofft (London, 1769), 6. The book contains an abstract by Gilbert of Locke's *Human Understanding.*

50. Huyler, *Locke in America,* 224–27; John Trenchard and Thomas Gordon, *Cato's Letters* (London, 1724), 2:55. There were several imprints of this popular work in book form throughout the eighteenth century. Caroline Robbins, *The Eighteenth-Century Commonwealthman: Studies in the Transmission, Development and Circumstance of English Liberal Thought* (Cambridge, Mass.: Harvard University Press, 1959). Trenchard and Gordon became familiar to students as carriers of the commonwealth tradition through the work of Bernard Bailyn, *The Ideological Origins of the American Revolution* (Cambridge, Mass.: Harvard University Press, 1967). The emphasis of the present essay on the individualistic implications of contract theory is in no way incompatible with that argument. But it is timely to direct attention to experience; neither version tells the whole story alone.

51. Ronald Hamowy, ed., *Cato's Letters, or Essays on Liberty, Civil and Religious, and Other Important Subjects,* 4 vols. (Indianapolis: Liberty Fund, 1995), vol. 2, no. 55.

52. Daniel Defoe, *Robinson Crusoe* (1719), ed. Michael Shinagel (New York: W. W. Norton, 1994), 86.

53. This theme will be developed in chapter 4.

54. Georges Lamoine, *Charges to the Grand Jury, 1689–1803,* Camden Society 4th series (London: Royal Historical Society, 1992), 34, 67, 142, 254–62.

55. Gillian Brown, *The Consent of the Governed: The Lockean Legacy in Early American Culture* (Cambridge, Mass.: Harvard University Press, 2001), 16–19, 30.

56. W. W. Hening, ed., *The Statutes at Large, being a collection of all the Laws of Virginia, 1619–1772,* 13 vols. (Richmond, 1809–1823), 9:110; and in J. R. Pole, ed., *The Revolution in America, 1754–1788: Documents and Commentaries* (London: Macmillan; Stanford: Stanford University Press, 1970), 519.

57. Massachusetts Archives, Boston, 276:30; and in Pole, *Revolution in America,* 481.

58. F. N. Thorpe, *Federal and State Constitutions, Charters and Organic Laws* (Washington, D.C.: Government Printing Office, 1909), 5:3081–90; also in Pole, *Revolution in America,* 530.

59. George Washington to the President of Congress, September 17, 1787, in Winton U. Solberg, ed., *The Federal Convention and the Formation of the Union* (Indianapolis: Bobbs Merrill, 1958), 363–64.

60. Locke, *Second Treatise,* chap. 9, sec. 131.

61. Saul Cornell, *The Other Founders: Anti-Federalism and the Dissenting Tradition in America, 1788–1828* (Chapel Hill: University of North Carolina Press, 1999), 29–30.

62. Locke, *Second Treatise,* chap. 13, secs. 149, 150. Cf. G. E. Aylmer, "Locke no Leveller," in *Soldiers, Writers and Statesmen of the English Revolution,* ed. Ian Gentles, John Morrill, and Blair Worden (Cambridge: Cambridge University Press, 1998), 304–22.

63. Pole, *Revolution in America.*

64. The powerful moral individualism developed by Kant might be held to make a reservation in the claims of the common law if there were any evidence of a Kantian influence on the American continent. But in the formative period, there appears to be virtually none.

65. John Hale, *The Civilization of Europe in the Renaissance* (New York: Atheneum, 1994), 89.

66. On which see in general Craig Evan Klafter, *Reason over Precedents: Origins of American Legal Thought* (Westport, Conn.: Greenwood Press, 1993).

67. In the most influential case, that of Jean-Jacques Rousseau, the current went the other way. *Du Contrat social* (1762) reflects a close reading of Locke. But even Rousseau is rarely cited by American colonial writers or introduced into their constitutional debates.

68. Macfarlane, *Origins of English Individualism*, 102–4, 121. Also citing Barbara Harvey, *Westminster Abbey and Its Estates in the Middle Ages* (Oxford: Clarendon Press, 1977), 300–301.

69. J. R. Pole, *The Pursuit of Equality in American History*, rev. ed. (Berkeley: University of California Press, 1993), 14.

70. 369 U.S. 186 (1962).

71. 377 U.S. 533 (1964).

72. J. G. A. Pocock, *The Machiavellian Moment: Florentine Political Thought and the Republican Tradition* (Princeton: Princeton University Press, 1975), 204–5.

3. Sedition and the Jury in London and New York

1. Anon., *The Fundamental Laws and Liberties of England* (1653), quoted in J. W. Gough, *Fundamental Law in English Constitutional History* (Oxford: Clarendon Press, 1955), 123.

2. Coke, *On Littleton*, 366; Thomas A. Green, *Verdict According to Conscience: Perspectives on the English Criminal Trial Jury, 1200–1800* (Chicago: University of Chicago Press, 1985), 175.

3. J. H. Baker, *An Introduction to English Legal History*, 3rd ed. (London: Butterworths, 1990), 6–7, 110.

4. Sir John Hawle, *The Englishman's Right: A Dialogue between a Barrister at Law and a Juryman* (London, 1680), 21, 23; J. M. Beattie, *Crime and the Courts in England, 1660–1800* (Oxford: Clarendon Press, 1986), 104. Exactly this point was crucial to Thomas Erskine's argument in his defense of the Dean of St. Asaph a century later.

5. Hawle, *Englishman's Right*, 14–15, 77, 31, 21.

6. Beattie, *Crime and Courts*, 211.

7. Hawle, *Englishman's Right*, 55–6.

8. *The Papers of John Marshall*, vol. 5: *Select Law Cases, 1784–1800*, ed. Charles F. Hobson, et al. (Chapel Hill: University of North Carolina Press, 1987), xliv.

9. Henry St. George Tucker, *Commentaries on the Laws of Virginia*, 2 vols. (Richmond, 1846; repr., Union, N.J.: Lawbook Exchange, 1998), 2:291.

10. Henry St. George Tucker, notebook VII, box 63, Tucker-Coleman Collection, Swem Library, College of William and Mary.

11. Donna J. Spindel, *Crime and Society in North Carolina, 1663–1776* (Baton Rouge: Louisiana State University Press, 1989), 95, 144.

12. George Fisher, "The Jury's Rise as Lie-Detector," *Yale Law Journal* 107 (1997): 669–70.

13. Morton J. Horwitz, *The Transformation of American Law, 1780–1860* (Cambridge, Mass.: Harvard University Press, 1977), 1–30.

14. Sir Charles Grant Robertson, *Select Statutes, Cases and Documents to Illustrate English Constitutional History, 1660–1832*, 8th ed. (London: Methuen, 1947), 388–406.

15. Patricia U. Bonomi, *A Factious People: Politics and Society in Colonial New York* (New York: Columbia University Press, 1971), 116–18; James Alexander, *A Brief Narrative of the Case and Trial of John Peter Zenger*, ed. Stanley Nider Katz (Cambridge, Mass.: Belknap Press of Harvard University, 1963); *Journal of the Legislative Council of New York* (Albany, N.Y., 1861), 642–43.

16. Thomas Hutchinson, *The History of the Colony and Province of Massachusetts-Bay, from the Charter of King William and Queen Mary, in 1691, Until the Year 1750*, ed. Lawrence Shaw Mayo, 3 vols. (Cambridge, Mass.: Harvard University Press, 1936), 2:330–33; Pauline Maier, *From Resistance to Revolution: Colonial Radicals and the Development of American Opposition to Britain, 1765–1776* (New York: Knopf, 1972), 6, 17.

17. John Philip Reid, *Constitutional History of the American Revolution: The Authority of Rights* (Madison: University of Wisconsin Press, 1986), 53–54.

18. New York Chancery Minutes, 1770–1776, October 26, 1774, 69–70, 326, John Tabor Kempe Papers, New-York Historical Society; Milton M. Klein, "Prelude to Revolution in New York: Jury Trials and Judicial Tenure," *William and Mary Quarterly*, 3rd ser., 17, no. 4 (October 1960): 456–57.

19. *Letters and Papers of Cadwallader Colden*, 9:205–6.

20. *The New-York Chronicle*, October 26, 1769; Reid, *Constitutional History*, 58.

21. *New-York Gazette*, January 21, 1765.

22. Reid, *Constitutional History*, 51.

23. William Kempe to [possibly the lieutenant governor], Lawsuits C–F, John Tabor Kempe Papers, New-York Historical Society.

24. "Cushing-Adams Correspondence," *Massachusetts Law Quarterly* 27, no. 4 (1942): 12.

25. James Oldham, *The Mansfield Manuscripts and the Growth of English Law in the Eighteenth Century*, 2 vols. (Chapel Hill: University of North Carolina Press, 1992), 2:792.

26. Howell, *State Trials*, 20:803.

27. Ibid., xxi, 946–55. My argument essentially converges with William Nelson, *The Americanization of the Common Law: The Impact of Legal Change on Massachusetts Society, 1760–1830* (Cambridge, Mass.: Harvard University Press, 1975).

28. James Oldham, "The Origins of the Special Jury," *University of Chicago Law Review* 50 (1983): 137–221; Oldham, *Mansfield Manuscripts*, 1:93–99. Oldham has persuasively argued that the special or "struck "jury represented a revival—even a con-

tinuation—of the specialist merchant juries of medieval times. A distinctive example of the same principle was the Jury of Matrons called on to determine a woman's claim to be pregnant. When verified, this claim would normally avert a death penalty and in civil cases would carry obvious implications for inheritance rights. James Oldham, *The Varied Life of the Self-Informing Jury* (London: Selden Society, 2005), 31–34.

29. *Mansfield Manuscripts*, 1:93–94.

30. Ibid., 2:783.

31. Jeremy Bentham, *The Elements of the Art of Packing, as applied to Special Juries, particularly in cases of Libel Law* (London: Effingham Wilson, 1821), 13, 26, 54, 75. According to Bentham, written in 1809.

32. Bonomi, *A Factious People*, 116–18.

33. *Colden Papers*, 9:201, 202, 291.

34. 32 Geo. 3 c. 6 (1792).

35. Herbert J. Storing, ed., *The Complete Anti-Federalist: Writings by Opponents of the Constitution* (Chicago: University of Chicago Press, 1981), 5:178, 179, 182, 207, 237–38, 20, 40, 285; Saul Cornell, *The Other Founders: Anti-Federalism and the Dissenting Tradition in America, 1788–1828* (Chapel Hill: University of North Carolina Press, 1999).

36. Winton U. Solberg, ed., *The Federal Convention and the Formation of the Union* (Indianapolis: Bobbs Merrill, 1958), 238–39.

37. Akhil Reed Amar, *The Bill of Rights: Creation and Reconstruction* (New Haven: Yale University Press, 1998), 94.

38. 5 U.S. 137, 1 Cranch (1803).

39. Amar, *Bill of Rights*, 98–104.

40. Cornell, *The Other Founders*, 134.

41. Amar, *Bill of Rights*, 70.

42. There is a complete record in Box 91-3562 R-2 Pos, New York Public Library. Christopher L. Tomlins, *Law, Labor and Ideology in the Early American Republic* (Cambridge: Cambridge University Press, 1993), 136–37.

43. The case is not discussed in Nelson, *Americanization of the Common Law*.

44. Donald H. Stewart, *The Opposition Press of the Federalist Period* (Albany: State University of New York Press, 1969), 471–86.

45. For a skeptical analysis of the issue in general: Norman L. Rosenberg, *Protecting the Best Men: An Interpretive History of the Law of Libel* (Chapel Hill: University of North Carolina Press, 1986).

46. *The Works of James Wilson*, ed. Robert Green McCloskey, 2 vols. (Cambridge, Mass.: Harvard University Press, 1967), 541–42.

47. Ibid., 547; Otto Gierke, *Natural Law and the Theory of Society, 1500 to 1800*, trans. Sir Ernest Barker (Cambridge: Cambridge University Press, 1958), 96–97, 128–31.

48. Wilson, *Works*, 542.

49. Holly Brewer, *By Birth or Consent: Children, Law, and the Anglo-American Revolution in Authority* (Chapel Hill: University of North Carolina Press, 2005), 141–48.

50. Francis Bacon, "Of Truth," in *The Essays*, ed. John Pitcher (London: Penguin, 1985), 61.

51. J. R. Pole, "Reflections on American Law and the American Revolution," *William and Mary Quarterly*, 3rd ser., 50, no. 1 (January 1993): 144–45.

52. John H. Langbein, "The Criminal Trial before the Lawyers," *University of Chicago Law Review* 45, no. 2 (1978): 298–300.

53. Helen Vendler, *The Art of Shakespeare's Sonnets* (Cambridge, Mass.: Harvard University Press, 1997), 233; in the original edition of 1609 it is No. 29.

54. As late as 1791 the federal grand jury for Georgia calls itself "We, the Grand federal Inquest for the district of Georgia," as instanced by Amar, *The Bill of Rights*, 86.

55. "But is this law?" "Ay, marry is't; crowner's quest law" (*Hamlet*, 5.1). The case is *Hales v. Petit* (8 Plowden), 1567.

56. Quoted in Barbara Shapiro, "Religion and the Law: Evidence, Proof and 'Matter of Fact,' 1660–1700," in *Law, Crime and English Society, 1660–1830*, ed. Norma Landau (Cambridge: Cambridge University Press, 2002), 191–93.

57. *The Letters of Frederic William Maitland*, ed. C. H. S. Fifoot (Cambridge, Mass.: Harvard University Press, 1965), 25.

58. There is strong evidence that the English monarchy's "blood line" was broken in 1441, where the ecclesiastical record book of Rheims Cathedral (where the English court was encamped) celebrates the birth to the queen of a child who was christened and baptized as Edward IV. However, the king, nine months previously, had been at the wars and the queen acknowledged an affair with an archer in the English army. The descendants to the true king have been traced to Australia. *Britain's Real Monarchy*, Channel 4 (U.K.), November 20, 2004.

59. William Walwyn (Walwin), *Juries Justified, or A Word of Correction to Mr Henry Robinson* (London, 1651), 2.

60. Patrick Wormald, *Legal Culture in the Early Medieval West: Law as Text, Image and Experience* (London: Hambledon Press, 1999), 61.

61. For the contribution of royal policy in creating the common law as a national institution and for later divergences between England and continental Europe, see R. C. Van Caenegem, *The Birth of the English Common Law* (Cambridge: Cambridge University Press, 1973).

62. Sir Frederick Pollock and F. W. Maitland, *The History of English Law before the Time of Edward I* (Cambridge: University Press, 1895), 1:143.

63. *Sir John Fortescue, On the Laws and Governance of England*, ed. Shelley Lockwood (Cambridge: Cambridge University Press, 1997), 36–40.

64. *F. W. Maitland, Selected Historical Essays*, ed. Helen M. Cam (Cambridge: Cambridge University Press, 1957), 129.

65. *The Rape of the Lock*, 3.21–22. E. P. Thompson, *Whigs and Hunters: The Origin of the Black Act* (New York: Pantheon Press, 1975), appendix 2: "Alexander Pope and the Blacks."

66. *Measure for Measure*, 2.1.18–21.

67. Roger D. Groot, "Petty Larceny, Jury Lenity and Parliament," in *The Dearest Birth Right of the People of England: The Jury in the History of the Common Law*, ed. John Cairns

and Grant McLeod (Oxford: Hart Publishing, 2002), 57–58; George Fisher, "The Jury's Rise as Lie Detector" *Yale Law Journal* 107, no. 575 (1997): 600–601.

68. Douglas Hay, "Property, Authority and the Criminal Law," and "Poaching and the Game Laws on Cannock Chase," in Douglas Hay et al., *Albion's Fatal Tree: Crime and Society in Eighteenth-Century England* (New York: Pantheon Press, 1975), 17–65.

69. Ibid., 211; and for the medieval history of lenity by juries who knew that the life or death of the accused was in their hands, Groot, "Petit Larceny," 58–61.

70. E. P. Thompson, *The Making of the English Working Class* (Harmondsworth: Penguin, 1974), 87.

71. George Lee Haskins, *Law and Authority in Early Massachusetts: A Study in Tradition and Design* (New York: Macmillan, 1960), 32.

72. Paul Samuel Reinsch, "English Common Law in the Early American Colonies," in *Select Essays in Anglo-American Legal History,* vol. 1 (Boston: Little, Brown, 1907), 386.

73. Mark de Wolfe Howe, "The Sources and Nature of Law in Colonial Massachusetts," in *Law and Authority in Colonial America,* ed. George Athan Billias (Barre, Mass.: Barre Publishers, 1965), 13–14. It would be premature to say that the principle was established definitively, however. Further comment on ibid., 11.

74. J. C. Holt, "The Ancient Constitution in Medieval England," in *The Roots of Liberty: Magna Carta, Ancient Constitution and the Anglo-American Tradition of the Rule of Law,* ed. Ellis Sandoz (Colombia: University of Missouri Press, 1993), 24–27.

75. Van Caenegem, *Birth,* 62–63; J. H. Baker, *An Introduction to English Legal History,* 3rd ed. (London: Butterworths, 1979), 6; Roger D. Groot, "Teaching Each Other: Judges, Clerks, Jurors and Malefactors Define the Guilt/Innocence Jury," in *Learning the Law: Teaching and the Transmission of English Law, 1150–1900,* ed. Jonathan A. Bush and Alain Wijjfels (London: Hambledon Press, 1999), 18–23.

76. Baker, *Introduction,* 110.

77. Mike McNair, "Vicinage and the Antecedents of the Jury," *Law and History Review* 17, no. 3 (1999): 546–48.

78. James Oldham, *The Varied Life of the Self-Informing Jury* (London: Selden Society, 2005).

79. Ibid., 57; for extensive documentation, see Oldham, *Varied Life,* 16–17.

80. Green, *Verdict According to Conscience,* 16, 18.

81. Barbara J. Shapiro, *"Beyond Reasonable Doubt" and "Probable Cause": Historical Perspectives on the Anglo-American Law of Evidence* (Berkeley: University of California Press, 1991).

82. Bushell's case in Howell, *State Trials,* 6:999. For a valuable comment, see also John Marshall Mitnick, "From Neighbor-Witness to Judge of Proofs: The Transformation of the English Civil Juror," *American Journal of Legal History* 32 (1988): 201–35. Mitnick argues (205) that "by the seventeenth century," when juries had come to rely solely on evidence presented in court, the practical transformation was complete; nevertheless, his exposition of Bushell's case (206–7) clearly recognizes the significance of the "neighbor-witness aspect" of the opinion. Mitnick argues per-

suasively that the development of a second trial in cases of perverse verdicts forced attention on objectively obtained evidence. While accepting this contribution, one may still raise the question of what was seen to constitute objective evidence, and why. And juries had not come to rely solely on evidence presented in court "by the seventeenth century." In the 1760s a New York jury seeking evidence in a civil land suit might go out of doors collectively to view the territory. (But this is a somewhat different thing from bringing evidence from one's neighborhood.) *The Letters and Papers of Cadwallader Colden* (New York: Printed for the New York Historical Society, 1937), 9:211.

83. Langbein, "Criminal Trial," 299.

84. James Oldham, "Truth-Telling in the Eighteenth Century English Courtroom," *Law and History Review* 12, no. 1 (Spring 1994): 106–7.

85. Sir John Hawle, *The Englishman's Right: A Dialogue between a Barrister at Law and a Juryman* (London, 1680), reprinted 1731, 1752, 1763, 1764, 1770, 1771, 1844.

86. Giles Duncombe, *Tryals per Pais* (Middle Temple, 1665), 151; (1695), 151; (1718), 151; (1739), 202–3.

87. Green, *Verdict According to Conscience,* 19.

88. J. H. Baker, *The Legal Profession and the Common Law: Historical Essays* (London: Hambledon Press, 1986), 286–88; Baker, *Introduction,* 82–83; Peter Charles Hoffer, *The Great New York Conspiracy of 1741: Slavery, Crime and Colonial Law* (Lawrence: University Press of Kansas, 2003), 20–21, 66, 57–58, 118. Perhaps incidentally, the fact that an accused slave's master was often allowed to speak for him in court (and was often reluctant to lose his labor) did constitute an elementary form of counsel for the defense.

89. David J. Seipp, "Jurors, Evidences and the Tempest of 1499," in Cairns and McLeod, *Dearest Birth Right,* 89, 91.

90. Cases determined in the constitutional courts of Charleston and Columbia 1796 to 1805 inclusive, *Moses Thompson v. James Mallet* (1796), University of South Carolina Library.

91. Philip Handler, "The Limits of Discretion: Forgery and the Jury at the Old Bailey, 1818–21," in Cairns and McLeod, *Dearest Birth Right,* 155–72.

92. Representativeness did not necessarily amount to fairness. In provincial New York, the notorious partiality of Dutch juries toward Dutch litigants in the Albany court made it difficult for an English litigant to win a case, while acquitting Dutchmen on the same charges. Where crown officers were concerned, consequences were politically significant. Deborah A. Rosen, "The Supreme Court of Judicature in Colonial New York: Civil Practice in Transition, 1691–1760," *Law and History Review* 5, no. 1 (Spring 1987): 218 n. 64.

93. Marianne Constable, *The Law of the Other: The Mixed Jury and Changing Conceptions of Citizenship, Law, and Knowledge* (Chicago: University of Chicago Press, 1994), 94–98; Cynthia Herrup, *The Common Peace: Participation and the Criminal Law in Seventeenth-Century England* (Cambridge: Cambridge University Press, 1987).

94. Herrup, *Common Peace,* 7.

95. Christopher W. Brooks, "The Place of Magna Carta and the Ancient Constitution in Sixteenth-Century English Legal Thought," in Sandoz, *Roots of Liberty*, 69.

96. Herrup, *Common Peace*, 53.

97. George Lamoine, ed., *Charges to the Grand Jury, 1689–1803*, Camden Society 4th series, 43 (London: Royal Historical Society, 1992), 34; J. S. Cockburn, ed., *Western Circuit Assize Orders, 1629–1848*, Camden Society 4th series, 17 (London: Royal Historical Society, 1976), no. 89 (1631), 21.

98. Cockburn, *Western Circuit Assize Orders*, no. 67 (Norfolk, 1709), no. 142 (Wiltshire, 1720).

99. Ibid., 254–62.

100. Ibid., 71.

101. Ibid., 254–62.

102. Ibid., 454.

103. Ibid., 468–70, 448–49, 469.

104. Ibid., 526.

105. Ibid., 587–91.

106. Ibid., 367.

107. Ibid., 376.

108. Gwenda Morgan, "Law and Social Change in Colonial Virginia: The Role of the Grand Jury in Richmond County, 1692–1776," *Virginia Magazine of History and Biography* 95, no. 4 (October 1987): 461. For a survey arguing the representational thesis, see Richard D. Younger, *The People's Panel: The Grand Jury in the United States, 1634–1941* (Providence: Brown University Press, 1981).

109. Morgan, "Law and Social Change," 464.

110. J. S. Morrill, *Cheshire 1630–1660: County Government and Society during the English Revolution* (Oxford: Oxford University Press, 1974), 12; J. M. Beattie, *Crime and the Courts in England, 1660–1800* (Oxford: Clarendon Press, 1986), 322 n. 24.

111. A Speech delivered by Frederick Smythe, Esq., Frederick Smythe Papers, American Philosophical Society, Philadelphia.

112. Lawsuits A–B, John Tabor Kempe Papers, New-York Historical Society.

113. Griffith J. McRee, ed., *Life and Correspondence of James Iredell* (New York: P. Smith, 1945), 180–82.

114. Ibid., 551–52.

115. Sarah Hadden, "Grand Jury Charges and Presentments of the Eighteenth Century: Regional and Temporal Comparisons," unpublished paper read at Cambridge, September 2000. I am much indebted to Dr. Hadden for letting me see this paper.

116. Constable, *The Law of the Other*, 7–8.

117. Herrup, *Common Peace*, 43.

118. Pole, "Reflections on American Law," 144. Judicial records, Jamaican Record Office, Spanish Town, Jamaica.

119. Carol J. J. Greenhouse, Barbara Yngvesson, and David M. Engel, *Law and Community in Three American Towns* (Ithaca: Cornell University Press, 1994), 2, 130.

120. Green, *Verdict According to Conscience*, 176.

121. G. R. Elton, *Policy and Police: The Enforcement of the Reformation in the Age of Thomas Cromwell* (Cambridge: Cambridge University Press, 1972); Anthony Holden, *William Shakespeare: His Life and Work* (London: Little, Brown, 1999), chap. 3.

4. American Independence and the Crisis of Sovereignty

1. 6 Geo. 3 c. 12.

2. Jack P. Greene, *Negotiated Authorities: Essays in Colonial Political and Constitutional History* (Charlottesville: University Press of Virginia, 1994), 16, 34, 390–91; Greene, *Peripheries and Center: Constitutional Development in the Extended Polities of the British Empire and the United States, 1607–1788* (Athens: University of Georgia Press, 1986).

3. William Blackstone, *Commentaries on the Laws of England*, 5th ed. (Oxford, 1773), 1:39, 49–51.

4. Greene, *Negotiated Authorities.*

5. In 1764 James Otis, groping for a satisfactory statement of Massachusetts's objections to the Revenue Act, accepted parliamentary supremacy, a statement which opened him to widespread criticism. Otis, *The Rights of the British Colonies Asserted and Proved* (1764), in *Pamphlets of the American Revolution*, ed. Bernard Bailyn (Cambridge, Mass.: Harvard University Press, 1966). Even John Dickinson, in his highly influential *Letters from a Farmer in Pennsylvania*, recognized that a power must exist somewhere to preside over the whole. *The Writings of John Dickinson*, ed. Paul Leicester Ford (Philadelphia, 1895), 2:312.

6. Dickinson, *Letters from a Farmer*, 2:370.

7. Jean Bodin, *Six Books of the Commonweale*, English trans. of 1606, ed. Kenneth Douglas McRae (Cambridge, Mass.: Harvard University Press, 1982), 159; Julian H. Franklin, *Jean Bodin and the Rise of Absolutist Theory* (Cambridge: University Press, 1973), 21; Quentin Skinner, *The Foundations of Modern Political Thought*, 2 vols. (Cambridge: Cambridge University Press, 1978), 2:254–75.

8. Jacques Godechot, *Les institutions de la France sous le Révolution et l'Empire* (Paris: Presses Universitaires de France, 1951), 4. This was a convention of royal speech for which Louis deserves no personal credit, and could be found as far back as Henri IV. Thus Loyseau had asserted that the sovereignty "consiste en puissance absolue. . . . Et comme la couronne ne peut estre, si son circle n'est entier, aussi la souveraineté n'est point si quelquechose y d'défaut" [consists of absolute power. . . . And as an imperfect circle cannot make a crown, so sovereignty is nothing if something is missing]. *Traité des Segneuries* (1609), chap. 11, no. 8. Roland Mousnier, *Les institutions de la France sous la Monarchie Absolue, 1598–1789* (Paris: Presses Universitaires de France, 1974), 512. Mousnier's own description is no less comprehensive: "La couronne de France est la fief suprême et le roi est le suprême seigneur. À la limite, tous les Français pourraient être considérés comme des vassaux. Le roi a sur tous le Français les droits de seigneur" [The French crown is the supreme fief and the king is the supreme lord. In sum, all the French could be considered as vassals. The king has rights of lordship over the French] (510). I am indebted to Peter Dickson for drawing this passage to my attention.

9. *Hamlet,* 4.5.

10. Jean-Jacques Rousseau, *Du Contrat sociale* (Paris, 1762).

11. Principally in [William Hicks], *The Nature and Extent of Parliamentary Power Considered* (repr. from *The Pennsylvania Journal* (New York, 1768); Philopolites [Benjamin Prescott], *A Free and Calm Consideration of the Unhappy Misunderstandings and Debates . . . Between the Parliament of Great Britain and these American Colonies . . .* (Salem, 1774); James Wilson, *Considerations on the Nature and Extent of the Legislative Authority of the British Parliament* (1774), in *Works of James Wilson*, ed. Robert Green McCloskey (Cambridge, Mass.: Harvard University Press, 1967), 721–46.

12. Paul H. Smith, ed., *Letters of Delegates to the Continental Congress* (Washington, D.C.: Government Printing Office, 1981), 8:435. Burke added that any state ought to be free to remain neutral in a war involving Congress. He did not consider the implications for the peace treaty in such a conflict.

13. Howell, *State Trials,* 18:60–61; Bertrand de Jouvenal, *Sovereignty* (Chicago: University of Chicago Press, 1957), 207–8.

14. The point is illustrated by an opinion recorded by the law firm of Duane and Scott in Kingston, New York, in 1783: "It is our opinion that the revolution has made no change in the judicial security to property and therefore judgements, costs taxed and every other process be had thereon as if the Revolution had not happened." Legal Misc., 1771–1866, Duane Papers, Massachusetts Historical Society. The principle was upheld by the Supreme Court in 1815. *Terrett v. Taylor,* 9 Cranch 43 (1815).

15. Merrill D. Peterson and Robert C. Vaughan, eds., *The Virginia Statute for Religious Freedom* (Cambridge: Cambridge University Press, 1988), 93.

16. J. H. Baker, *An Introduction to English Legal History,* 3rd ed. (London: Butterworths, 1990), 122–33; James Oldham, ed., *The Mansfield Manuscripts and the Growth of English Law in the Eighteenth Century,* 2 vols. (Chapel Hill: University of North Carolina Press, 1992), 1:57, 204.

17. Baker, *Introduction,* 232.

18. Peterson and Vaughan, *Virginia Statute,* ix.

19. Francis Newton Thorpe, ed., *The Federal and State Constitutions, Colonial Charters, and other Organic Laws of the States, Territories and Colonies Now or Heretofore Forming the United States of America,* 7 vols. (Washington, D.C.: Government Printing Office, 1909). Examples of specific declarations are South Carolina, Article XXIX (4:3247); Delaware, Article XXV (1:566–67); New York, Article XXXV (5:2635–36); New Jersey, Article XXII (5:2598). Examples of states where declarations were less specific: Georgia, Article VII (2:779); Virginia, sec. 2 (7:3813–14). This principle had a long life.

20. Joseph Story, *Commentaries on the Constitution of the United States,* 5th ed. (Boston, 1891), secs. 210–15; *Debates in the House of Representatives of South Carolina on the Constitution framed for the United States* (Charleston, 1788).

21. Gordon S. Wood, *The Creation of the American Republic, 1776–1787* (Chapel Hill: University of North Carolina Press, 1969), 527–36. Wood is inclined to take Federalist rhetoric literally, but, as we shall see, their tune soon changed.

22. Alexander Hamilton, James Madison, and John Jay, *The Federalist*, ed. J. R. Pole (Indianapolis: Hackett, 2005), 76–77, 109.

23. Ibid., 168–69.

24. Ibid., 251.

25. Ibid., 47n.

26. Woodrow Wilson, "Political Sovereignty," in *An Old Master, and Other Political Essays* (New York: Scribner's, 1893), 62–63, 81–82.

27. Ibid., 77.

28. John Austin, *Lectures on Jurisprudence* (London, 1880).

29. Wilson, "Political Sovereignty," 94–95.

30. Arthur F. Bentley, *The Process of Government* (Chicago: University of Chicago Press, 1908).

31. Alexander Passerin d'Entrèves, *The Notion of the State* (Oxford: Oxford University Press, 1967), 59–60.

32. John R. Commons, *A Sociological View of Sovereignty, 1899–1900* (repr., New York: A. M. Kelley, 1965), 51–52, 61.

33. Wilson, "Political Sovereignty," 52, 53, 73.

34. Ibid., 136, 143; and for a similar analogy, J. R. Pole, "Enlightenment and the Politics of America Nature," in *The Enlightenment in National Context*, ed. Ray Porter and Mikulás Teich (Cambridge: Cambridge University Press, 1981), 211.

5. Inferences and Continuities

1. George Lee Haskins, *Law and Authority in Early Massachusetts: A Study in Tradition and Design* (New York: Macmillan, 1960), 135–36; Alexis de Tocqueville, *Democracy in America; and Two Essays on America*, trans. Gerald E. Bevan (London: Penguin, 2003), 313.

2. Haskins, *Law and Authority*, 135–36.

3. 8 Anne c. 19.

4. J. H. Baker, *An Introduction to English Legal History*, 3rd ed. (London: Butterworths, 1990), 515.

5. Christine MacLeod, *Inventing the Industrial Revolution: The English Patent System, 1660–1800* (Cambridge: Cambridge University Press, 1988), 58.

6. Baker, *Introduction*, 516.

7. Herbert L. Osgood, *The American Colonies in the Eighteenth Century* (1925; repr., Gloucester, Mass.: Peter Smith, 1958), 1:382–83.

8. N. A. M. Rodger, *The Command of the Ocean: A Naval History of Britain, 1649–1815* (London: Allen Lane, 2004).

9. Ibid.

10. James Oldham, ed., *The Mansfield Manuscripts and the Growth of English Law in the Eighteenth Century*, 2 vols. (Chapel Hill: University of North Carolina Press, 1992), 1:450.

11. Olwen Ufton, *Europe: Privilege and Protest, 1730–1789*, 2nd ed. (Oxford: Black-

well, 2000), 1–27; C. B. A. Behrens, *The Ancien Régime* (London: Thames and Hudson, 1967), chap. 1.

12. Alexander Hamilton, James Madison, and John Jay, *The Federalist*, ed. J. R. Pole (Indianapolis: Hackett, 2005), 240.

13. Alice Hanson Jones, *Wealth of a Nation to Be: The American Colonies on the Eve of the Revolution* (New York: Columbia University Press, 1980), 302, 303; John J. McCusker and Russell R. Menard, *The Economy of British America, 1607–1789* (Chapel Hill: University of North Carolina Press, 1985), 57, 85–88, 351.

14. Zepheniah Swift, *A System of Laws for the State of Connecticut* (Windham, Conn., 1795), 446.

15. DuPonceau Notebook, MSS, 1785–91, Historical Society of Pennsylvania. The transcript in DuPonceau's handwritten notes is more detailed than in Alexander James Dallas, *Reports of Cases . . . of Pennsylvania, Before and Since the Revolution* (Philadelphia, 1790), 1:16–17, but Dallas's is well worth noting. The importance of this case is attested by the fact that it was one of the very few colonial cases which Dallas chose to reproduce along with the first report of the Supreme Court of the United States.

16. 5 Geo. 2 c. 7 (1732), in W. W. Hening, ed., *The Statutes at Large, being a collection of all the Laws of Virginia, 1619–1772*, 13 vols. (Richmond, 1809–23).

17. John Dickinson, *Letters from a Farmer in Pennsylvania* (New York, 1895), letter 9. Dickinson also deplored the prevailing uncertainty as to what parts of the common law were in force and what were not. He insisted on the urgent necessity for "an act settling the extent of the English laws" without saying whether it was to be a British or a Pennsylvania act; he wanted the courts to adopt a general set of rules for the regulation of legal practice.

18. William Blackstone, *Commentaries on the Laws of England*, 4 vols. (Oxford, 1765–69), 1:39, 53; R. Hunt, MS Student Notebook of lectures by Judge Gould, p. 11, Johnson Collection, Columbia University Law Library.

19. Winthrop D. Jordan, *White over Black: American Attitudes toward the Negro, 1550–1812* (Chapel Hill: University of North Carolina Press, 1968), 78, 80, 82.

20. Tocqueville, *De la démocratie en Amérique*, 1:286–87.

21. *The People v. Crosswell*, 3 *Johnson's Cases* 1803, 3:354–55.

22. Ibid., 375; 3 Dall. 4.

23. Norman L. Rosenberg, *Protecting the Best Men: An Interpretive History of the Law of Libel* (Chapel Hill: University of North Carolina Press, 1986), 112.

24. Ibid., 115.

25. Ibid., 119–20.

26. *The Commonwealth of Massachusetts v. Buckingham*, Boston, 1822.

27. The process of law reform was uneven, and its principal focus was on the continued status of the common law. For a survey, see Charles M. Cook, *The American Codification Movement: A Study in Antebellum Legal Reform* (Westport, Conn.: Greenwood Press, 1981); Lorraine Smith Pangle and Thomas L. Pangle, *The Learning of Liberty: The Educational Ideas of the American Founders* (Lawrence: University Press of Kansas Press, 1993), 218–22.

28. *Georgia v. Brailsford* (1974), 3 Dall. 1, 1 L. Ed. 483; Chief Justice's Jay's reference to it as "the good old rule" suggests that he had not kept up with his subject since moving to the bench. *The Carolina Law Journal*, ed. A. Blanding and D. J. McCord (Columbia, S.C., 1832), 38–92.

29. Adapted from William E. Nelson, "The Eighteenth-Century Background of John Marshall's Constitutional Jurisprudence," *Michigan Law Review* 76 (1978): 893; Nelson, "The Jury and Consensus Government in Mid-Eighteenth-Century America," in *The Bill of Rights: Original Meaning and Current Understanding*, ed. Eugene W. Hickok Jr. (Charlottesville: University of Virginia Press, 1991), 333–50.

30. *Sioux City and Pacific R.R. Co. v. Stout*, 84 U.S. 657 (1873), cited in Stephen A. Weiner, "The Civil Trial Jury and the Law-fact Distinction," *California Law Review* 54, no. 5 (December 1966): 1880–81.

31. Weiner, "The Civil Trial Jury," 1884–85.

32. *Hughes v. Wabash RR*, 342 Ill. App. 159, 167–68 (1950), cited in Weiner, "The Civil Trial Jury," 1886.

33. Andrew Geddes, "Juries Aren't Delivering Justice," *Guardian* (London), March 27, 2002. Lord Justice Auld's recent inquiry had reported serious defects in the jury system with the opinion of many experienced trial judges that the jury gets it wrong in one case out of four.

34. Blackstone, *Commentaries*, 3:360.

35. The authentication of this observation can be had in conversation with members of appropriate law firms, which need not be named here.

36. *Ash v. United States ex. Rel. Valotta*, 270 U.S. 424, 425 (1926). The number of permitted challenges has been varied from time to time by the Supreme Court.

37. George Fisher, *Plea Bargaining's Triumph: A History of Plea Bargaining in America* (Stanford: Stanford University Press, 2003), 223; reviewed by Michael Willrich, *Reviews in American History* 31, no. 3 (September 2003): 430–39.

38. The author was told by the assistant district attorney in Cook County, Chicago, in 1969 that the figure for plea-bargain settlements was 80 percent, which he explained on the ground that there was no other way of getting through the docket. For an argument on the origins of the practice in the need to mitigate ethnic conflicts, see Mary Elizabeth Vogel, "The Social Origins of Plea Bargaining: Conflict and the Law in the Process of State Formation, 1830–1860," *Law and Society Review* 33, no. 1 (1999): 161–246.

39. Baker, *Introduction*, 109–10.

6. Some Problems of a Colonial Attorney General in a Multicultural Society

Reprinted from Thomas Angerer, Birgitta Bader-Zaar, and Margarete Grandner, eds., *Geschichte und Recht: Festschrift für Gerald Stourzh zum 70. Geburtstag* (Vienna: Böhlau, 1999).

1. The story is here reconstructed from Sorted Legal mss., BSW/3, John Tabor Kempe Papers, New-York Historical Society. The complete folder is entitled "Case

of Juan Miranda, a slave who claimed to be a free Spanish citizen, 1759." (Juan more probably said "subject.") The official title of the case that follows is *Juan Miranda v. The Widow Van Rans*, also appearing as Van Rantz; Cornelius Van Ranst [*sic*] later becomes the defendant. The date of the last entry is 1759; the first deposition, of Lucas Farfan, is dated October 5, 1754, and others appear from 1756 and 1758.

2. There is no indication in the records as to whether Juan's friends were white or black.

3. A. Leon Higginbotham, *In the Matter of Color: Race and the American Legal Process: The Colonial Period* (New York: Oxford University Press, 1978), 118–25. The boundaries were not always clear, and it was not unknown for slaves to defend themselves in court. But an action *by* a slave for assault seems incompatible with the ethos of the slave code.

4. Memorial of William Kempe, Attorney General of the Province of New York to the Rt. Hon. The Lords Commissioners of Trade and Plantations, September 20, 1752. Public Record Office, London, CO, 1068:180. This was a request to disallow an act to prevent malicious prosecutions, which Kempe claimed would affect the greater part of his income.

5. Minutes of the Supreme Court of Judicature, April 14, 1757–August 2, 1760, New York Division of Old Records, Manhattan. See pp. 151, 167, 181, 231, and 258 for proceedings of October 26, 1758, January 20, 1759, August 3, 1759, and finally October 5, 1759.

6. Sir William Blackstone, *Commentaries on the Laws of England*, 4 vols. (London, 1765–69), 3:357.

7. Letter from Armando Gomez Ortiz, Coordinator, Carrera de Historia, Universidad Industrial de Santander, Bucaramanga, Colombia, to J. R. Pole, July 26, 1988.

8. E. B. O'Callaghan, *List of Inhabitants of Colonial New York* (Baltimore: GPC, 1979).

9. Howell, *State Trials*, 20:82; Simon Schama, *Rough Crossings: Britain, the Slaves and the American Revolution* (London: BBC Books, 2006), 72. Usually quoted as "The Black must be discharged." But it appears that Mansfield approved this version.

10. There is no indication in the records as to whether Jalla was black or white.

11. J. W. Sweet, "Bodies Politic: Colonialism, Race and the Emergence of the American North: Rhode Island, 1730–1830" (PhD diss., Princeton University, 1995), 242, citing MS-L, Massachusetts Historical Society. I am indebted to Dr. Sweet for supplying me with this information, which now appears in his book *Bodies Politic: Negotiating Race in the American North, 1730–1830* (Baltimore: John Hopkins University Press, 2003).

12. Sweet, *Bodies Politic*, 243, citing George Thomas to Gideon Wanton, April 17, 1746, Rhode Island Historical Society; W. Greene to Don Juan Franzo de Inumes and Harristitas to George Thomas, June 14, 1746, in Gertrude Selwyn Kimball, ed., *The Correspondence of the Colonial Governors of Rhode Island: 1723–1775* (Boston: Houghton, Mifflin, 1902), 1:425–26; Edward Freelawny to Gideon Wanton, June 22, 1746; and Joseph Espinosa to Gov. of R.I., August 22, 1746, Rhode Island Historical Society.

13. Patricia U. Bonomi, *A Factious People: Politics and Society in Colonial New York* (New York: Columbia University Press, 1971), 111, 172–73.

14. De Lancey to B.o.T., July 31, 1759; B.o.T. documents, November 27, 1759, Public Record Office, CO/5, 1068:283, 314.

15. Petition of William Smith to B.o.T., July 26, 1759, Public Record Office, CO/5, 1068:310.

16. *Journal of the Commissioners of Trade and Plantations* (London, 1932), 61:386, 387, 390. The Privy Council acted within days.

17. *Documents Relating to the Colonial History of New York* (Albany, 1856), 7:399.

18. This account has been reconstructed from the case of the above title in Sorted Legal mss., BSW/3, John Tabor Kempe Papers, New-York Historical Society. The Domine's name is also spelled Myer. Most of the prolonged correspondence and other documentation is reproduced in Hugh Hastings, ed., *Ecclesiastical Records, State of New York* (Albany, 1905), vol. 6.

19. Hastings, *Ecclesiastical Records,* 6:4070 (October 6, 1766). The classis had already noted Meyer's independent disposition in commenting that he had passed through Amsterdam without making himself known to them (ibid., 6:3896).

20. Alison Gilbert Olsen, *Making the Empire Work: London and American Interest Groups, 1690–1790* (Cambridge, Mass.: Harvard University Press, 1992), 86–87.

21. Twenty-four signatures are appended in the version printed in Hastings, *Ecclesiastical Records,* 6:4040.

22. Blackstone, *Commentaries,* 1:474; Matthew Bacon, *A New Abridgement of the Law* (1736–59, and many reprints), 1:506.

23. For an excellent analysis and summary, see James Oldham, *The Mansfield Manuscripts: Lord Mansfield and the Growth of English Law in the Eighteenth Century,* 2 vols. (Chapel Hill: University of North Carolina Press, 1992), 1:223–25. There is considerable and controversial literature, to which Oldham provided illuminating commentary (see his chap. 5).

24. Department of Old Records, Chambers Street, New York City: Province of New York Court of Chancery: Copies of Equity Judgments, 373:273–85.

25. Hastings, *Ecclesiastical Records,* 6:4268, 4328, 4355.

26. Lawsuits A–B, John Tabor Kempe Papers, New-York Historical Society.

7. Bicameralism and Republican Government in the British American Colonies and in the United States

Reprinted from H. W. Blom, W. P. Blockmans, and H. de Schepper, eds., *Bicameralisme: Tweekamerstelsel Vroeger En Nu* (The Hague: Sdu Uitgeverij Koninginnegracht, 1992).

1. Sir Thomas Smith, *De Republica Anglorum* (1583), ed. Mary Dewar (Cambridge: Cambridge University Press, 1982), 78–79.

2. The leading exponents are Bernard Bailyn, *The Ideological Origins of the American Revolution* (Cambridge, Mass.: Harvard University Press, 1967); Gordon S. Wood, *The Creation of the American Republic* (Chapel Hill: University of North Carolina Press, 1969); J. G. A. Pocock, *The Machiavellian Moment* (Princeton: Princeton University Press, 1975). There have been followers of lesser note.

3. E.g., Jack P. Greene, *The Quest for Power: The Lower Houses of Assembly in the Southern Royal Colonies, 1689–1776* (Chapel Hill: University of North Carolina Press, 1963); Greene, "Political Mimesis: A Consideration of the Historical and Cultural Roots of Legislative Behavior in the British Colonies in the Eighteenth Century," *American Historical Review* 75 (1969): 337–60; J. R. Pole, *Political Representation in England and the Origins of the American Republic* (1966; Berkeley: University of California Press, 1971).

4. A more powerful version of this thesis could be developed with reference to the dynamics of representative institutions in general, and especially the lower houses; but that is not the purpose of this paper.

5. Joyce Oldham Appleby, *Economic Thought and Ideology in Seventeenth-Century England* (Princeton: Princeton University Press, 1978).

6. David Hume, "That Politics May be Reduced to a Science; Of the First Principles of Government," in *Essays* (London, 1777); Edmund Burke, *Thoughts on the Causes of the Present Discontents* (1770), in *Works*, 2 vols. (London: Holdsworth and Ball, 1834), 1:148.

7. For development of this theme, see Pole, *Political Representation*, 442–57.

8. The incident is naturally a favorite with historians; an account can be found in George Lee Haskins, *Law and Authority in Early Massachusetts: A Study in Tradition and Design* (New York: Macmillan, 1960), 38–39.

9. Richard R. Johnson, *Adjustment to Empire: The New England Colonies, 1675–1715* (Leicester: Leicester University Press, 1981), 215–16, 230, 395–96.

10. Pole, *Political Representation*, 130.

11. See Greene, *Quest for Power*, for this trend; also Bailyn, *Ideological Origins*.

12. *The Letters of Richard Henry Lee*, ed. James Curtis Ballagh, 2 vols. (New York: 1911–14), 1 (1762–78): 18–22.

13. Wood, *Creation*, 211.

14. Jackson Turner Main, *The Upper House in Revolutionary America, 1763–1788* (Madison: University of Wisconsin Press, 1967), 188–89; Willi-Paul Adams, *The First American Constitutions: Republican Ideology and the Making of the State Constitutions in the Revolutionary Era* (Chapel Hill: University of North Carolina Press, 1980), 293–307.

15. [Theophilus Parsons], *The Result of a Convention Holden at Ipswich in the County of Essex . . . .* (Newburyport [Mass.], 1778).

16. *Works of John Adams*, ed. Charles Francis Adams, 9 vols. (Boston, 1856–61), 1:243, quoted by Main, *The Upper House*, 206.

17. Adams, *Works*, 4:290. Adams got this idea directly from Jean de Lolme; see Joyce Appleby, "The New Republican Synthesis and the Changing Political Thought of John Adams," *American Quarterly* 25 (1973): 578–95.

18. W.-P. Adams, *The First American Constitutions*, 1:271–75, goes a little way to resuscitate the powers of state governors, but not very far.

19. Main, *The Upper House*, 188–190.

20. Leonard W. Levy, *Constitutional Opinions: Aspects of the Bill of Rights* (New York: Oxford University Press, 1986), 111. State bills of rights seemed to have been somewhat

randomly drawn up, and were full of serious omissions (111–12). Several states, including New York, did not have a bill of rights. A research project worth pursuing would be to trace the record of civil rights on a state-by-state basis to compare the record in states with and without bills of rights.

21. Popular senatorial elections were a much later development in response to the rise of a more popular form of democracy.

22. The word "senate" derives from the Latin *senex;* note also our "senile."

23. Wood, *Creation,* 500.

24. *The Federalist,* ed. J. R. Pole (Indianapolis: Hackett, 2005), No. 62, p. 334.

25. *Federalist,* No. 62, 331–36.

26. *Federalist,* No. 63, 422–31.

27. Particularly *Federalist,* No. 6, 22–27.

28. *Works of the Rt. Hon. Edmund Burke,* ed. Henry Rogers (London, 1842), 1:180. Almost identical language had, however, been used as early as 1721 by the *Freeholders Journal.* For discussion, see J. R. Pole, *The Gift of Government: Political Responsibility from the English Restoration to American Independence* (Athens: University of Georgia Press, 1983), 103–4.

29. *Federalist,* No. 44, 244.

30. John Adams, *A Defence of the Constitutions of the United States,* in *Works,* 4:434.

31. Wood, *Creation,* 254.

32. *Federalist,* No. 62, 333.

33. Turgot's letter to Dr. Richard Price, March 22, 1778, to which Adams responded, is published (in substance) in Adams, *Works,* 4:278–81.

34. For discussion of bicameralism and the social order, see Pole, *The Gift of Government,* 214–26; and Wood, *Creation,* 197–255.

35. Main, *The Upper House,* 214–15.

8. The Individual, the Region, the Nation

Adapted from Waldemar Zacharasiewicz and Michael Draxlbauer, eds., *Remembering the Individual/Regional/National Past* (Vienna: Stauffenberg Verlag, 1999), and reproduced by the permission of the publisher.

1. *Chisholm v. Georgia* (1973), 2 Dall. 418–79, at 454. John Austin, lecturing at Oxford in the 1830s, struggled to produce this tortuous definition: "Sovereignty . . . resides in the states' governments *as forming the aggregate body: meaning by a state government, not its ordinary legislature, but the body of its citizens which appoints its ordinary legislature, and which (the union apart) is properly sovereign therein.*" Austin, *Lectures on Jurisprudence* (London, 1880), part 1, vol. 6, p. 103. (This was written in 1830–32.)

2. *Wickard v. Filburn,* 317 U.S. 111 (1942).

3. *Garcia v. United States,* 476 U.S. 1186 (1985).

4. Frederick Jackson Turner, *The Frontier in American History* (1893; New York: Holt, 1950).

5. The best modern study is William E. Nelson, *The Fourteenth Amendment: From*

Political Principle to Judicial Doctrine (Cambridge, Mass.: Harvard University Press, 1988).

6. J. R. Pole, *The Pursuit of Equality in American History,* rev. ed. (Berkeley: University of California Press, 1993), 246–50.

7. This refers to continuous use; it may be found occasionally during the years of the French Revolution.

8. Alexis de Tocqueville, *De la démocratie en Amérique,* ed. J.-P. Mayer, 2 vols. (Paris: Gallimard, 1961), 2:105–12.

9. David Riesman, *The Lonely Crowd* (New Haven: Yale University Press, 1950).

10. Robert E. Lane, *Political Ideology: Why the American Common Man Believes What He Does* (New York: Free Press, 1962), 57–82.

9. Nation-Making and the American Constitutional Process

From Gary L. McDowell and Johnathan O'Neill, eds., *America and Enlightenment Constitutionalism* (New York: Palgrave Macmillan, 2006).

1. David A. J. Richards, *Foundations of American Constitutionalism* (New York: Oxford University Press, 1989), 294–95.

2. Paul M. Angle, ed., *Created Equal? The Complete Lincoln-Douglas Debates* (Chicago: University of Chicago Press, 1958), 1–9.

3. Which is the underlying theme of Jacob E. Cooke in his edition of *The Federalist* (Middletown, Conn.: Wesleyan University Press, 1961).

4. John Marshall, *Life of George Washington,* 5 vols. (New York: William H. Wise, 1925), 5:279–306, on 283.

5. Ibid., 285.

6. Ibid., 284–85.

7. Andrew W. Robertson, "'Look at this picture . . . And on this!': Nationalism, Localism and Partisan Images of Otherness in the United States, 1787–1820," *American Historical Review* 106 (2001): 1263–80.

8. 6 Cranch 87 (1810).

9. J. J. Powell, *Essay Upon the Law of Contracts and Agreements,* 2 vols. (London: For J. Johnson and T. Whieldon, 1790).

10. 4 Wheat. 518 (1819).

11. Walker P. Mayo, "The Federal Bill of Rights and the States before the Fourteenth Amendment," DPhil thesis, Oxford University, 1993, 223–27.

12. Letter from Charles C. Jones Jr. to Rev. C. C. Jones, May 30, 1854, in *The Children of Pride: A True Story of Georgia and the Civil War,* ed. Robert Manson Myers (New Haven: Yale University Press, 1972), 37–38.

13. The leading work is James H. Kettner, *The Development of American Citizenship, 1608–1870* (Chapel Hill: University of North Carolina Press, 1978), esp. 213–46. The right to citizenship and related duties were matters of heated party debate.

14. J. G. A. Pocock, *The Machiavellian Moment: Florentine Political Thought and the Atlantic Republican Tradition* (Princeton: Princeton University Press, 1975), 204–5.

15. *Federalist*, No. 37 (Pole ed., 192–98).

16. Mayo, "Federal Bill of Rights," 1–26, appendix D; William W. Crosskey, *Politics and the Constitution in the History of the United States*, 2 vols. (Chicago: University of Chicago Press, 1953), 2:1070; attacked by Charles Fairman, "The Supreme Court and the Constitutional Limitations on State Governmental Authority," *University of Chicago Law Review* 21 (1953): 40–78; Crosskey's reply: "Charles Fairman, 'Legislative History,' and the Constitutional Limitations on the State Authority," *University of Chicago Law Review* 22 (1954): 1–143; Fairman's rejoinder: "A Reply to Professor Crosskey," ibid., 144–56; J. R. Pole, "The Individualist Foundations of American Constitutionalism," in *"To Form a More Perfect Union": Critical Ideas of the Constitution*, ed. Herman Belz, Ronald Hoffman, and Peter J. Albert (Charlottesville: University Press of Virginia, 1992), 98–101.

17. The contract clause did restrain the states but hardly on the grounds applied in *Fletcher v. Peck* (1810) or *Dartmouth College v. Woodward* (1817).

18. Mayo, "Federal Bill of Rights," 155.

19. William Rawle, *A View of the Constitution of the United States of America* (Philadelphia: H. C. Carey and I. Lea, 1825); Mayo, "Federal Bill of Rights," 256–57. These remarks represent an attempt to reconcile the dissenting views expressed in my essay "The Individualist Foundations," with the persuasive Marshallian argument of Akhil Reed Amar, *The Bill of Rights* (New Haven: Yale University Press, 1998), 140–71.

20. The issues are analyzed in J. R. Pole, *The Pursuit of Equality in American History*, rev. ed. (Berkeley: University of California Press, 1993), 180–85. See Don E. Fehrenbacher, *The Dred Scott Case: Its Significance in American Law and Politics* (New York: Oxford University Press, 1978), for comprehensive cover.

21. 83 Wall. 16 (1873).

22. Nelson, *Fourteenth Amendment*, 156–59; Pole, *Pursuit of Equality*, 224–26.

23. *The Civil Rights Cases*, 109 U.S. 3 (1883).

24. *Plessy v. Ferguson*, 163 U.S. 357 (1896).

25. *The Writings of James Madison*, ed. Gaillard Hunt, 9 vols. (New York: Putnam's Sons, 1910), 5:294.

26. Ibid., 565.

27. The practice of reversal is in fact known in Congress and among certain special interest lobbies, but not in connection with such constitutional or public policy issues as we are concerned with.

28. Angle, *Created Equal?* 306.

29. Noel T. Dowling and Gerald Gunther, *Constitutional Law: Cases and Materials*, 7th ed. (Brooklyn: Foundation Press, 1965), 49–50.

30. *Constitution of the United States, Analysis and Interpretation*, 82nd Cong., 2nd sess., 1951, S.Doc 170, 513.

31. United States, *Statutes at Large of the United States of America, 1789–1873*, vol. 12 (Boston, 1863), 432.

32. United States, *Statutes at Large of the United States of America, 1789–1873*, vol. 14 (Boston, 1866), 27.

33. James Bryce, *The American Commonwealth* (London: Macmillan, 1891), 1:27.

34. Ibid, 390.

35. Alan Cromartie, *Sir Matthew Hale: Law, Religion and Natural Philosophy* (Cambridge: Cambridge University Press, 1995), 36, 107.

10. Representative Institutions, 1776–1876

1. See Fritz Stern, *Gold and Iron: Bismarck, Bleichröder, and the Building of the German Empire* (New York: Knopf, 1977).

2. For a discussion of "virtual representation," see J. R. Pole, *Political Representation in England and the Origins of the American Republic* (1966; Berkeley: University of California Press, 1971). See also Jenyns Soame, *The Objections to the Taxation of Our American Colonies, by the Legislature of Great Britain, Briefly Consider'd* (London, 1765).

3. See Ian R. Christie, *Crisis of Empire, Great Britain and the American Colonies, 1754–1783* (London: Edward Arnold, 1966).

4. Edmund Burke, *Thoughts on the Cause of the Present Discontents*, 2nd ed. (London, 1770), 98.

5. David Hume, "Politics Reduced to a Science," in *Essays, Moral and Political* (London, 1741).

6. See Ian R. Christie, *Wilkes, Wyvill and Reform: The Parliamentary Reform Movement in British Politics, 1760–1785* (London: Macmillan, 1962).

7. "C'est en ma personne que réside la puissance souveraine . . . c'est à moi seul qu'appartient le pouvoir législatif, sans dépendance et sans partage, c'est par ma seule autorité que les officiers de mes cours procèdent non à la formation, mais à l'enregistrement et à la publication de ma loi. . . . L'ordre public tout entier émane de moi, j'en suis le gardien suprême; mon people n'est qu'un avec moi, et les droits et les intérêts de la nation . . . sont nécessairement unis avec les miens et ne reposent qu'en mes mains." Louis XV, March 3, 1766, before the Parlement of Paris, in Jacques Godechot, *Les institutions de la France sous la Révolution et l'Empire*, 3rd ed. (Paris: Presses Universitaires de France, 1985), 4.

8. "La nation existe avant tout, elle est l'origine de tout, sa volonté est toujours légale, elle est la loi elle-même. Avant-elle et au-dessus d'elle, il n'y a que le droit *naturel*." "L'assemblé des représentants du people ne doit tenir aucun comte de la division en 'ordres,' vestige de la féodalité; le vote doit avoir lieu par tête." E. J. Sieyès, *Qu'est-ce que le tiers état?* (1789), new ed. by l'abbé Morellet (Paris, 1822), 159.

9. For details of the French Revolution, see William Doyle, *The Oxford History of the French Revolution*, 2nd ed. (Oxford: Oxford University Press, 2002).

10. See F. A. Simpson, *Louis Napoleon and the Recovery of France, 1848–1856*, 2nd ed. (London: Longmans Green, 1930).

11. *The Recollections of Alexis de Tocqueville*, trans. Alexander Teixeira de Mattos (New York: Doubleday, 1971), 6.

12. Ibid., 12.

13. See Robert Gildea, *Barricades and Borders: Europe 1800–1914* (Oxford: Oxford University Press, 1987).

14. James J. Sheehan, *German Liberalism in the Nineteenth Century* (Chicago: University of Chicago Press, 1978), 10.

15. Theodore S. Hamerow, *The Social Foundations of German Unification, 1858–1871*, vol. 1 (Princeton: Princeton University Press, 1969), 165.

16. Ibid., 207.

17. Ibid., 234.

18. Otto von Bismarck, *Die gesammelten Werke* (Berlin, 1924), quoted in Gordon A. Craig, *Germany, 1866–1945* (Oxford: Oxford University Press, 1981), 45.

19. Hamerow, *Social Foundations*, 136.

20. Sheehan, *German Liberalism*, 159.

21. Stern, *Gold and Iron*, 93.

22. Pole, *Political Representation*, 486.

23. Lord Durham during the debates in the House of Lords on the First Reform Bill, in Norman Gash, *Politics in the Age of Peel: A Study in the Technique of Parliamentary Representation, 1830–1850* (London: Longmans, Green, 1953), 16.

24. As argued in Pole, *Political Representation*; but for a more proleptically Whiggish view, see John Cannon, *Parliamentary Reform 1640–1832* (Cambridge: Cambridge University Press, 1973).

25. See Walter Bagehot, *The Political Essays*, ed. Norman St. John-Stevas, vols. 5–8 of *The Collected Works of Walter Bagehot* (London: The Economist, 1974).

26. Maurice Cowling, *1867: Disraeli, Gladstone and Revolution: The Passing of the Second Reform Bill* (London: Cambridge University Press, 1967), 52.

27. Ibid.

Index